Specialty Competencies in Clinical Health Psychology

D1715256

Series in Specialty Competencies in Professional Psychology

KEVIN T. LARKIN
ELIZABETH A. KLONOFF

Specialty Competencies in Clinical Health Psychology

OXFORD
UNIVERSITY PRESS

Oxford University Press is a department of the University of Oxford.
It furthers the University's objective of excellence in research, scholarship,
and education by publishing worldwide.

Oxford   New York
Auckland   Cape Town   Dar es Salaam   Hong Kong   Karachi
Kuala Lumpur   Madrid   Melbourne   Mexico City   Nairobi
New Delhi   Shanghai   Taipei   Toronto

With offices in
Argentina   Austria   Brazil   Chile   Czech Republic   France   Greece
Guatemala   Hungary   Italy   Japan   Poland   Portugal   Singapore
South Korea   Switzerland   Thailand   Turkey   Ukraine   Vietnam

Oxford is a registered trademark of Oxford University Press
in the UK and certain other countries.

Published in the United States of America by
Oxford University Press
198 Madison Avenue, New York, NY 10016

Library of Congress Cataloging-in-Publication Data
Larkin, Kevin T.
Specialty competencies in clinical health psychology / Kevin T. Larkin, Elizabeth A. Klonoff.
    pages cm.—(Specialty competencies in professional psychology)
Includes bibliographical references and index.
ISBN 978-0-19-977913-0
1. Clinical health psychology.   2. Clinical competence.   3. Core
competencies.   I. Klonoff, Elizabeth A.   II. Title.
R726.7.L37 2015
616.89—dc23
2014012125

9 8 7 6 5 4 3 2 1
Printed in the United States of America
on acid-free paper

SELECTED EVENTS IN THE HISTORY OF CLINICAL HEALTH PSYCHOLOGY

Early 1950s   Neal Miller's pioneering research on conditioning of physiological processes led to an interest in biofeedback

1950   Four psychologists in the US Public Health Service (Godfrey Hochbaum, S. Stephen Kegeles, Howard Leventhal, and Irwin Rosenstock) developed the health belief model in an effort to explain why people were not being vaccinated against tuberculosis

1953   Guze, Matarazzo, and Saslow first published an article in the *Journal of Clinical Psychology* on the biopsychosocial model

1969   William Schofield published his landmark paper, "The Role of Psychology in the Delivery of Health Services" in *American Psychologist*

1973   The APA Board of Scientific Affairs established a Task Force on Health Research. Chaired by William Schofield, the task force included Claus Bahnson, Edward and Miriam Kelty, John Rasmussen, Lee Sechrest, Lisa Schusterman, and Walter Wilkins

1974   The Task Force on Health Research holds an open meeting at the 1974 APA Convention in New Orleans, during which the decision to seek division status was put on hold

1975   Division 18 (Psychologists in Public Service) establishes a new Section on Health Research, Section 2

1976   The Task Force on Health Research published a summary of its work, "Contributions of Psychology to Health Research: Patterns, Problems, and Potentials" in *American Psychologist*

1977   Physician George Engel popularized the biopsychosocial model

1977   Stephen Weiss named head of the new Behavioral Medicine Branch at the National Heart, Lung, and Blood Institute

1977   The Yale Conference on Behavioral Medicine was held and the first definition of that interdisciplinary field was developed

1977   The Society of Behavioral Medicine (SBM) was established

1978   The beginning of APA Division 38 (Health Psychology)

1978   The first issue and volume of *Journal of Behavioral Medicine* was published

1979   The initial edition of the Division 38 newsletter, *The Health Psychologist*, was published, edited by John Linton, who served as editor for 15 years

1979   George Stone, Frances Cohen, and Nancy Adler publish the first handbook in the field of health psychology

1980   The Health Research Section (Section 2 of Division 18) officially dissolved; its activities were subsumed under the newly created Division 38

1980   Joseph Matarazzo puts forward the first formal definition of *health psychology* in an article in *American Psychologist*

1982   The journal, *Health Psychology*, began quarterly publication, with George Stone serving as the inaugural editor

1983   The National Working Conference on Education and Training in Health Psychology, also known as the Arden House conference, was held, May 23–27. The conference proceedings were published as a supplement to Volume 3 of *Health Psychology* that year

1983   The Council of Health Psychology Training Directors was established

1984   A joint task force representing the Council of Health Psychology Training Directors and Division 38 established the American Board of Health Psychology as the credentialing body for the specialty practice of health psychology

1988   The National Working Conference on Research in Health and Behavior was held at Harpers Ferry, West Virginia, May 15–17.

1992   The National Conference on Behavioral and Sociocultural Perspectives on Ethnicity and Health, cosponsored by APA Divisions 38 and 45, Duke University Medical Center, Howard University School of Medicine, NHLBI, NIMH, the Upjohn Corporation, and the Office of Minority Health in the Department of Health and Human Services, was held in Washington, D.C., September 17–20.

1993   The American Board of Health Psychology became fully affiliated with the American Board of Professional Psychology (ABPP) such that specialty practice was now recognized through ABPP

1993   *Health Psychology* became an official APA publication

1996   *The Health Psychologist* became a quarterly publication

1997   Clinical Health Psychology was first recognized as a specialty by the APA Commission for the Recognition of Specialties and Proficiencies in Professional Psychology (CRSPPP); it has been re-recognized for the full 7 years every time it has come up for review

2000   The Future of Health Psychology Conference was held in Pittsburgh, Pennsylvania

2007   The Tempe Summit on Education and Training in Clinical Health Psychology was the first to describe the distinctive competencies essential for the practice of the specialty; the summary of these competencies was published in 2009

2008   The Council of Clinical Health Psychology Training Programs (CCHPTP) was reinvigorated with the support of the Council of University Directors of Clinical Psychology (CUDCP); CCHPTP has met consecutively with CUDCP since

2010   The Riverfront Conference on Education and Training in Health Psychology was held in Jacksonville, Florida, reaffirming many of the guidelines established during the Arden House Conference

CONTENTS

ABOUT THE SERIES IN SPECIALTY COMPETENCIES IN PROFESSIONAL PSYCHOLOGY

This series is intended to describe state-of-the-art functional and foundational competencies in professional psychology across extant and emerging specialty areas. Each book in this series provides a guide to best practices across both core and specialty competencies as defined by a given professional psychology specialty.

The impetus for this series was created by various growing movements in professional psychology during the past 15 years. First, as an applied discipline, psychology is increasingly recognizing the unique and distinct nature among a variety of orientations, modalities, and approaches with regard to professional practice. These specialty areas represent distinct ways of practicing one's profession across various domains of activities that are based on distinct bodies of literature and often addressing differing populations or problems. For example, the American Psychological Association (APA) in 1995 established the Commission on the Recognition of Specialties and Proficiencies in Professional Psychology (CRSPPP) in order to define criteria by which a given specialty could be recognized. The Council of Credentialing Organizations in Professional Psychology (CCOPP), an interorganizational entity, was formed in reaction to the need to establish criteria and principles regarding the types of training programs related to the education, training, and professional development of individuals seeking such specialization. In addition, the Council on Specialties in Professional Psychology (COS) was formed in 1997, independent of the APA, to foster communication among the established specialties, in order to offer a unified position to the pubic regarding specialty education and training, credentialing, and practice standards across specialty areas.

Simultaneously, efforts to actually define professional competence regarding psychological practice have also been growing significantly. For example, the APA-sponsored Task Force on Assessment of Competence in Professional Psychology put forth a series of guiding principles for the assessment of competence within professional psychology, based, in part, on a review of competency assessment models developed both within (e.g., Assessment of Competence Workgroup from Competencies Conference— Roberts et al., 2005) and outside (e.g., Accreditation Council for Graduate Medical Education and American Board of Medical Specialties, 2000) the profession of psychology (Kaslow et al., 2007).

Moreover, additional professional organizations in psychology have provided valuable input into this discussion, including various associations primarily interested in the credentialing of professional psychologists, such as the American Board of Professional Psychology (ABPP), the Association of State and Provincial Psychology Boards (ASPBB), and the National Register of Health Service Providers in Psychology. This widespread interest and importance of the issue of competency in professional psychology can be especially appreciated given the attention and collaboration afforded to this effort by international groups, including the Canadian Psychological Association and the International Congress on Licensure, Certification, and Credentialing in Professional Psychology.

Each volume in the series is devoted to a specific specialty and provides a definition, description, and development timeline of that specialty, including its essential and characteristic pattern of activities, as well as its distinctive and unique features. Each set of authors, long-term experts and veterans of a given specialty, were asked to describe that specialty along the lines of both functional and foundational competencies. Functional competencies are those common practice activities provided at the specialty level of practice that include, for example, the application of its science base, assessment, intervention, consultation, and where relevant, supervision, management, and teaching. Foundational competencies represent core knowledge areas that are integrated and cut across all functional competencies to varying degrees, and dependent upon the specialty, in various ways. These include ethical and legal issues, individual and cultural diversity considerations, interpersonal interactions, and professional identification.

Whereas we realize that each specialty is likely to undergo changes in the future, we wanted to establish a baseline of basic knowledge and principles that comprise a specialty highlighting both its commonalities with other areas of professional psychology, as well as its distinctiveness. We look forward to seeing the dynamics of such changes, as well as the emergence of new specialties in the future.

In this volume, Larkin and Klonoff provide an important description of the evolution of the clinical health psychology specialty, which uniquely integrates multidisciplinary and interdisciplinary research, practice, knowledge, and experience. They provide important insights regarding the areas of overlap and/or collaboration with other specialties such as cognitive and behavioral psychology, as well as the specialty's unique foundational and functional competencies. One particularly salient insight for readers is the intentional aim of the specialty to impact and improve the health care system. Thus, the professional identity of clinical health psychologists can potentially have a profound impact on both national and global health. To promote such changes toward comprehensive and integrated health care, maintaining one's professional identity within the culture of Western medicine can be daunting. Larkin and Klonoff use their knowledge and expertise to provide practical support and advice for clinical health specialists entering this challenging specialty area. Finally, the authors provide a comprehensive understanding of the biopsychosocial model that serves as a foundation for this important specialty as well as prescriptions for continued professional development and self-care. This is an important book that is not limited to individuals who aspire to specialize in clinical health psychology but all psychologists and behavioral health practitioners who work in health care systems.

Arthur M. Nezu
Christine Maguth Nezu

PART I

Introduction to Clinical
Health Psychology Practice
in Professional Psychology

ONE

Health Psychology and Clinical Health Psychology

In recent decades, the leading causes of death in the United States have come to parallel closely causes of death observed around the world (Centers for Disease Control and Prevention [CDC], n.d.; Murphy, Xu, & Kochanek, 2012; World Health Organization [WHO], 2013). As shown in Table 1.1, similar but not identical causes of death are reflected in the most recent reports of the CDC and WHO. Contrast that to the beginning of the 20th century, when the top three causes of death in the United States were (1) pneumonia and influenza; (2) tuberculosis; and (3) diarrhea, enteritis, and ulceration of the intestines (CDC, n.d.). What is striking when one compares the causes of death in 1900 with the causes of death today is that behavioral or psychosocial factors now play a more substantial role in the etiology, progression, and outcomes of morbidity and mortality, not only in the United States but around the world as well.

For most of the history of the field of medicine, health, typically thought of as the mere absence of disease, was conceptualized solely as a biological or a biomedical phenomenon. This no doubt was due to the nature of the illnesses and diseases that impaired health and led to disease states and death in past centuries. As a consequence of advances in medical science, death from infectious diseases dropped dramatically during the 20th century (CDC, 1999). This decline was attributed to three major interventions. First, as the science of medicine led to an increased emphasis upon sanitation and hygiene, social practices evolved to improve water treatment and sewage disposal, the safety of food preparation, and animal and pest control (e.g., animal vaccination, mosquito control, and rodent and vector control).

TABLE 1.1 **The 10 Contemporary Leading Causes of Death in the United States and Worldwide**

UNITED STATES (CDC, 2010)	WORLDWIDE (WHO, 2011)
Heart disease	Heart disease
Cancer	Stroke and other cerebrovascular diseases
Chronic lower respiratory diseases	Lower respiratory infections
Cerebrovascular diseases/stroke	Chronic obstructive pulmonary disease
Accidents	Diarrheal diseases
Alzheimer's disease	HIV/AIDS
Diabetes mellitus	Cancer of the trachea, bronchus, and lung
Nephritis, nephrotic syndrome, and nephrosis	Diabetes mellitus
Influenza and pneumonia	Road injury
Intentional self-harm/suicide	Prematurity

Second, vaccination campaigns, coordinated and supported through the Vaccination Assistance Act, were implemented to reduce exposure to previously common diseases such as diphtheria, tetanus, poliomyelitis, smallpox, measles, mumps, and rubella. Vaccination has virtually eliminated these diseases; for example, smallpox was deemed eradicated worldwide in 1977, and continuing efforts are being made to eradicate polio. Finally, the emergence of the use of antibiotics in the 1940s resulted in a decrease in deaths from streptococcal and staphylococcal infections, gonorrhea and syphilis, and many other infections. The shift toward increased efforts to prevent the emergence of illness was aided by improved methods to detect and monitor a range of infectious diseases. Other improvements in medical diagnosis and treatment were also relevant. For example, the development of anesthesia made it possible for the surgeons of the time to begin to develop what has become a highly specialized and technologically based way of treating everything from gunshot wounds to tumors. The ultimate consequence of these advances in medicine is that people are living longer, and as a result, people are increasingly dying of chronic illnesses rather than acute infectious diseases. Many of these chronic illnesses are influenced significantly by behavioral factors or lifestyle choices.

Recent calls for health care reform and emerging debates about the influence of lifestyle and behavioral factors in health and illness might lead one to conclude that psychology has only recently entered into the field of health. In fact, psychologists have been active in developing assessments and interventions related to a broad range of health problems for many decades. In addition, organized psychology has had a major focus on health for a while. A brief history of psychology's interest in health will serve to clarify this.

THE BIRTH OF DIVISION 38 (HEALTH PSYCHOLOGY)

In his detailed history of the American Psychological Association (APA) Division 38 (Health Psychology), Wallston (1996) noted that a 1969 paper in the *American Psychologist* (Schofield, 1969) caught the attention of members of the Committee on Newly Emerging Areas of Research (NEAR) of the APA. Accepting the role of psychology as a health profession, NEAR prompted the Board of Scientific Affairs of the APA to establish a Task Force on Health Research in 1973, chaired by William Schofield and including Claus Bahnson, Edward and Miriam Kelty, John Rasmussen, Lee Sechrest, Lisa Schusterman, and Walter Wilkins. In 1976, this Task Force concluded that much of the science of psychology could be applied to the prevention and treatment of physical illnesses (APA Task Force on Health Research, 1976).

The Task Force held an open meeting at the 1974 APA Convention, and a major topic of the meeting was discussion of the formation of a new division within the APA to focus on health research. Although the decision to create a new APA division was postponed at that time, a number of the Task Force members who were active in Division 18 (Psychologists in Public Service) sought permission to institute a new section on Health Research within that Division, and in 1975, Section 2 of Division 18 was formed. William Schofield and Wilbert Fordyce served as the first two chairs. When Stephen Weiss was elected to serve as chair-elect in 1977, he made it clear that his goal was to establish a new independent division within the APA. With the assistance of Joseph Matarazzo, a group (that by then included Joseph Brady, Richard Evans, Wilbert Fordyce, W. Doyle Gentry, David Glass, Irving Janis, Neal Miller, Gary Schwartz, Jerome Singer, and George Stone as well) petitioned the APA to establish a Division of Health Psychology. Supported by the leadership of the Medical Psychology Network (led by David Clayman and John Linton) and the Society of Pediatric Psychology (led by Logan Wright, Lee Salk, and Dorothea Ross), the petition was approved in 1978. Following creation of the formal Division of Health Psychology, the Health Research Section of Division 18 was dissolved in 1980.

The official definition of health psychology was originally written by Matarazzo (1980) and then later modified prior to the final vote in 1980 (Wallson, 1996). That definition was as follows:

> Health psychology is the aggregate of the specific educational, scientific, and professional contributions of the discipline of psychology to the promotion and maintenance of health, the

prevention and treatment of illness, and the identification of etiologic and diagnostic correlates of health, illness and related dysfunction and to the analysis and improvement of the health care system and health policy formation. (Wallston, 1996, p. 10)

That original definition remains fairly much intact today. On its Web site, Division 38 (Health Psychology), the APA division formed as a consequence of these actions, identifies the following tripartite mission:

- Advancing contributions of the psychology discipline toward understanding health and illness through basic and clinical research and by encouraging the integration of biomedical information about health and illness with current psychological knowledge;
- Promoting education and services in the psychology of health and illness; and
- Informing the psychological and biomedical community, as well as the general public, on the results of current research and service activities in this area. (Division 38, http://www.health-psych.org/AboutMission.cfm)

THE BIRTH OF THE SOCIETY OF BEHAVIORAL MEDICINE

According to Kennerly (2002), the term "behavioral medicine" first appeared in the published work *Biofeedback: Behavioral Medicine* (1973) by Lee Birk. Only 5 years later, in the first volume and first issue of the *Journal of Behavioral Medicine*, Weiss described the following "news and developments of actions that had already occurred" since the inception of the field in 1973:

1. Harvard Medical School created its Behavioral Medicine Section and Clinic at Beth Israel Hospital in September 1977.

2. Johns Hopkins University established its Behavioral Medicine Center, which included a Behavioral Medicine Clinic, Cardiovascular Learning Clinic, and Behavior Therapy Clinic.

3. Clinical psychology internship and psychiatry residency training programs in behavioral medicine were available at the University of Mississippi Medical Center.

4. After initially developing programs to treat problem drinking and smoking, John Paul Brady and Ovide Pomerleau founded the Center for Behavioral Medicine at the University of Pennsylvania in 1973.

5. The Laboratory for the Study of Behavioral Medicine was established in the Department of Psychiatry and Behavioral Sciences at Stanford University around 1975.

6. Spring of 1977 brought the Yale Center for Behavioral Medicine into existence, operated through the cooperative efforts of the Departments of Psychology, Psychiatry, and Epidemiology and Public Health.

These events represented just a few of the many laboratories and departments that were inaugurated coast to coast during the 1970s whose names included the term "behavioral medicine." In an effort to define this emerging field of specialized focus on health and to coordinate efforts that were occurring across the United States, a working conference, the Yale Conference on Behavioral Medicine, was held on February 4–6, 1977. Four major conclusions were drawn from the proceedings of this conference. The first conclusion centered on developing a definition of "behavioral medicine" that would be acceptable to a broad array of researchers in the area. Even at this early stage, an effort was made to distinguish between this emerging field and existing mental health–related ones; the definition included the premise that "Psychosis, neurosis, and substance abuse are included only insofar as they contribute to physical disorders as an end point" (Schwartz & Weiss, 1978a, p. 7). The second conclusion attempted to expand and clarify the scope of problems of concern to behavioral medicine. A cube-type matrix involving discipline (e.g., psychology, internal medicine), point in the illness process (e.g., prevention, treatment), and type of disease (e.g., hypertension, asthma) was proposed, along with a list of nine problems in behavioral medicine that could be applied to any physical disorder (e.g., sociocultural influences, cognitive determinants of health and disease). The third conclusion was that there was a need for an interdisciplinary journal that could serve as an outlet for theory and research conducted in the study of behavioral medicine, broadly conceptualized. Finally, the group involved in the conference concluded that it should "explore the feasibility of forming a Society for Behavioral Medicine," with an emphasis "in basic research. . . as well as controlled investigations dealing with clinical application" (Schwartz & Weiss, 1978a, p. 11). As a result, seeds were sown for the development of the Society of Behavioral Medicine (SBM), and the *Journal of Behavioral Medicine*, which was formally established in July of 1977.

Currently, SBM has an active, interdisciplinary membership that assembles once a year for a highly successful meeting. The formal definition of "behavioral medicine," as taken from the SBM Web site, is as follows:

> Behavioral Medicine is the interdisciplinary field concerned with the development and integration of behavioral, psychosocial, and biomedical science knowledge and techniques relevant to the understanding of health and illness, and the application of this knowledge and these techniques to prevention, diagnosis, treatment and rehabilitation. (Schwartz & Weiss, 1978b; http://www.sbm.org/resources/education/behavioral-medicine)

Note that while health psychology and its applied clinical health psychology counterpart both represent specializations within the science of psychology, behavioral medicine is interdisciplinary in nature. Thus, when one attends a Division 38 meeting or conference, the attendees would invariably be trained as psychologists; in contrast, when one attends an SBM meeting, participants come from a variety of health professions—medicine, nursing, pharmacy, dentistry, and public health, to name a few.

SIGNIFICANCE OF THE ARDEN HOUSE CONFERENCE

After the Yale Conference in 1977 and the creation of the SBM, perhaps the most significant meeting with respect to the development of health psychology per se was the National Working Conference on Education and Training in Health Psychology, or what has come to be called the Arden House Conference, held in 1983. The result of over 2 years of planning, the meeting brought together 57 participants for 4 days of activities funded by the Carnegie Foundation, the MacArthur Foundation, and the Kaiser Family Foundation. Consensus was reached on virtually all decisions, and the report on the conference itself was divided into four major sections: (1) how the conference was developed, including the working agenda; (2) the major addresses that were presented during plenary sessions; (3) task group reports prepared prior to the meeting, including three position papers developed during the conference itself; and (4) the reports from the working groups, which constituted the endorsed output from the meeting itself (for a comprehensive report of the conference proceedings, see Stone et al., 1987).

Neal Miller (1983) summarized some of the primary themes and highlights that were developed during the meeting. There was unanimous agreement that there was value to both aspects of the scientist-practitioner model and that education and training of practitioners had to include both training as scientists and as practitioners. Similarly, attendees agreed that virtually all of psychology was relevant to functioning as a health psychologist and so a broad foundation in the discipline of psychology was seen as a prerequisite knowledge base for those desiring training to be health psychologists. The importance of breadth of interdisciplinary knowledge was noted. In addition to the more obvious need to understand how the health care system works, elementary knowledge of clinical symptoms and pathophysiology, exposure to the mores and vocabulary of the health care setting, and knowledge concerning public health and health policy also were highlighted.

The fundamental training competencies and curriculum guidelines established at the Arden House Conference were reaffirmed in 2010 at the Riverfront Conference, a small meeting held for the purposes of preparing clinical health psychology's petition to maintain clinical health psychology as a specialty by the APA's Commission for the Recognition of Specialties and Proficiencies in Professional Psychology. During this meeting, the field reaffirmed the Arden House themes and highlights noted by Miller (1983); most notably among these was that health psychologists and clinical health psychologists needed to be able to actually do research (i.e., reaffirming the importance of the scientist-practitioner model). What the Arden House attendees referred to as scientist and scientist-practitioner tracks in graduate training programs are more commonly referred to as health psychology and clinical health psychology training programs in contemporary educational settings. In addition, the attendees of the Riverfront Conference reaffirmed that specialty training in clinical health psychology occurred largely at the postdoctoral level; there was consensus not to pursue the goal of accreditation of doctoral programs in clinical health psychology because health psychology training optimally occurs after basic training in health service provision has already been completed. There is growing recognition, however, that foundational elements of clinical health psychology (particularly knowledge-based competencies and basic applied skills) are commonly acquired concurrent to basic training in health service provision, and that such practices for preparing trainees for advanced competency acquisition at the postdoctoral level are now routine (Nash & Larkin, 2012).

A variety of training conferences have continued the dialog regarding competencies to practice as clinical health psychologists since Arden

House. For example, in 2000, the Future of Health Psychology Conference was held in Pittsburgh, Pennsylvania. Six working groups (evolution of the biopsychosocial model; advances in medicine and technology; changes in demographics; health care economics and the health care marketplace; prevention; and health psychology interventions) were constituted and prepared articles that summarized the state of the field at that time.

In more recent years and consistent with general movement in the health care professions, there has been an increased focus on the identification of distinctive competencies essential for the effective practice of clinical health psychology (e.g., France et al., 2009; Masters, France, & Thorn, 2009). The initial step in this direction was the planning and implementing of the Tempe Summit on Education and Training in Clinical Health Psychology in 2007. Due to the importance of the work that was launched at the Tempe Summit, comprehensive coverage of its role will be described in more detail in Chapter 3.

Unlike many other specialties in professional psychology, clinical health psychology as a field made an active decision to define itself as having only two training options at the Arden House Conference: scientist and scientist-practitioner. Because the nature of the field requires that all health psychology practitioners be able to, at a minimum, provide basic program or treatment evaluation services or share methods for doing so with their interdisciplinary colleagues, training in research is essential. Clinical health psychologists stand out as the only profession uniformly and routinely trained to conduct empirical studies or program evaluations among all other professions encountered in the modern health care environment. Additionally, clinical health psychology has a strong allegiance to the science of health psychology. This professional camaraderie, fostered by an APA division that fully appreciates both the science and its applications, facilitates communication between those who focus only on scientific inquiry and those who blend science with its application. Thus, a practitioner-only model, where individuals are not trained to conduct research but rather only to "consume" it, does not provide some of the unique contributions that make clinical health psychologists such useful members of health care teams; this view has been put forward by others as well (HSPEC, 2013). These contributions have become even more critical as psychologists are increasingly integrated into primary care settings. In those settings in particular, it has become important (both to health care funders and to the public) to be able to demonstrate empirically that having a behavioral health practitioner on site makes a difference regarding both health outcomes and the costs of achieving those outcomes. A hallmark feature of the Affordable Care Act that is now guiding the development of the United States' future health care system is a focus upon conducting research that distinguishes cost-effective health care approaches from either those that fail to work or those whose cost outweighs potential benefits. As scientist-practitioners, clinical health psychologists are uniquely positioned to conduct this type of research.

One additional issue needs to be mentioned. This book was written primarily to focus on clinical health psychology with adults. While many of the competencies described here apply to work regardless of the age of the patient, obviously not all do. In 2012, the Board of Directors of the Society of Pediatric Psychology established a task force to "develop core competencies applicable from initial entry level to practicum training to readiness for entry to practice in pediatric psychology" (Palermo, Janicke, McQuaid, Mullins, Robins, and Wu, 2014, p. 5); that Task Force has now produced a document. Readers interested in competencies that are specific to the implementation of clinical health psychology with pediatric patients should consult this document in addition to the comments and observations provided here (Palermo, Janicke, McQuaid, Mullins, Robins, and Wu, 2014).

SUMMARY AND CONCLUSIONS

In the almost four decades since "health psychology" was defined and recognized as a specialty area, the field has evolved from one where it seemed as if its time had come to one that may help to redefine the nature of all of professional practice. Many believe that the future of health service provision rests on the shoulders of clinical health psychologists, and that, in the future, all professional psychologists will require training as "health psychologists," that is, psychologists competent to function in the health care environment, broadly defined. As the APA has moved toward defining psychology as a health care profession, it would appear that professional psychology is moving in this direction. Even the revision of the *Guidelines and Principles for Accreditation of Programs in Professional Psychology* (2009) that went out for public comment in 2014 has been renamed *Standards of Accreditation in Health Service Psychology*. Despite significant movement in this direction, our training programs and credentialing systems are languishing, still tied to the traditional view of psychologists as mental health providers. As such, the professional psychologists of tomorrow, those we are currently training, may not be obtaining the necessary knowledge, values, and skills they will need in their future careers. The primary purpose of this volume is to elucidate the competencies associated with the professional practice of clinical health psychology, so that those in training and those doing the training are armed with a blueprint regarding what the outcome of training should be.

Traditionally, clinical health psychologists constituted only a fraction of the total number of professional psychologists being trained. Most commonly, training occurred in clinical psychology training programs, although several counseling psychology programs also provide training in clinical health psychology. In this regard, the profession of psychology evolved based on this view of the education and training community depicted in the left panel of Figure 1.1; basically, all students received training as mental health professionals, and those who chose to pursue training as clinical health psychologists acquired the extra competencies to enter their profession as a clinical health psychologist. However, as the full integration of behavioral and medical health care approaches, as advocated by the Institute of Medicine (1972), it now appears that the figure depicted in the right panel of Figure 1.1 reflects more accurately our profession in the future. All professional psychologists will need training in health care provision, and a subset of them will choose to practice in a given specialty area (e.g., clinical health psychology, clinical psychology, etc.). Of course, such a shift would require a substantial rethinking of what else should be in the required knowledge base of the health care provision, who else should be involved in providing the education and training for future health care providers, and where that training should occur; such deliberations have already begun (HSPEC, 2013), but in no way are they universally accepted. In this new conceptualization of our profession and

FIGURE 1.1 **Clinical health psychology: a distinctive health service profession.**

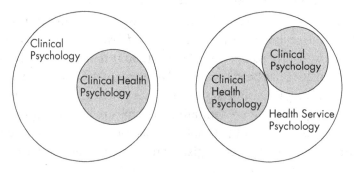

the health care system, mental health service provision is viewed as but one subset of health service provision. As the term "health service psychologist" becomes more universally used to describe individuals who historically have characterized themselves solely as clinical, counseling, or school psychologists, exactly what constitutes a "specialty" will need to be reconceptualized as well. While it remains to be seen whether the profession elects to reconceptualize itself in this way, this book provides an introduction to the basic skills and competencies one would need to acquire in order to function as a clinical health psychologist, regardless of how narrow or broad that definition might be.

TWO

Conceptual and Scientific Foundations
of Clinical Health Psychology

The practice of psychology stands out among other professions for its firm foundation upon a recognized scientific discipline. Students who enter the medical profession commonly obtain undergraduate degrees in biology and chemistry, and students who enter law often obtain their degrees in the fields of political science or philosophy. In reality, there is no science of medicine or law; these professions represent the application of scientific principles learned in interrelated underlying scientific disciplines. When undergraduates in these professional tracks are queried regarding their major area of study, they will claim to be pre-med or pre-law rather than claiming allegiance to their actual scientific disciplines. And certainly, upon completion of their doctorates, they no longer introduce themselves as biology or political science majors. Although other professions, like social work, counseling, or education, employ evidence-based practices, students who pursue degrees in these professions are not typically trained nor thought of as scientists.

The professional practice of psychology is unique among health care professions in its reliance on the underlying scientific discipline of psychology. Due to the special connection between the basic and applied aspects of our discipline, all professional psychologists are expected not only to master the applied skills of professional practice but also the content of the underlying science of psychology itself. Even accreditation standards acknowledge the importance of gaining competence in knowledge of the breadth of the discipline of psychology among all students in professional training programs through the requirement that all students are exposed to several core domains of knowledge, including biological aspects of behavior, cognitive-affective aspects of behavior; social aspects of behavior; and research methodology, human development, and techniques of data collection (Commission on Accreditation, 2009).

Although psychology's distinction of being both a scientific discipline and an area of professional practice is unique among health professions, and some might claim laudable, this phenomenon is not without complication. Foremost among these complications is the distinct difference between the primary goal of science (i.e., the pursuit of knowledge) and the primary goal of an applied profession (i.e., to define and implement standards of practice to protect the public). In their continuous effort to bring order out of chaos, scientists require free reign regarding pursuit of knowledge, determining which hypotheses to test, selecting appropriate methods for scientific inquiry and data analysis, and determining the extent to which their findings relate to specific theoretical perspectives. In fact, some of the most recognized advances in science (e.g., Darwin's theory of natural selection; Einstein's theory of relativity) resulted from "out of the box" reasoning and observation afforded to those who engage in scientific inquiry. To establish rules and regulations through which science must operate almost seems antithetical to its purpose, and as such scientists typically eschew efforts to set such standards. In contrast, professional practices associated with scientific disciplines aim to set standards, procedures, and principles so that practitioners who purport to engage in professional practice can somehow be categorized into those who possess the competence for practice in a scientifically informed manner and those who do not. Without such standards, practitioners would have free reign to engage in professional activities regardless of whether the practices had a scientific foundation. As such, we might as well return to peddling snake oil, dispensing specially formulated elixirs and tonics, and submerging patients into magnetic troughs!

This tension between scientific freedom and regulated practice is commonly detected in our roles as professional psychologists, and we would argue it is more palpable for those trained in professional psychology because of our training as *both* scientists and practitioners. If we were trained solely as scientists, we could easily reject efforts aimed at regulating what we study and what conclusions we choose to draw in the spirit of maintaining academic freedom. In contrast, if we were trained solely as practitioners, academic freedom would be of lesser concern to us, but we certainly would desire strict guidelines regarding competencies, restrictions, and requirements for entry-level practice to assure that all those who practice are competent to do so. As such, individuals who practice in professions that are not as fundamentally based on a scientific discipline experience this tension to a far lesser extent than the tension experienced by professional psychologists. Balancing academic freedom of the scientist with the desire for adopting uniform training guidelines, the Working Group on Predoctoral Education/Doctoral Training at Arden House was the first group to articulate the required scientific foundations for both health psychologists and clinical health psychologists.

SCIENTIFIC FOUNDATIONS ARTICULATED AT ARDEN HOUSE

Shortly following the inception of the fields of health psychology and behavioral medicine, educators concerned that psychologists possessed the requisite competencies for practicing as health psychologists and clinical health psychologists met at the Arden House Conference to articulate training guidelines. As mentioned in Chapter 1, participants at the conference outlined two training pathways—scientist and professional—now called health psychology and clinical health psychology. Depicted in Table 2.1 are the scientific foundations enumerated by the Arden House participants. For anyone familiar with the current accreditation standards of the Commission on Accreditation of the American Psychological Association, these areas will be easily recognizable. The Arden House participants used the accreditation standards as a launching point for their discussion and consideration of these issues, and through their careful deliberation of these issues, they contributed to the advancement and promulgation of accreditation standards for all of professional psychology.

As shown in Table 2.1, the biopsychosocial model provides the scientific foundation for the discipline of clinical health psychology. Core knowledge and skill-based competencies in the biological, psychological, and social realms are required for all psychologists who desire to call themselves clinical health psychologists. According to Arden House participants and those who continued this tradition during the decades that followed, this biopsychosocial model provides the foundation for both general psychology and health psychology. Regarding competencies in general psychology, the breadth of knowledge assured by the biopsychosocial model typically informs the foundation of the area of professional practice rather narrowly. For instance, in clinical psychology, the biological, psychological, and social bases of behavior focus on elements of these areas of breadth as they relate to psychopathology and the various

TABLE 2.1 **Minimum Knowledge and Skill in Three Areas of Psychology Necessary for Clinical Health Psychology Training**

AREA TRAINING	1. GENERAL PSYCHOLOGY	2. HEALTH PSYCHOLOGY	3. PROFESSIONAL
Knowledge and skill	Statistics Research design Professional issues History and systems	Social bases of health and disease Biological bases of health and disease Psychological bases of health and disease Health policy and organization Health assessment and intervention	Assessment Intervention Consultation Evaluation
3-semester-hour course in each	Biological bases of behavior Social bases of behavior Cognitive and affective bases of behavior Individual differences and psychological bases of behavior		
Practica—professional (min. 400 hours) and research Internship—professional (1 year)			

Note. Students not seeking to provide direct service and/or professional credentialing need not receive training in area 3.

Source: Reprinted from Working Group on Predoctoral Education/Doctoral Training (1983). *Health Psychology, 2* (Supplement), p. 128.

interventions used to treat them. After all, these are the areas that will assist clinical psychologists who work with patients suffering from these various mental disorders. Accordingly, it is fairly common that such courses in their curricula focus almost exclusively on the nervous system, psychopharmacology, theories of psychopathology for mental health conditions, and mental health policy. Clinical or counseling psychologists in training rarely acquire knowledge about other organ systems in the body (e.g., circulatory, respiratory, gastrointestinal systems), drugs that are used to treat general health problems (e.g., anti-arrhythmia, antihypertensive, and antibiotic medications), psychological theories of health conditions that extend beyond mental health, or health policy for both mental health and general physical health conditions. Training in clinical health psychology, in contrast, was conceptualized as extending beyond the nervous system to the other systems of the body and the disorders and diseases that occurred in them. The Arden House participants were keenly aware of this aspect of training, and they added an entire second tier of breadth requirements for students who pursued specialty training in this area (see Area 2 of Table 2.1).

In addition to acquiring knowledge in the biological, psychological, and social bases of health and disease, clinical health psychologists are exposed to the scientific foundation of the practice of psychology, including ethical and legal issues, as well as psychological assessment, intervention, and consultation (see Area 3 in Table 2.1). In fact, Arden House participants distinguished training in health psychology from clinical health psychology using these areas. Students in both types of programs were required to be trained in the breadth of scientific knowledge in both general and health psychology, but only those in clinical health psychology programs were required to obtain hands-on training in these applied areas. Additionally, Arden House participants endorsed the addition of a full-time 1-year internship experience for students in clinical health psychology training programs, much like their peers in clinical, counseling, and school psychology programs.

THE BIOPSYCHOSOCIAL MODEL

The foundation of the science of health psychology and the scientific practice of clinical health psychology is the biopsychosocial model. Initially articulated by Engel in 1977 as a replacement for the biomedical model for comprehending the etiology of disease processes, the biopsychosocial conceptualization broadens the examination of realms of knowledge pertinent to understanding disease and health that were not traditionally taught in medical schools or schools of allied health professions at that time. Although the biomedical model had served us well in uncovering the causes of death and disease in the earlier part of the 20th century (as described in Chapter 1), the chronic conditions responsible for most death and disability occurring during the latter half of the 20th century (e.g., cardiovascular diseases, cancer, respiratory diseases) could not be easily understood or treated without acknowledging behavioral and social factors. Consequently, health providers and health professionals-in-training began to acknowledge the contributions of behavioral and social sciences in addition to the biomedical sciences with which they were already familiar. The recent decision to develop and employ a test of knowledge of psychological, social, and biological foundations of behavior as part of the Medical College Admissions Test (MCAT) indicates that the biopsychosocial model has now been embraced by all health care professions.

Although Engel was the first to call for the broad adoption of the bio-psychosocial model, there were many important precursors to it stemming from the fields of epidemiology and public health, medical sociology and anthropology, and psychosomatic medicine in the earlier years of the 20th century (Friedman & Adler, 2007). In particular, the laboratory investigations of Walter Cannon (1932), Hans Selye (1956), and Neal Miller (1957) all contributed greatly to our knowledge of how the body responds to exposures to environmental stress and how physiological responses to chronic stress damage body organs and systems. A complete description of the biopsychosocial model, as it has been articulated by the specialty of clinical health psychology, is as follows:

> Biological, cognitive, affective, social, and psychological bases of health and disease are bodies of knowledge that, when integrated with knowledge of biological cognitive-affective, social and psychological bases of behavior, constitute the distinctive knowledge base of Clinical Health Psychology. This includes broad understanding of biology, pharmacology, anatomy, human physiology and pathophysiology, and psychoneuroimmunology. Clinical health psychologists also have knowledge of how learning, memory, perception, cognition, and motivation influence health behaviors; are affected by physical illness/injury/disability; and can affect response to and recovery from illness/injury/disability. Knowledge of the impact of social support, culture, physician-patient relationships, health policy, and the organization of health care delivery systems on health and help-seeking is also fundamental, as is knowledge of diversity and minority health issues, individual differences in coping, emotional and behavioral risk factors for disease/injury/disability, developmental issues in health and illness, and the impact of psychopathology on disease, injury, disability and treatment. (American Psychological Association, 2011, p. 10)

Two features of this description are notable. First, the term "biopsycho-social" does not suggest that any of these bodies of knowledge (i.e., bio-logical, psychological, or social bases of health and disease) is conceived as having a greater role than the others in attempting to understand the etiology of disease processes; all are given equal weight and special emphasis is given to their integration (Belar, 2003). In this regard, the biopsychosocial conceptualization fully appreciates the contributions of the biomedical model that preceded it, but it adds to it by adding the important social and behavior factors that had previously been overlooked. Second, Belar (2003) noted an additional feature of the biopsychosocial model, namely that it focuses on maintenance of health in addition to reducing and managing disease processes. As such, clinical health psychologists possess skills in health promotion and prevention of disease in addition to caring for those already afflicted with the disease. As seen in Figure 2.1, it is now largely acknowledged that the absence of symptoms is not equivalent to being healthy. The historically prominent disease model has been replaced with a more comprehensive wellness model. Although many psychological interventions have been devised and shown to be efficacious using the disease model, the addition of this emphasis on prevention assures that we are in the midst of taking what we know regarding interventions and integrating them into community wellness programs and other efforts aimed at health promotion. Specific relaxation strategies devised for use with patients with anxiety disorders and cognitive restructuring strategies devised for use with patients suffering from depressive episodes have their place in these broader wellness initiatives. It goes without saying that with the emergence of advances in technology, more and more of these tools will be available in community settings, at kiosks in malls, Web sites, and as applications for smartphones of whatever devices are developed in the future. Consequently, clinical health psychology has a significant role in assuring the quality and integrity of dissemination of these potentially

FIGURE 2.1 **Continuums of health: the disease and wellness models.**

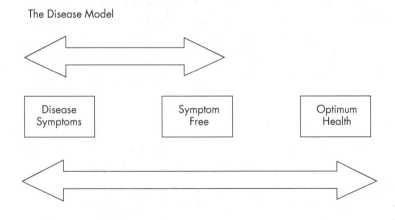

useful tools for implementing changes in health behaviors for patients, their families, or entire communities.

MODELS OF BEHAVIORAL HEALTH CARE PRACTICE

As the Affordable Care Act becomes reality, exciting new opportunities are emerging for clinical health psychologists to function in health care facilities, particularly in primary care settings (i.e., family medicine, internal medicine, pediatrics, obstetrics and gynecology). In particular, because the accountable care organizations that will serve as the backbone of the health care system count on "one-stop" health care provision, behavioral health care is being integrated into primary care clinics and other health provision agencies. This is nothing new for clinical health psychologists who are familiar with working in interdisciplinary health care teams. What is new, and remains to be seen, is that more efficient models of health care will purportedly be encouraged via financial incentives for agencies that deliver the most affordable, evidence-based care. This suggests that the days when clinical health psychologists worked autonomously in health care environments may give way to environments in which behavioral health care is fully integrated with concurrent care for physical ailments. Using an integrative approach, all patients in primary care settings have immediate access to behavioral health care at the time they are receiving medical care. Patients with diabetes mellitus can have glucose levels checked at the same time that exercise adherence plans are implemented and monitored. Children receiving immunization shots can have immediate access to behavioral health care experts armed with the latest information regarding management of acute episodes of pain. Not all clinical health psychologists will operate in primary care settings, but within the evolving health care system, these opportunities are becoming increasingly available to those clinical health psychologists who are interested and have been appropriately trained to work in these kinds of environments.

For those clinical health psychologists who desire to practice in primary care settings, a range of models of provision of behavioral health services in primary care settings have been described by Peek (2011):

- *Specialty Mental Health or Chemical Dependency Care*—behavioral health provider accepts referrals from primary medical provider and provides services at a different mental health facility (e.g., clinic, hospital) with little contact with primary medical provider.

- *Co-located Behavioral Health Care*—behavioral health provider accepts referral from primary medical provider and provides services within the primary care facility with minimal contact with primary medical provider.

- *Coordinated Behavioral Health Care*—behavioral health and primary medical providers practice separately within their respective systems (not necessarily in the same system). Information on mutual patients is shared as needed, but collaboration is limited following the initial referral (Blount, 2003).

- *Collaborative Behavioral Health Care*—behavioral health and primary medical providers collaborate in providing care for patients with regular communication between clinicians.

- *Integrated Behavioral Health Care*—tightly integrated on-site teamwork including both behavioral health and medical providers with a unified care plan for shared patients (Blount, 2003). Because most patients arrive at primary care settings with both behavioral and medical problems, or their medical problem is influenced by behavioral factors (e.g., stress, health behaviors, psychological disorders), cost-effective treatments require access to providers with expertise in both behavioral and medical health provision.

The nature of the model of health service provision chosen will clearly dictate the specific competencies required for functioning in the primary care work environment. Adopting either specialty mental health or co-located models of health care provision will require acquisition of fewer specialized competencies in contrast to those who engage fully in integrated behavioral health care teams. Because of the vast range of problems seen and the brevity of patient appointments in primary care settings, a separate set of competencies has recently been articulated for professional psychologists who desire to seek employment in these settings (McDaniel et al., 2014).

THEORETICAL CONSIDERATIONS AND CONCLUSIONS

Much controversy over training models (e.g., scientist-practitioner vs. practitioner-scholar models) and theoretical perspectives (e.g., psycho-analysis vs. behaviorism) has plagued professional psychology for over a century and, for the most part, has limited advancement in the profession of psychology. As a consequence of our professional disagreements, our credentialing systems and standards of training languish behind all of the other health professions. Professional psychology continues to accept the fact that trainees from nonaccredited training programs can become licensed psychologists and our training community lacks a common vision regarding the specific knowledge- and skill-based competencies that graduates of all training programs should possess prior to entry into the profession. In some respects, clinical health psychology has suffered these negative consequences less than other specialty areas of professional psychology, likely because (1) all clinical health psychologists embrace the biopsychosocial model as the foundation of our practice, and (2) our marriage with the underlying science of health psychology has kept us focused on employing evidence-based psychological assessments and interventions. Regarding the former, Kuhn (1962) argued convincingly that the existence of a shared belief system (i.e., a scientific paradigm) is a characteristic of a mature science; recognizing that the biopsychosocial model possesses paradigmatic status among health and clinical health psychologists, we communicate with one another with a more-or-less common language. Regarding the latter, clinical health psychology's adherence to supporting our professional practice with evidence has permitted us to avoid professional disagreements based solely on theoretical perspectives.

The biopsychosocial model not only provides a foundation for the profession of clinical health psychology but for all contemporary health care professions. The primary diseases that cause death and disability today as well as throughout the latter half of the 20th century reflect problems that cannot be easily explained using the biomedical model. Engagement in healthy lifestyles, coupled with a range of other behaviors (e.g., identifying risk factors for disease, engaging in preventive screening programs, functioning within a social network), are needed to explain the etiology of these chronic conditions more completely. Additionally, behavioral scientists have devised and tested many social or behavioral interventions that have been shown to have positive health benefits and lead to prolonged lives. Although clinical health psychologists are not the only behavioral health professionals who can be trained to provide these services, they are uniquely suited for developing and testing them, training those who use them, and consulting with other members of the health care teams regarding patients with complicated medical presentations. It is up to the trainers comprising professional training programs to assure that the next generation of clinical health psychologists acquires the requisite competencies for effective practice in these types of positions.

THREE

Competency-Based Education in Clinical Health Psychology

For well over a decade, professional psychology has grappled with questions regarding the identification of the fundamental competencies required for entry into practice as a licensed psychologist. The initial effort in articulating these competencies was conducted by the National Council of Schools and Programs of Professional Psychology (Peterson, Peterson, Abrams, & Stricker, 1997), which was followed by a national conference focusing entirely on examining and identifying the competencies required for the professional practice of psychology (see Kaslow, 2004; Kaslow et al., 2004). Building upon these efforts to define competencies in professional psychology, Rodolfa and colleagues (2005) developed a conceptual framework for defining professional competencies across the life span of professional psychologists. Using the geometric configuration of a cube, they described six foundational (reflective practice/self-assessment, scientific knowledge and methods, relationships, ethical and legal standards/policy issues, individual and cultural diversity, and interdisciplinary systems) and six functional competencies (assessment/diagnosis/conceptualization, intervention, consultation, research/evaluation, teaching/supervision, and management/administration) comprising the first two dimensions of the cube. Foundational competencies were conceptualized as the bedrock principles that underlie all we do as professional psychologists, and functional competencies were seen as the activities in which professional psychologists engage on a regular basis. The third dimension of the cube, stage of professional development, depicted foundational and functional competency development over the career of professional psychologists from their training in doctoral programs through the internship experience and postdoctoral period that followed to the ultimate level of being continuously educated as lifelong learners. The distinction between foundational and functional competencies has served the profession well until now and provided the foundation for considerable work in the articulation of professional competencies (including the organization of the remaining chapters of this book and others in this series). However, as we will describe later, there are emerging concerns about this artificial dichotomy between what practitioners "know" from science and what they "do" in practice.

The most comprehensive effort in defining competencies in professional psychology was conducted by the Competency Benchmarks Work Group (Fouad et al., 2009), an assembly of educators representing all levels of the entire training community. Using the cube model as a guide, this work group fully defined the specific competencies associated with seven foundational and eight functional competency areas outlined in prior work in the field (depicted in the left column of Table 3.1). Additionally, each competency area was carefully defined by describing the essential components of the knowledge/skills/attitudes that comprised it as well as providing several examples of observable behavioral anchors of what the specific competency would look like in practice. Three distinct levels of behavioral anchors were created by the work group to reflect competencies at critical transition periods of professional development: (1) readiness for practicum, (2) readiness for internship, and (3) readiness for entry into professional practice. To assist educators and training programs in assessing competencies of their students, a competency assessment toolkit that outlined various methods for measuring the acquisition of competencies was published in the same volume (Kaslow et al., 2009). Together, these articles reflect the evolution of defining professional competency acquisition as it occurs throughout doctoral and internship training as well as providing the training community with useful tools for assessing student progress in their development as professional psychologists. Although the efforts of the Competency Benchmarks Work Group were aimed at identifying the competencies required for all professional psychologists (i.e., clinical, counseling, and school psychologists), specialty areas began using these documents to launch comparable efforts to articulate the professional competencies associated with their distinctive specialty practices.

THE TEMPE SUMMIT ON EDUCATION AND TRAINING
IN CLINICAL HEALTH PSYCHOLOGY

As described in Chapters 1 and 2, the Arden House Conference was an extremely influential meeting with respect to delineating training

TABLE 3.1 **Foundational and Functional Competencies Identified by the Competency Benchmarks Work Group, the Health Service Psychology Education Collaborative (HSPEC), and the Inter-Organizational Work Group on Competencies for Primary Care Psychology Practice**

BENCHMARK COMPETENCIES	HSPEC COMPETENCIES	PRIMARY CARE COMPETENCIES
	FOUNDATIONAL COMPETENCIES	
	Professionalism	**Professionalism**
Professionalism	Professional values and attitudes	Professional values and attitudes
Reflective practice, self-assessment, and self-care	Reflective practice, self-assessment, and self-care	Reflective practice/ self-assessment/self-care
Individual and cultural diversity	Individual and cultural diversity	Individual, cultural, and disciplinary diversity
Ethical legal standards and policy	Ethical legal standards and policy	Ethics in primary care
Relationships	**Relational: Interpersonal Skills and Communication**	**Relationships**
		Interprofessionalism
		Building and sustaining Relationships in primary care
	Science*	**Science***
Scientific knowledge and methods	Scientific knowledge and methods	Science related to the biopsychosocial model
	Systems*	**Systems***
Interdisciplinary systems	Interdisciplinary/interprofessional systems	Interdisciplinary systems
	FUNCTIONAL COMPETENCIES	
	Applications	**Application**
	Evidence-based practice	Practice management
Assessment	Assessment	Assessment
Intervention	Intervention	Intervention
Consultation	Consultation	Consultation
	Science*	**Science***
Research/evaluation	Research/evaluation	Research/evaluation
	Education	**Education**
Supervision	Supervision	Supervision
Teaching	Teaching	Teaching
	Systems*	**Systems***
Management/administration	Professional leadership development	Leadership/administration
Advocacy	Advocacy (local, state, and national)	Advocacy

*Science and Systems clusters contain both foundational and functional competencies according to HSPEC and the Inter-Organizational Work Group on Competencies in Primary Care Psychology Practice.
Sources: Competency lists from Fouad et al. (2009); Health Service Psychology Education Collaborative (2013); and Inter-Organizational Work Group on Competencies in Primary Care Psychology (2013).

guidelines for the sciences of health psychology and clinical health psychology. The recommendations from the Arden House Conference, reaffirmed at the Riverfront Conference, continue to serve as the fundamental guidelines for training in health psychology and clinical health psychology. As the area of specialty training became aware of the growing momentum in defining competencies within the broader profession of psychology (e.g., the Benchmark Competencies Working Group) and recognizing that the training guidelines devised at Arden House (see Table 2.1 in Chapter 2) were in need of updating, clinical health psychology became the first specialty to tackle the task of defining the specialty competencies needed in order to call oneself a clinical health psychologist. The initial step in this direction occurred during the Tempe Summit on Education and Training in Clinical Health Psychology in 2007 (see France et al., 2008).

Sharing responsibilities in planning this meeting, Christopher France, Kevin Masters, and Sonia Suchday approached the Board of Directors of Division 38 (Health Psychology) of the American Psychological Association (APA) to support an educational summit to revise and update the standards of graduate curricula and training in clinical health psychology and bring the work of Arden House into the 21st century. Two goals of the meeting were identified: "(1) bring interested parties together to begin a dialogue on issues of curriculum and training, and (2) explore the possibility of establishing a standing Council of Clinical Health Psychology Training Directors" (France et al., 2008, p. 575). The Board approved the proposal to plan this meeting in December of 2005, assuming sufficient interest could be generated. In 2006, representatives from programs that conducted training in clinical health psychology at all levels were contacted and endorsed the idea, expressing a willingness to participate in this effort.

Considering a balance of participants across program level and type, geographic representation, and diversity of race, ethnicity, and gender, 20 participants were selected to attend the Tempe Summit on Education and Training in Clinical Health Psychology on March 1–2, 2007. Conference participants familiarized themselves with the existing literature on defining competencies prior to the meeting, including a preliminary rendering of the Benchmarks document. Additional readings pertinent to the practice of clinical health psychology were provided as well.

Following introductory remarks by Dr. Cynthia Belar, the remaining portion of the conference involved small group work aimed at defining the functional competencies for the specialty practice of clinical health psychology. Conference participants were divided into three groups, with one group assigned to work on defining competencies in assessment/diagnosis/case conceptualization and intervention (chaired by Kevin Larkin), one group assigned to work on competencies in research/evaluation and consultation (chaired by Timothy Smith), and the final group assigned to work on supervision/teaching and management/administration (chaired by Elizabeth Klonoff). Although a complete description of the meeting and its outcomes were reported by France et al. (2008), a synopsis is provided in the following paragraphs.

FOUNDATIONAL COMPETENCIES IN CLINICAL HEALTH PSYCHOLOGY

Upon review of the Competency Benchmarks document, Tempe Summit participants fairly quickly concluded that all of the foundational and functional competencies contained in that document were equally applicable to the practice of clinical health psychology (France et al., 2008). Four foundational competency areas were identified, however, that were unique to the practice of clinical health psychology and represented competency areas that clinical health psychologists acquired above and beyond those enumerated in the Benchmarks document. First, engagement in reflective self-assessment regarding one's degree of competency for working in health systems was considered a unique foundational competency of clinical health psychologists. Because of the diversity of positions clinical health psychologists hold in addition to the range of settings in which they provide services (e.g., primary care settings, pain clinics, public health departments, cardiac rehabilitation programs, cancer centers), it became quite clear to Tempe participants that not every clinical health psychologist was competent to practice in every health care setting. Consequently, competency in self-assessment of knowledge, skills, and attitudes to practice in a specific health care environment was considered an entry-level credential for all clinical health psychologists. Further elaboration of this area of competency occurs in Chapter 5.

The second foundational competency area unique to clinical health psychology involves basing our practice on the biopsychosocial model using the best available evidence and by considering the individual differences, values, and preferences of the patients we treat. As mentioned in Chapter 2, in contrast to other areas of professional psychology, clinical health psychology was founded on the biopsychosocial model, and this conceptual paradigm continues to serve our profession well as a distinctive knowledge-based area of competence.

The third foundational competency area identified by Tempe Summit participants as being distinctive to clinical health psychology was the reliance on interdisciplinary collaboration in providing care to patients as well as implementing practice-based research. Although more thoroughly discussed in Chapter 7, clinical health psychologists do not operate in isolation. Because we work with health care professionals from numerous educational backgrounds, it is critical that we acquire foundational skills in developing effective and meaningful interprofessional relationships.

Finally, the last foundational area of competence uniquely associated with the practice of clinical health psychology was comprehension of the ethical and legal standards specifically associated with the health care system. In contrast to psychology departments and counseling centers, there are several ethical and legal issues clinical health psychologists confront on a weekly if not daily basis (e.g., making end-of-life decisions, determining capacity to make informed consent for medical treatments, determining who will or who will not be approved for receiving medical treatments). Consequently, we need to be well prepared to respond appropriately when confronting situations in which our ethical principles are challenged by the differing ethical principles of other health care professionals and the broader health care system. These foundational competencies will be discussed further in Chapter 9.

FUNCTIONAL COMPETENCIES IN CLINICAL HEALTH PSYCHOLOGY

The bulk of the time at the Tempe Summit was devoted to articulating functional competencies of entry-level clinical health psychologists. Six tables of both knowledge-based and skill-based competencies were drafted during this 2-day meeting in the following areas: assessment, intervention, consultation, research, supervision-training, and management-administration. These functional competencies were derived from the existing literature dating back to the Arden House conference, updated to reflect the contemporary practice of clinical health psychology, and published in 2008 (France et al., 2008). Attesting to the quality of the work done at Tempe, all of the items generated at this meeting continue to be included in the most recent listing of competencies for specialty practice in clinical health psychology. Because each of these functional competency areas is covered in detail in Part III of this book, no further description of them will be offered here.

One additional outcome of the Tempe Summit warrants mention. Although the Council of Health Psychology comprised of directors of all training programs in this specialty area was established shortly after the Arden House meeting for purposes of regular contact among educators involved in health psychology training programs, the council had become functionally dormant over the decade prior to the Tempe Summit. In their wisdom, Tempe Summit participants believed that a reinvigorated council should emerge with the primary goal of facilitating an ongoing discussion and collaboration of educators involved in training clinical health psychologists in doctoral, internship, and postdoctoral fellowship programs. Based upon the vision of those who participated in the Tempe Summit, the training council was revived and reincorporated under the new name of the Council of Clinical Health Psychology Training Programs (CCHPTP, acronym pronounced "chip-tip").

WORK OF CCHPTP IN DEFINING CLINICAL
HEALTH PSYCHOLOGY COMPETENCIES

CCHPTP was incorporated as a nonprofit educational agency in 2007, just a few short months after the Tempe Summit. Since that time, CCHPTP has been the vehicle through which ongoing work in defining competencies in clinical health psychology has been done. As shown in Table 3.2, CCHPTP has conducted annual midwinter meetings every year since 2008. In the spirit of Arden House and the Tempe Summit, each meeting is a working meeting that aims to capture information from the educational community and synthesize it into meaningful documents that inform the broader community regarding guidelines for training the next generation of clinical health psychologists. Typically, only a few presentations are made and the bulk of the meeting involves small group work focused on specific assignments designed to move the specialty area forward in articulating the distinctive competencies that define clinical health psychology. Much of the work conducted at CCHPTP meetings has been published and has served to move the specialty of clinical health psychology forward (Kerns, Berry, Frantsve, & Linton, 2009; Larkin, 2009; Masters, France, & Thorn, 2009; Nash & Larkin, 2012; Nash, McKay, Vogel, & Masters, 2012; Nicholas & Stern, 2011).

Although it is beyond the scope of this chapter to provide a detailed account of all that occurred during these seven meetings, a brief overview is warranted to describe the sequence of events that took place that led to the creation and dissemination of competencies required for practice as a clinical health psychologist. The inaugural meeting of CCHPTP in San Antonio introduced the entire specialty area to the work from the Tempe Summit.

TABLE 3.2 **Themes of the Annual Midwinter Meetings of the Council of Clinical Health Psychology Training Programs (CCHPTP)**

YEAR	THEME	LOCATION
2008	New Directions: Competencies in Clinical Health Psychology	San Antonio, TX
2009	Assessing Competencies in Clinical Health Psychology	Albuquerque, NM
2010	Clinical Health Psychology: Just When Does Specialized Training Begin?	Orlando, FL
2011	Training in Integrated Behavioral Health Care in Primary Care Settings: Emerging Roles for Clinical Health Psychologists	Nashville, TN
2012	Primary Care Psychology: Is Training in Clinical Health Psychology Necessary?	San Diego, CA
2013	Promoting Quality in the Profession of Clinical Health Psychology	Austin, TX
2014	The Future of Clinical Health Psychology Training: Opportunities and Challenges	New Orleans, LA

Participants reviewed the lists of competencies derived in Tempe and considered each entry with the goal of obtaining input from the broader community of clinical health psychologists. The work of the Tempe Summit was warmly received, and while some minor modifications were made by meeting participants (see Masters, France, & Thorn, 2009), the competencies were largely endorsed by the field and plans were made to disseminate the resulting product to educators and students comprising training programs in clinical health psychology. The following year, CCHPTP highlighted presentations on state-of-the-art methods for assessing competencies and meeting participants developed matrices of optimal methods for measuring the various CCHPTP competencies among students at all levels of training (i.e., doctoral program, internship, and postdoctoral fellowship). Using the Joint Conference of Training Councils in Psychology in 2010 as a venue, the next CCHPTP meeting focused on categorizing the specialty competencies into those that were typically acquired during the doctoral training years, those that were normally developed on internship, and those that were generally obtained during postdoctoral study. Not surprisingly, in all cases the knowledge-based competencies identified in Tempe 3 years earlier preceded the acquisition of skill-based competencies in the normal sequence of the developing clinical health psychologist.

Recognizing the growing interest among clinical health psychologists in the practice of psychology in primary care settings, CCHPTP focused on brainstorming and generating lists of competencies needed to practice in these fast-paced health care environments during the fourth and fifth annual midwinter meetings. Following informational presentations by clinical health psychologists who worked in primary care settings, significant progress was made in developing a list of competencies that would serve the field well in distinguishing those who are competent to work in primary care settings from those who are not (Nash, McKay, Vogel, & Masters, 2012). During the most recent CCHPTP meetings, the field returned to refining the list of competencies for practice in clinical health psychology, by incorporating the recent work of the Inter-Organizational Work Group on Competencies for Primary Care Psychology Practice (APA, 2013) and the Health Service Psychology Education Collaborative (HSPEC).

INTERORGANIZATIONAL WORK GROUP ON COMPETENCIES FOR PRIMARY CARE PSYCHOLOGY PRACTICE

Recognizing the unique skill set that was needed for practicing in primary care settings that was evident in the literature, during recent discussions at the CCHPTP meetings, and through conversations with practitioners functioning in these settings, Suzanne Bennett Johnson, president of the American Psychological Association in 2012, assembled a group of psychologists from numerous professional organizations to create a definitive list of essential competencies for the practice of primary care psychology. Included were representatives from APA Division 20 (Adult Development and Aging), APA Division 38 (Health Psychology), APA Division 54 (Society of Pediatric Psychology), the Association of Psychologists in Academic Health Centers, the Collaborative Family Healthcare Association, CCHPTP, the Society of Behavioral Medicine, the Society of Teachers of Family Medicine, and the VA Psychology Training Council.

Under the direction of Susan McDaniels, an aggressive time line was adopted that led this group to read and consider all relevant literature before breaking into smaller groups to draft lists of primary care competencies in the following areas: science, systems, professionalism, relationships, applications (including practice management, assessment, intervention, and consultation), and education (see right column of Table 3.1). Following the format adopted by the Competency Benchmarks Work Group, careful attention was paid to defining the essential components of each competency as well as creating several behavioral examples of what each competency would look like in the daily practice of primary care psychology. The final document was made available on the APA Web site in March of 2013 (see http://www.apa.org/ed/resources/competencies-practice.pdf).

HEALTH SERVICE PSYCHOLOGY EDUCATION COLLABORATIVE

At approximately the same time that the Inter-Organizational Work Group was meeting and discussing competencies for primary care psychology, another group comprised of representatives from the Council of Chairs of Training Councils (CCTC), the Board of Educational Affairs (BEA) at APA, and the Council of Graduate Departments of Psychology (COGDOP) met to examine the Competency Benchmarks document with the goal of devising a standard set of competencies that were expected of any psychologist claiming to provide health services to the public. With an eye toward the future of professional psychology, this group was charged with devising a blueprint that would guide the field forward in its effort to become an important and recognized health service profession (see Health Service Psychology Education Collaborative, 2013). In contrast to other health professions, professional psychology has suffered from the fact that numerous models of training existed and no standard set of competencies had been defined for program credentialing and the licensing of individual practitioners. To assure integrity of any health profession, professional standards are needed to define competencies that every health care provider exhibits, and guidelines are required to define the educational courses and related experiences required in order to assure that only competent health providers enter the profession. Furthermore, the existence of nonaccredited programs in professional psychology that graduate students who are eligible for licensure in most states and provinces is a blemish on the profession that prevents us from gaining the stature psychology could possess if the only route to becoming a health service provider was by attending an accredited training program. With the vision of improving our stature among the health professions in mind, the HSPEC focused considerable energy on articulating the essential competencies required for practicing as health service providers.

It is important to note that the term "health service provider" was adopted by HSPEC instead of "professional psychologist" based on the recognition that not all "professional psychologists" provide health services (e.g., educational psychologists or industrial-organizational psychologists), and that credentialing via licensing is only needed among those who provide health services. Consequently, the blueprint document developed by HSPEC pertains only to graduates who desire to become health service providers and the programs that claim to train them. It should also be noted that health services refers to all types of health, including the services of psychologists who only work with patients with mental health problems as well as those who only work with specific types of medical patients. The term "health service provision" should not be confused with clinical health psychology. They are not synonyms. While all clinical health psychologists are trained as health service providers and possess the requisite competencies outlined in this book, all health service providers are not clinical health psychologists and should not attempt to assume positions in clinical health psychology settings without the proper training.

It is probably not surprising that the competencies defined by the HSPEC closely parallel those depicted in the earlier Competency Benchmarks document (see the middle column of Table 3.1). Organized into clusters of competencies on Professionalism, Science, Relationships, Application, Education/Training, and Systems, the HSPEC competencies reflect the most succinct listing of competencies to date. Although no attention was paid to defining behavioral anchors for each competency area by the HSPEC, the Blueprint document is destined to serve the profession well in aligning psychology among all existing health professions.

OVERVIEW OF THE REMAINDER OF THIS BOOK

Because draft documents of the HSPEC (2013) and the Competencies for Psychology Practice in Primary Care document from the Inter-Organizational Work Group on Competencies in Primary Care Psychology Practice (2013) were available for participants of the sixth CCHPTP meeting, a primary goal of the Austin meeting was to update the existing clinical health psychology competencies using the format and structure being disseminated by the most contemporary work on competencies depicted in Table 3.1. To these ends, working groups were constructed and each was assigned a cluster of competencies to review using (a) the Competency Benchmarks document (Fouad et al., 2009), (b) the Blueprint document of the HSPEC (2013), and (c) the Competencies for Psychology in Primary Care (2013). Existing clinical health psychology competencies from earlier lists (France et al., 2008; Masters, France, & Thorn, 2009) were restructured to match the formats of these other contemporary documents. To make the list more useful for trainees and training programs that use them for purposes of tracking competency acquisition, essential components were defined for entry into practice and behavioral anchors were derived as examples of each area of competence. This work by CCHPTP provides the most current description of the specialty competencies in clinical health psychology and serves as the foundation for the remaining chapters of this book.

The Competency Benchmarks document (Fouad et al., 2009) is structured around the foundational and functional competencies that were identified by earlier definitions of entry-level competencies (i.e., Rodolfa et al., 2005). The more recent works by the HSPEC and the Inter-Organizational Work Group have deviated somewhat from this approach. This modification has resulted in part from a growing recognition that distinguishing "foundational" from "functional" competencies implies that they can be acquired separately. In other words, to take this position might suggest that one could learn *how* to implement an intervention (a functional competency) without knowing *why* or *how* the intervention was derived (a foundational competency). In fact, this has occurred with many interventions initially developed by clinical health psychologists but now offered by social workers or individuals working in public health settings. Clinical health psychology has prided itself on the success of the interventions it has developed, and these interventions for such health concerns as smoking, excess weight, and physical sedentariness have been disseminated to many environments and have become part of organized wellness programs. When these interventions are applied to typical patients who present without any complications and who are highly motivated to change, indeed practitioners with varying levels of education can implement these types of "manualized" treatments successfully. However, if the patient is atypical, has other diagnoses or problems complicating the clinical picture, or does not seem to be responding to the treatment, the provider needs to know and understand the scientific bases underlying the treatment so that it can be modified to be effective. Typically, responding appropriately in these cases involves a close integration between knowledge and understanding of the scientific "foundational" competencies underlying the treatment and the "functional" skill-based competencies associated with treatment delivery. Thus, for doctoral-level clinical health psychologists, there is no clear separation between foundational and functional competencies, and for practical purposes, this means that science and practice are inextricably intertwined. Nonetheless, for the rest of this volume, we have elected to utilize the distinction between foundational and functional competencies in order to allow for an easy comparison between the competencies required for all professional psychologists and the competencies required for specialty practice.

In Part II of this book, six foundational competency areas (professionalism, reflective practice/self-assessment/self-care, scientific knowledge and methods, relationships, individual and cultural diversity, and ethical and legal standards/policy) will be presented in detail. Next, in Part III of this book, six areas of functional competency (assessment, intervention, consultation, research, teaching/supervision, and management/administration/advocacy) will be presented. In the chapters comprising both Parts II and III, attention is paid to both describing how essential competencies identified in the Competency Benchmarks document would appear in clinical health psychology settings (i.e., behavioral anchors for clinical health psychology) as well as delineating professional competencies unique to the practice of clinical health psychology that were not included in prior efforts to list the benchmark competencies that applied to all professional psychologists. In brief, each chapter describes how benchmark competencies might look in the practice of clinical health psychology *and* enumerates new competencies distinctive to the specialty area of clinical health psychology.

PART II

Foundational Competencies of
Clinical Health Psychology

FOUR

Professionalism as a Clinical Health Psychologist

Professional values and ethics serve as the foundation for individuals aspiring to enter any type of profession, including those with ambitions to work in positions in health care, teaching, law, pastoral ministry, engineering, and technology settings. Because professions are self-regulating bodies, ones that might have emerged without paying attention to defining standards of professional behavior, values, and ethics would have been very short-lived professions. Members of a given profession share the responsibility of acquiring a common set of competencies and behaviors through which they distinguish themselves from members of other professions and present themselves to the public in a way that assures integrity and accountability. We all have heard instances of damage that a rogue member of a profession created for the entire group when appropriate standards for professional behavior were not upheld.

Although the terms "occupation" and "profession" are often treated synonymously in dictionaries and in colloquial conversation, it is more accurate to consider a profession as an occupational subtype that requires acquisition of advanced competencies and pays considerable attention to credentialing and oversight. To address the unique characteristics regarding which occupations can be categorized as professions, Cruess, Johnston, and Cruess (2004) developed the following comprehensive definition:

> A profession is an occupation whose core element is work based
> upon the mastery of a complex body of knowledge and skills. It
> is a vocation in which knowledge of some department of science

or learning or the practice of an art founded upon it is used in the service of others. Its members are governed by codes of ethics and profess a commitment to competence, integrity and morality, altruism, and the promotion of the public good within their domain. These commitments form the basis of a social contract between a profession and society, which in return grants the profession a monopoly over the use of its knowledge base, the right to considerable autonomy in practice and the privilege of self-regulation. Professions and their members are accountable to those served and to society. (p. 74)

Several components of this definition warrant mention. First, a profession is based on "mastery of a complex body of knowledge and skills" that is based upon scientific foundations (see Chapter 6). This certainly describes the profession of psychology in general and its specific application in clinical health psychology. Accreditation criteria for training programs in professional psychology require broad coverage of the scientific foundations of the discipline of psychology in addition to covering the range of knowledge and skills in the specialty area of practice. Second, it is important to note that workers characterized as professionals are employed to directly serve others. To do so, occupations characterized as professions develop ethical codes, practice standards, and credentialing systems to assure all within their realm possess the necessary competencies to serve needs of the public. Finally, this definition recognizes that professions are granted autonomy to regulate themselves, a critical distinction between occupations that can and cannot be categorized as professions. Although Cruess et al. devised this definition by considering its application to the profession of medicine, it can be easily extended to describe the profession of psychology, and clinical health psychology in particular.

The importance of professionalism as a foundational competency was recognized by the Competency Benchmarks Work Group (Fouad et al., 2009), who identified five domains of professionalism: integrity-honesty; deportment; accountability; concern for the welfare of others; and professional identity. Because clinical health psychology is a recognized specialty area in professional psychology, there is no doubt that these domains apply to individuals whose professional paths have led or are leading them to careers in this specialty area. However, like other specialty areas, there are encounters or situations that clinical health psychologists or clinical health psychologists in training experience that call for the elaboration of competencies in professionalism unique to clinical health psychology.

Using the Competency Benchmarks Document (Fouad et al., 2009) as a guide, we will address each domain of professionalism with specific reference to the science and practice of clinical health psychology.

INTEGRITY-HONESTY

Politicians and used car salespersons are often seen as two peas in the same pod. One has only to glimpse the mistrust people have in their elected governmental representatives or the salesperson attempting to get them to buy the lemon on the lot to realize the magnitude of problems encountered when an occupation loses its reputation for integrity. It goes without saying that the profession of clinical health psychology is based upon the integrity we all share as clinical health psychologists and clinical health psychologists in training. As a group, we typically enjoy the positive appraisals by others for our integrity and ability to rely on empirical evidence to support our positions.

As clinical health psychologists, it is not uncommon to encounter situations in which patients as well as other health care providers hope we can provide answers to pressing clinical questions when we simply are unable to do so. For example, patients with cancer might ask whether participation in psychological interventions will help prevent cancer cells from metastasizing, or patients with coronary heart disease and depression might wonder whether treatment for their depression will decrease their risk for subsequent cardiac problems. Although we might consider endorsing these commonly held beliefs to encourage engagement in psychological interventions, doing so makes us no different than politicians or used car salespersons. Competency in this domain requires us to base our assertions upon evidence and to deliver information to the patient or health care team accurately but sensitively. Sometimes that means we need to say we simply do not have sufficient information to answer the question.

Defining integrity-honesty is fairly simple. Essentially, integrity is the label we assign to the trait of consistently matching verbal behaviors with either observable behaviors or some other externally verifiable data. Integrity is enhanced, for example, when the clinical health psychologist informs a patient he or she will visit the patient the next day, and he or she actually makes time to stop by the patient's hospital room the next day. Or when the clinical health psychologist informs a patient that there is evidence that progressive muscle relaxation is an effective treatment for insomnia, and this is verified through a literature search. Although defining integrity may be easy, living it consistently on a day-to-day basis can be challenging. This is true of all professionals, but it is particularly problematic in today's health care environments, where multitasking is the norm and taking shortcuts is a regularity that is often encouraged or rewarded by health care payers.

There are some unique situations regarding integrity-honesty that confront clinical health psychologists. For example, patients or family members of patients occasionally misunderstand the role of the clinical health psychologist and believe he or she is medically trained. This is understandable, given that the clinical health psychologist is referred to as a doctor and is working in a medical environment. In these circumstances, it is very important that the clinical health psychologist correct this misperception promptly, but sensitively; otherwise he or she runs the risk of losing a good bit of credibility when expected to perform tasks that require medical training (e.g., prescribing medicines, intubating a patient, or cleaning an infusion port). In these types of conversations, it is important to draw the distinction between those who are doctors and those who are physicians. This approach permits clinical health psychologists to retain the doctoral-level credentials they rightfully earned while distinguishing them from professionals trained in medicine or other related medical professions.

Another task that confronts clinical health psychologists from time to time is the request to conduct a presurgical psychological evaluation, typically for the purpose of screening appropriate candidates for surgery. In this role, the clinical health psychologist is really not working for the patient, but instead he or she is working for the medical treatment team. Failure to communicate this role clearly to the patient can result in significant problems, particularly in cases where the results of the evaluation include recommending a surgery the patient very much wants to have done not be performed. In this regard, a solid informed consent process is essential to maintaining integrity prior to conducting the evaluation.

Finally, clinical health psychologists, because of their unique roles on medical treatment teams, are often asked for their input on decisions that fall outside their boundaries of competence. Recommendations regarding appropriateness of pharmacotherapy come to mind as a very common occurrence. It is important to develop an appropriately worded way to "dodge this bullet" and to use it consistently; otherwise one can easily shape the team to employ the clinical health psychologist as an unofficial psychiatric consultant and to be practicing outside one's area of competence. Relatedly, as a mental health professional, one may be requested to assist the team in making end-of-life decisions. Although the interpersonal skills of a clinical health psychologist may facilitate these sorts of discussions, it is important to remember that the decisions are to be made by the patient and family, not team members. In fact, the presence of clinical health psychologists with specialty training in end-of-life decision making could be assets to a hospital staff as they attempt to navigate this difficult time in their work with patients.

DEPORTMENT

Deportment refers to professional conduct, including appropriate attire and personal hygiene as well as appropriate communication and use of language. It goes without saying that first impressions count, and patients and other professionals encountered in health care settings learn a lot during their very first interaction with the clinical health psychologist on the team; in fact, in these times of rapidly expanding settings and opportunities for clinical health psychologists, the first impression the initial clinical health psychologist makes in a setting often sets the stage for the success of those who follow. Additionally, in this time of rapid advancement in technology and digital communication, professional conduct also extends to how clinical health psychologists portray themselves through electronic means, including e-mail messages, Web pages, voicemail greetings, blogs, or social networking sites.

There is a significant literature that demonstrates the importance of attire on how an individual is perceived (e.g., Dacy & Brodsky, 1992; Gosling & Standen, 1998). Put simply, if we want to be perceived professionally and be respected by others around us in the work environment, we need to dress professionally. Unfortunately, standards for what is considered appropriate professional attire are not easily located, and they are inconsistently applied across various professions and settings. For example, pediatricians may have different standards for professional attire in clinical settings than cardiologists, and child care teachers have different standards for attire than physicians. There are certain types of clothing that would be considered inappropriate in any professional setting, including clothing that reveals one's underwear, is too form-fitting or revealing, or portrays offensive words or pictures. In many environments, "offensive" can include visual demonstrations of support for various political causes; types of advertising; or even clothing that shows support for athletic teams, movies, or singing groups. Similarly, shorts, low-cut blouses/shirts/sweaters, beachwear, and tank, halter, and midriff tops are never appropriate when functioning in a professional capacity, nor is wearing flip-flops. In most hospital or clinic settings, in fact, wearing open-toed footwear of any type is forbidden. The typical attire for most health care settings where clinical health psychologists work ranges from categories of business-casual to professional. However, one must be cautious when purchasing clothing for a professional wardrobe, because the range of what is called business-casual or even professional can be quite broad across various clothing establishments.

As clinical health psychologists often work in settings alongside members of other health care disciplines, aspects of attire unique to this setting warrant mention. It is well known that other health care providers wear white coats in clinical or hospital environments. For example, in medical education, donning the white coat demarcates the important transition from learning based in the laboratory to applied clinical work. Indeed, there is some empirical work demonstrating that wearing a white coat endows physicians with increased levels of perceived authority and expertise (Brase & Richmond, 2004). To achieve comparable status in the health care setting, the question of whether clinical health psychologists should wear white coats must be considered. Although donning the white coat may enhance perceived status of the provider, it could be argued that clinical health psychologists' expertise and contributions to the team come largely through their unique training in both science and practice and in their ability to develop rapport with a range of patients. There is no evidence that wearing a white coat facilitates either of these roles. Indeed, nowhere in the training of clinical health psychologists do we make the transition from laboratory learning to clinic-based learning. As clinical health psychologists, we are required to integrate these two facets of our upbringing throughout our training and professional lives. That said, there may be specific instances in which donning a white coat may be important (e.g., assessing a patient for or studying the phenomenon of white coat hypertension; supervising [precepting] medical students or residents on how to improve doctor–patient communication), but for the most part, the daily functions of a clinical health psychologist are not facilitated by wearing a white coat. Relatedly, wearing hospital scrubs is not likely to enhance the credibility of a clinical health psychologist engaging in his or her profession. However, there are instances when this type of attire may actually need to be worn. For example, if the clinical health psychologist is asked to assist with a medical procedure for an anxious patient, he or she might find himself or herself wearing scrubs or even scrubbing and gowning to enter a surgical suite from time to time. Likewise, visiting an immunocompromised patient will require wearing a hospital mask and full body gown, regardless of the profession of the team member working with the patient.

The type of clothing one chooses to wear is not the only aspect of personal grooming that falls into the category of professional conduct. Professionals in clinical health psychology need to be attentive to careful selection of appropriate styles of haircuts, hair color, and location of body art and piercings. Although individuals certainly have the right to express how they adorn and display their bodies, they need to be aware of how these choices may influence their portrayals as professionals and patients' reactions to them as professionals. When functioning as a clinical health psychologist in a health care environment, it is best to select more conservative styles of haircuts, to use naturally occurring hair colors, and to cover body art and piercings.

Professional conduct also pertains to the language one chooses to use. Although use of colloquialisms and slang terms can be useful in relating to some patients, use of degrading terms, discriminatory slurs, and foul language is always considered inappropriate. This applies to electronic forms of communication as well as oral statements. Electronic communication is particularly vulnerable; because anything stated on the Internet is potentially accessible to anyone who bothers to look, electronic communications must be carefully crafted and transmitted. Many health care systems will regulate how and to whom you may communicate electronically (including adherence to standards stipulated by HIPAA), and it is important for clinical health psychologists and clinical health psychologists-in-training to abide by these policies. As a general rule, if you would not want the communication ending up on the front page of the newspaper, it is better left unsent.

Proximity to the patient and touch are features of deportment that impact clinical health psychologists differently than other types of professional psychologists, and often very differently than other members of the health care team. Most training as professional psychologists involves face-to-face interaction at a comfortable distance from one another in an office or clinic setting. Clinical child psychologists have long recognized that modifications in these general rules of proximity and touch are crucial to their success in interacting with a child. It probably goes without saying that if you cannot envision yourself sitting at a child-sized table and coloring with a child, you would be a very poor clinical child psychologist. The same can be said when working with a hospitalized patient—only in this type of environment, the patient is typically lying prone in bed or on an examination table and the clinical health psychologist is standing in the room. The patient may be in pajamas or a hospital gown rather than the street clothes worn in more traditional mental health settings. Recognizing the discomfort associated with this degree of proximity, clinical health psychologists may find themselves adopting atypical positions for ongoing interaction, including crouching next to the bed to make eye contact or even sitting on the edge of the bed when there are a number of medical devices taking up floor space. Touching the patient (e.g., holding the back of his or her hand) can be very therapeutic in many of these situations, particularly during visits in which bad news is being conveyed. Likewise, it would not be necessarily inappropriate for a clinical health psychologist to hold the hand of a patient who is dying or undergoing a painful medical procedure.

ACCOUNTABILITY

President Harry Truman had a carving prominently sitting on his desk in the Oval Office that said, "The buck stops here." This attitude reflects the key attribute of the component of professionalism called accountability. Clinical health psychologists who demonstrate competence in accountability accept credit humbly for services well done and do not lay blame on others or become defensive when services they are providing are not operating well. Basically, two attributional errors of accountability can be made: (a) accepting credit for something not earned or deserved; and (b) deflecting responsibility for errors in which one was responsible. Although Truman's credo focused on the second type of error, the first type can be equally problematic for establishing oneself professionally. The bottom line is that professional accountability involves appropriately and accurately accepting responsibility for one's actions (or inactions). This is particularly important when functioning as part of a health care team; in those instances it is better that the entire team takes the credit for successes (or blame for failures) in order to continue to build relationships among those working together.

Some other core features of being accountable include demonstrating a good work ethic (i.e., working until the job is completed, not ending prematurely just because the end of your typical work day has occurred), having effective organizational skills, operating within the boundaries of one's competence, and completing assigned tasks and procedures in a timely fashion. Like other professions, clinical health psychology is rarely practiced in isolation. Most clinical health psychologists work in health care systems alongside other health care providers, each with their designated roles and responsibilities. The clinical health psychologist is often the primary person on the team responsible for addressing the emotional, psychological, and behavioral needs of patients being seen by the team. As such, a competent professional accepts these responsibilities, completes assessments and interventions expeditiously, and anticipates problems the team may encounter before they occur.

CONCERN FOR THE WELFARE OF OTHERS

A core ethical principle of psychologists is "respect for people's rights and dignity" (American Psychological Association, 2002). Although important in all professional interactions, it is particularly relevant when working with vulnerable individuals or communities characterized by being less capable of autonomous decision making. The compassion and desire to help others is not typically a difficult competency to master. After all, many individuals choose to enter the applied fields of psychology, clinical health psychology included, to help those who have struggled with behavioral or emotional problems throughout their lives. Where this foundational competency becomes more challenging is through its translation from intention to action.

Translating compassion to action is often complicated by other elements of the ethical code that define the nature of the helping relationships between clinical health psychologists and their patients. For example, numerous patients who most certainly would enjoy improved health status if they engaged in regular exercise report having no access to exercise programs and/or equipment. It probably would not pass ethical muster to give them guest passes to your health club, to go on a daily walk with them, or to buy them exercise equipment with your money. Although these options may all result in increased success at engaging in exercise behavior, they complicate the nature of the professional relationship between the clinical health psychologist and patient. However, these actions would not seem to be problematic if they were conducted through an existing community program (e.g., getting a local health club to donate guest passes for you to give to patients with low incomes; getting a patient to join a local walking group). In this regard, many communities have plenty of activities organized by nonprofit agencies in which patients and their care providers could participate without compromising the nature of their helping relationship. For example, numerous patients and professionals walk concurrently in the American Cancer Society's Relay for Life on an annual basis. Here the distinction is between you arranging for a service to be provided that could be available to all patients in similar circumstances, and you personally providing a service to an individual patient for some reason. In this example, the former is acceptable, but the latter is not.

There is one area pertaining to respect for people's rights and dignity that uniquely impacts clinical health psychologists. In contrast to other types of professional psychologists, clinical health psychologists frequently encounter patients enduring medical procedures or in medical environments in which they are more vulnerable to being perceived in less than dignified ways. For example, clinical health psychologists will see patients when they are vomiting; using a bedpan; bleeding; delivering a baby; or being poked or prodded for purposes of dialysis, bone marrow aspiration, or transfusion. It is not uncommon to see patients, or at least portions of them, unclothed. Unlike other health care professionals, professional psychologists are typically trained to interact only with patients who are completely dressed, from a safe distance, with the emphasis on eye contact. In this regard, clinical health psychologists need to desensitize themselves to interacting with patients in hospital settings who may not always be entirely clothed. We do not share the advantage of other health care professionals-in-training of taking courses in anatomy, which can be very useful in shaping one's reactions to the naked human body, allowing one to observe body parts and processes with a degree of objectivity. To be effective in these settings, clinical health psychologists need to monitor these reactions, desensitize any discomfort that might be caused by the situation, and maintain one's professional demeanor throughout the procedure or interaction. In general, professional decorum stipulates that we primarily maintain face-to-face contact with the patient during interactions, unless specifically invited to do otherwise (e.g., "Look at this incision" or "I can't see what is going on; can you tell me how it looks?") to facilitate the patient's more appropriate reaction to what is occurring.

PROFESSIONAL IDENTITY

Development as a professional clinical health psychologist involves establishing an identity as such. This is a critical aspect of professional training that requires regular interaction with a cohort of peers and explains why professional training cannot easily be done through an online learning environment. The most recent enumeration of professional competencies of clinical health psychologists by the Council of Clinical Health Psychology Training Programs (CCHPTP) highlights the professional

TABLE 4.1 **Competencies and Behavioral Anchors in Professionalism Unique to Clinical Health Psychology**

1. Professional identity as a clinical health psychologist[a]
   - Conveys to others the added value that the clinical health psychologist brings to the setting
   - Participates in professional groups regarding the development and advancement of clinical health psychology
2. Flexibility in approaching problems and issues in the health care setting[b]
   - Modifies interventions and approaches to patients to deal with emergent issues in the health care setting (e.g., "Code Blue")
   - Willingly assists with patient problems when encountered by members of the treatment team (e.g., uncooperative patient, patient in pain)
   - Depending on the setting, adapts to the physical environment (e.g., hospital room, intensive care unit) to meet the needs of the patient and family
3. Knowledge to address issues and challenges unique to working in health care settings[b]
   - Displays competence in dealing with issues associated with death and dying
   - Modifies approach in response to infection control procedures

[a]Adapted from Competencies for Psychology Practice in Primary Care. Interorganizational Workgroup on Competencies for Primary Care Psychology Practice (2013, p. 24).
[b]Adapted from Competencies in Clinical Health Psychology. France et al. (2008, p. 579).

identity as a clinical health psychologist as a distinctive area of competency development (see Table 4.1). Although there is little doubt that knowledge can be acquired using online instructional environments, acquisition of the complex skills and professional attitudes comprising clinical health psychology requires regular face-to-face contact that allows for observation of others more senior to the trainee, and appropriate role modeling and discussion of the behaviors being displayed, both of which are required to ensure eventual acquisition of the skills themselves. During the early formative years in training, this learning is done in the context of the cohort of peers comprising graduate school or internship classes. Later on, this is accomplished through regular contact with others at professional meetings, membership in professional organizations, or continuing education opportunities.

Given the multidisciplinarity of clinical health psychology, the number of organizations professionals could join is too many to list. However, some of the organizations with significant foci devoted to clinical health psychology are briefly described as follows:

- *Division 38 (Health Psychology)—American Psychological Association (APA).* One of the largest divisions of APA, Division 38 is comprised of members devoted to the broad field of health psychology, including clinical health psychology. Division 38 publishes the journal *Health Psychology* as well as a division newsletter, *The Health Psychologist.*

- *The Society of Behavioral Medicine (SBM).* Spawned from a special interest group of the Association for Advancement of Behavior Therapy in the 1970s, SBM is an interdisciplinary organization with significant membership by clinical health psychologists. Individuals from other health-related professions (e.g., medicine, nursing, public health, and epidemiology) are also represented in its membership. SBM publishes the journal *Annals of Behavioral Medicine* and a newsletter, *The Outlook.*

- *The American Psychosomatic Society (APS).* Originally designed to link developments in psychology and psychiatry with medicine, physiology, and other disciplines, this organization was originally funded by the Josiah Macy, Jr. Foundation in 1936. Now it also includes members representing pediatrics, neuroanatomy and neurophysiology, sociology, clinical psychology, and public health. APS publishes the journal *Psychosomatic Medicine* nine times a year.

- *Council of Clinical Health Psychology Training Programs (CCHPTP).* In contrast to other organizations comprised of individuals as members, CCHPTP is an organization of training programs as members. Although initially incorporated following the Arden House conference, it currently is more narrowly defined as a council of doctoral, internship, and postdoctoral training programs in clinical health psychology. Directors of programs are representatives to the council, which meets twice a year.

- *American Board of Professional Clinical Health Psychology (ABPP).* ABPP is the organization that board-certifies licensed clinical psychologists as specialists across a range of specialty areas, including clinical health psychology. To be board certified and a member of ABPP, the applicant must possess adequate credentials in clinical health psychology, demonstrate work samples of his or her areas of competence, and pass an oral examination in his or her competency area as well as ethical principles.

- *European Health Psychology Society (EHPS).* Considered the European complement to Division 38 of APA, EHPS publishes *Psychology and Health* as well as *Health Psychology Review.* Additionally, *The European Health Psychologist* is their quarterly newsletter that promotes ongoing discussion of issues pertinent to clinical health psychology in Europe.

- *International Society of Behavioral Medicine (ISBM)*. As an international federation of societies devoted to behavioral medicine, ISBM sponsors periodic international congresses to promote international collaboration and dissemination of scholarship. ISBM also publishes the *International Journal of Behavioral Medicine* and a newsletter.

The professional identity of a clinical health psychologist involves both domestic and foreign policy components. Their domestic policy operates within the field of professional psychology. The peer group consists of other clinical health psychologists with whom we share a common background in the knowledge base of psychology as our scientific discipline. We interact with one another at professional meetings of psychologists and publish in journals edited and reviewed by other psychologists. On the other hand, our foreign policy is dependent upon the health-related area in which we work or the health-related professionals with whom we collaborate. Some of us interact with cardiologists, present papers at the American Heart Association meetings, and publish articles in medical journals in that area. Others interact with anesthesiologists, present papers at the American Pain Society meetings, and publish in journals focusing on topics related to research on pain. In this regard, the professional identity of a clinical health psychologist involves maintaining one's fundamental training as a psychologist while collaborating with professionals trained in entirely different fields of scientific inquiry and related practices.

Two additional areas of competency development in professional identity are unique to clinical health psychology and were highlighted in the original list of competencies defined at the Tempe Summit (France et al., 2008) as well as the most recent listing of competencies by CCHPTP: (1) flexibility in approaching problems in the health care setting and (2) knowledge to address issues that arise in health care settings. As depicted in the behavioral anchors associated with these competencies shown in Table 4.1, the former focuses upon adapting to emergent issues in the health care setting, such as what to do when a "Code Blue" is called to resuscitate a failing patient. In contrast, the latter area of competence focuses upon knowledge of issues unique to the health care environment, such as working with a dying patient or modifying one's professional behavior to work with a patient who has an infectious disease like tuberculosis. Suffice it to say that most doctoral programs in the broader field of professional psychology do not train their students how to behave during these types of situations, many of which are frequently encountered in health care settings. As such, they represent unique professional competencies required for the effective practice of clinical health psychology.

One other issue regarding our identification as clinical health psychologists warrants attention: the title we choose to use in introducing ourselves to our patients. Although in professional circles we easily claim titles of being clinical health psychologists, we may often choose other titles when introducing ourselves to our patients, including behavioral health consultants, smoking cessation experts, or even the "pain relief" gal or guy. Given the mental health stigma associated with the term "psychologist," many patients express some reluctance to meet with a clinical health psychologist but would gladly talk to the stress expert. Except in rare exceptions, the patients we evaluate and treat are seeking help for medical not psychological problems. In this regard, we may carry a variety of titles in the medical work environment; these titles are more likely to represent what we treat more than the specialty we represent. Again, professionalism requires that you be clear with patients regarding what your specialty training is in (i.e., psychology not medicine) to ensure that there is no miscommunication or misunderstanding.

ACQUISITION OF PROFESSIONAL COMPETENCIES
IN CLINICAL HEALTH PSYCHOLOGY

As a foundational competency, elements of professionalism are acquired fairly early in the sequence in training. In fact, one could argue that several of the elements of professionalism (e.g., integrity, accountability, concern for the welfare of others) are already fairly well developed during the undergraduate preparatory years. These professional values are the sorts of things that are written about in letters of recommendation by undergraduate advisors and instructors and the pieces of information that doctoral program selection committees weigh heavily in determining which students are invited to interview and which are eventually offered admission to training programs. Undergraduate students who approach their academic work with integrity, who are accountable for their behavior both in the classroom and their lives, and who express a genuine desire to help those less fortunate are already developing these fundamental competencies before they pursue graduate training. For these competencies, the primary aims of doctoral programs, and the internship and postdoctoral programs that follow, is to maintain the professional attitudes and behaviors that were partly acquired before entering graduate school. In this regard, it is important for these programs to reinforce these professional attributes and create learning environments conducive to their further development.

The early years of doctoral training should also promote the development of professional conduct, behavior, and attire as well as lay the foundation for the emerging professional identity as clinical health psychologists. In contrast to integrity, accountability, and concern for the welfare of others, fundamental skills in deportment and professional identity are often less well developed at the time of admission to graduate programs and may require more attention from faculty and other supervisors within graduate program settings. As students make the transition from their undergraduate to graduate years in training, it is not unusual to see students persist in behaviors and standards of attire that may be appropriate during undergraduate training but are no longer functional or appropriate in their developing professional world. New wardrobes are acquired and professional organizations joined, and these professional competencies are typically acquired early during graduate training.

It goes without saying that competencies in professionalism, then, are displayed on a daily basis throughout the remainder of one's career as a professional clinical health psychologist. Through establishment of one's professional identity in this domain of specialty practice, clinical health psychologists regularly interact with one another at conferences, read professional journals to keep up with the ever-changing literature, and consult with our peers when confronting situations that challenge the bounds of our competencies. By doing so, we continually reinforce the competencies in professionalism that provide a solid foundation for development of subsequent competencies in scholarship, education, and practice within the field of clinical health psychology.

FIVE

Reflective Practice, Self-Assessment, and Self-Care

Like virtually all other professions, the professional practice of psychology influences areas of one's life that typically fall outside the boundaries of the work environment. Physicians, for example, are bound to offer assistance to others wherever medical care is needed, both within their work environment and in a wide range of nonwork environments, including while dining out at a restaurant, attending church, on a plane, driving by a car accident, or spending time at a favorite vacation spot. Similarly, those trained in educational or health care settings are obligated to take action and report instances of child or elder abuse whether it is observed in work, neighborhood, or other public settings. In this regard, entering a profession involves some sacrifice to one's personal life. Many personal decisions regarding health habits, how you interact with family and friends, and which organizations to join and establishments to patronize are of lesser consequence to those employed in nonprofessional jobs, but they can have significant consequences for professionals. Work performance of those in nonprofessional positions is unlikely to be affected by one's choice to use tobacco products, cheat on his or her spouse, join fascist organizations, or visit strip clubs. Professionals, including clinical health psychologists, however, need to be aware of how these presumably personal decisions will impact their ability to function as professionals. In essence, by entering a profession, the professional ethical standards of that profession define behavior in both one's professional and personal lives.

Although the initial foundational competency domain in this area defined by Rodolfa et al. (2005) included competencies in reflective practice and self-assessment, subsequent work in defining core competencies in professional psychology (Fouad et al., 2009) fully addressed the influence of personal health and well-being on professional functioning by adding self-care to this domain of competence. Using the Competency Benchmarks Document (Fouad et al., 2009) as a guide, we will address each of these areas in this domain with reference to the science and practice of clinical health psychology.

REFLECTIVE PRACTICE

The science of psychology was founded in Wilhelm Wundt's laboratory in Leipzig, Germany, in 1879, largely upon an experimental technique known as classical introspection. Using this methodology, Wundt and colleagues trained participants in their early studies how to observe cognitive functioning as various types of stimuli were presented. Participants not only paid attention to various aspects of sensory stimulation but also to the emotional and motivational properties each stimulus elicited in them. In this regard, the foundations of the science of psychology depended upon humans' ability to look inward and observe the internal processes that have fascinated psychologists for well over a century. A few decades later, Carl Jung (1921) touted the importance of this aspect of human behavior, which he conceptualized as falling into two types: introversion (i.e., focusing on internal stimuli) and extraversion (i.e., focusing on external stimuli). Accordingly, Jung believed cognitive activity of humans was dominated by the propensity to observe internal processes subjectively or the propensity to attend to contexts in the external environment objectively. Regardless of whether reflection is conceptualized as a trainable experimental technique à la Wundt or a personality dimension à la Jung, it has been a topic of interest since the inception of the science of psychology.

What exactly is reflective practice? Although terms like self-awareness and mindfulness are often used synonymously with reflective practice, our understanding of professional competence in reflective practice is largely based upon the work of Schön in 1983. In his effort to describe how experienced professionals think quickly to integrate the vast knowledge of their scientific discipline with characteristics of the applied context in which they were operating, Schön described two types of reflective thinking: reflection-in-action and reflection-on-action. Reflection-in-action occurred in the moment and often was characterized as "thinking on one's feet," whereas reflection-on-action occurred as one reviewed his or her decision making after an encounter had passed. Both represent cognitive processing of the situation with careful review of the various options the trained professional considered, the course of action that was chosen, and an appraisal of one's skills in implementing the course of action. In essence, both types of reflection are akin to conducting a scientific appraisal of a specific professional encounter. Developmentally, for professional psychologists in training, acquiring solid competencies in reflection-on-action typically precedes competencies in reflection-in-action. For example, reflective practice is typically first modeled by supervisors following review of patient encounters with the aim of moving toward shaping the trainee to engage in reflective practice that occurs more proximally during patient encounters.

The professional practice of psychology, including clinical health psychology, involves mastering some very complicated critical thinking skills within interpersonal contexts. Rote actions occur rarely and each professional encounter possesses its own unique issues and challenges. It goes without saying, then, that rote memorization of psychological facts does little to prepare one for careers in professional psychological practice. Instead, solid critical thinking skills are at the core of competence in reflective practice. Acknowledging the importance of critical thinking, Fouad et al. (2009) listed the presence of good problem-solving skills, organized reasoning skills, and intellectual curiosity and flexibility among core elements comprising reflective practice.

Given the importance of critical thinking skills for the professional practice of clinical health psychology, it is implied that our methods of instruction need to optimize opportunities for evaluating students' critical thinking skills. Although rote memorization of factual knowledge may have its place during the undergraduate preparatory years, trainees should be fully capable of advanced critical thinking by the time they enter graduate school. Unfortunately, our methods for assessing critical thinking at the time of admissions lags behind our methods for evaluating applicants' abilities to retain information; and knowledge of one's grade point average or Graduate Record Examination (GRE) scores does little to assist us in this regard. Given the importance of critical thinking skills during graduate education, it goes without saying that our predominant modes of assessing graduate-level competence should tap into these domains. The Competency Assessment Toolkit (see Kaslow et al., 2009) provides a good description of several strategies for assessing competencies using a broad range of methods for evaluating critical thinking skills.

SELF-ASSESSMENT

Monitoring one's behavior and reflecting on it during or following patient encounters is an essential competency, but by itself it does little to improve overall professional competence. In addition to reflecting on various professional encounters, it is important to assess what went well and what did not go so well. In this regard, the competencies of reflective practice and self-assessment are dependent upon one another. It does no good to engage in reflection without the ability to evaluate what went well and what could be improved, and conversely, professional competence could not be acquired if one possessed the ability to assess his or her strengths and weaknesses but lacked the capacity for reflection. In some respects, acquiring the combined competencies of reflective practice and self-assessment is similar to setting up a self-control intervention, during which patients need to exhibit good self-monitoring skills (reflection) and self-evaluation (self-assessment) skills. We need to do both to succeed.

Throughout development and life as professional psychologists, we get asked periodically to declare our levels of competence for the wide range of professional behaviors in which clinical health psychologists engage. It happens during the licensure process, while requesting hospital privileges, when applying for board certification, and even when applying to various insurance and health maintenance organization provider panels. These represent important steps in our professional lives, and we should be thoroughly competent in the process of self-assessment when called upon to perform one. Coupled with competencies in integrity, our self-assessments need to be accurate reflections of what we can and cannot do. For each competency claimed, evidence describing the educational and experiential foundation of the area of competence should be available.

The sweet spot in self-assessment occurs when one's actual competence matches one's perceived competence. In this case, the psychologist is providing an accurate self-assessment of his or her professional competencies. Unfortunately, actual and perceived competencies are occasionally not congruent. One instance of a mismatch between actual and perceived competencies occurs when the professional psychologist perceives himself or herself as less competent than he or she really is. Although problematic because the psychologist in this situation lacks competencies in self-assessment, this type of mismatch is likely not to harm anyone; psychologists with this sort of self-assessment problem rarely engage in professional behaviors outside the narrow view of their own competencies. These cases can be difficult, however, as the psychologist will not be of much help to his or her peers when attempting to expand areas of service or providing coverage to colleagues when they are out of the office or on vacation. The other type of mismatch between actual and perceived competence is far more dangerous. In this case, the professional psychologist perceives himself or herself as being competent in an area in which he or she is not. Psychological practices conducted by psychologists in this category are often fertile grounds for ethical complaints and malpractice lawsuits.

In clinical health psychology, there is a growing recognition that a full array of specialized competencies is required before declaring oneself a clinical health psychologist (France et al., 2008; Masters et al., 2009). While the profession is comprised of a multitude of clinical health psychologists who actually possess competencies as articulated by the field, there are, unfortunately, some who identify themselves as clinical health psychologists but lack these specialized competencies. Some of these individuals claim that taking a course or two in health psychology during graduate training and doing a rotation on internship is sufficient training to become a clinical health psychologist. Others have claimed that their training in clinical or counseling psychology has prepared them broadly enough to accept positions as clinical health psychologists in health care settings without any additional course work or practical training. As you will see in the chapters that comprise this book, there is an extensive list of competencies associated with the specialty of clinical health psychology, and neither of these two case examples is likely to have acquired the necessary knowledge, skills, and values to identify themselves as clinical health psychologists.

Clinical neuropsychology encountered a similar problem in the 1990s in which clinical psychologists would attend weekend workshops in neuropsychological assessment and begin advertising their services in neuropsychological assessment the following week. This situation resulted in the Houston conference, during which basic training requirements for those who identify with this specialty area were outlined (Hannay, 1998). Foremost among these recommendations was the endorsement of the position that competence in the specialty area should be recognized by the receipt of board credentialing through the American Board of Professional Psychology (ABPP). Additionally, a 2-year postdoctoral training experience has become the standard method for assuring competence in clinical neuropsychology. Clinical health psychology has yet to adopt this position for acknowledging competence in our specialty area, although increasing demands are being heard to do so.

Clinical health psychologists operate in a variety of health care settings, and although we are trained using a biopsychosocial model, we do not have degrees in other health care professions, and we cannot possibly possess the foundational knowledge bases that they learn in their graduate training. Nonetheless, clinical health psychologists are often asked to extend their expertise into unfamiliar areas. Due to the location of our work, one area of competency in self-assessment is unique to clinical health psychology: knowledge of the importance of self-assessment in health care settings (see Table 5.1). Clinical health psychologists who work with patients experiencing pain can easily find themselves working with patients diagnosed with fibromyalgia, migraine, cancer, phantom limb pain, and angina. As such, these patients often turn to us to ask questions regarding their medical treatment that could be better answered by other members of the treatment team. In these situations, it is critical that we only give information that we are competent to provide. To complicate matters, the knowledge of the physiology of various medical conditions as well as the treatments known to be efficacious for each is continually changing, and the information we have will inevitably change quickly. In this regard, it is essential that clinical health psychologists acquire excellent skills in self-assessment. Otherwise we run the risk of conducting assessments and interventions in areas in which we lack the requisite knowledge and skill, or for which our knowledge and skills are woefully outdated. Belar and colleagues (2001) developed a self-assessment template for clinical health psychologists to use when considering readiness to provide services in a health care setting. Using this approach, the clinical health psychologist considers 13 questions regarding the basic knowledge and skill-based competencies needed to deliver clinical services in a

TABLE 5.1 **Competencies and Behavioral Anchors in Self-Assessment and Self-Care Unique to Clinical Health Psychology**

1. **Knowledge of importance of self-assessment in clinical health settings[a]**
   - Evaluates one's own competencies in the context of the entire health care team
   - Refrains from attempting to answer questions outside of one's areas of professional competence
   - Recognizes the inability to work with certain medical conditions or procedures (e.g., practitioners who cannot view blood drawings; practitioners with overactive gag reflexes)
2. **Facilitation of self-care, including health lifestyles, of health professionals in clinical health settings**
   - Models self-care to patients and other health professionals in clinical health settings (e.g., appropriate nutrition and exercise behavior, limited alcohol consumption, no tobacco use)
   - Facilitates the development and implementation of wellness programs in health care settings

[a]Adapted from Competencies for Psychology Practice in Primary Care. Interorganizational Workgroup on Competencies for Primary Care Psychology Practice (2013, p. 27).

TABLE 5.2 **Self-Assessment of Readiness to Delivery of Services to Patients With Medical-Surgical Problems**

1. Do I have knowledge of the biological bases of health and disease as related to this problem? How is this related to the biological bases of behavior?
2. Do I have knowledge of the cognitive-affective bases of health and disease as related to this problem? How is this related to the cognitive–affective bases of behavior?
3. Do I have knowledge of the social bases of health and disease as related to this problem? How is this related to the social bases of behavior?
4. Do I have knowledge of the developmental and individual bases of health and disease as related to this problem? How is this related to developmental and individual bases of behavior?
5. Do I have knowledge of the interactions among biological, affective, cognitive, social, and developmental components (e.g., psychophysiological aspects)? Do I understand the relationships between this problem and the patient and his or her environment (including family, health care system, and sociocultural environment)?
6. Do I have knowledge and skills of the empirically supported clinical assessment methods for this problem and how assessment might be affected by information in areas described by Questions 1–5?
7. Do I have knowledge of, and skill in implementing, the empirically supported interventions relevant to this problem? Do I have knowledge of how the proposed psychological intervention might impact physiological processes and vice versa?
8. Do I have knowledge of the roles and functions of other health care professionals relevant to this patient's problem? Do I have skills to communicate and collaborate with them?
9. Do I understand the sociopolitical features of the health care delivery system that can impact this problem?
10. Do I understand the health policy issues relevant to this problem?
11. Am I aware of the distinctive ethical issues related to practice with this problem?
12. Am I aware of the distinctive legal issues related to practice with this problem?
13. Am I aware of the special professional issues associated with practice with this problem?

Source: Reprinted from Belar, C. D., Brown, R. A., Hersch, L. E., Hornyak, L. M., Rozensky, R. H., Sheridan, E. P., Brown, R. T., & Reed, G. W. (2001). Self-assessment in clinical health psychology: A model for ethical expansion of practice. *Professional Psychology: Research & Practice, 32,* 135–141 (p. 137).

specific area of practice (see Table 5.2). Should the self-assessment reveal deficiencies, courses of action for acquiring the requisite competency are recommended, including using online sources, continuing education events, and peer consultation or mentoring. Through systematic application of self-assessment strategies, clinical health psychologists will find it much easier to navigate multifaceted health sciences center environments successfully throughout their professional careers.

SELF-CARE

To assure competent professional functioning as psychologists, Fouad et al. (2009) include competencies in maintaining personal health and well-being. After all, if we do not take adequate care of our own physical and mental health, how can we be expected to have any credibility as health care professionals? Attesting to the importance of the topic of self-care, Rodolfa (2010) recently reported that by far the single most frequently downloaded article published during the first 4 years in the journal *Training and Education in Professional Psychology* focused on provision of a self-care program for students during graduate training. In contrast to other professional psychologists, the range of health behaviors expected from clinical health psychologists is much broader. For the most part, consuming a high-fat diet or failing to exercise regularly would probably not interfere with a clinical psychologist's ability to conduct psychological evaluations or psychotherapy or a counseling psychologist's ability to counsel a person in need. However, clinical health psychologists' expertise in promoting health behaviors almost requires that we engage in a wide range of appropriate health behaviors ourselves. To not do so would certainly result in failing to "practice what we preach," harming our credibility as well as that of our profession. With the aim of modeling appropriate health behaviors for our patients, Table 5.3 depicts a sample of the sorts of health behaviors in which clinical health psychologists should engage. Granted, one could argue that these health behaviors comprise personal choices and should not be prescribed by one's profession. However, given that adherence to appropriate self–health care influences

TABLE 5.3 **Appropriate Self-Care Health Behaviors of Clinical Health Psychologists**

Not smoking or consuming other tobacco products
Consuming a balanced diet
Exercising regularly
Regulating alcohol consumption (and avoiding it altogether when driving automobiles or boats or operating heavy equipment)
Using protective clothing and lotions when exposed to sunlight
Wearing seat belts
Avoiding illegal drugs or substances
Limiting caffeine use
Obtaining annual physical examinations by health care professionals
Avoiding indoor tanning salons
Maintaining an appropriate weight
Visiting dental hygienists for regular teeth cleaning
Brushing and flossing teeth daily
Taking medications as prescribed by one's health care provider
Wearing protective equipment when engaged in potentially dangerous activities (e.g., motorcycling, skateboarding, skydiving)
Engaging in safe sexual practices

functioning in both one's work and home environments, acquiring competence in self-care cannot be ignored. Consequently, facilitation of effective self-care by modeling adoption of positive health behaviors represents another competency area unique to clinical health psychologists (see Table 5.1).

An additional reason to maintain appropriate self–health care behaviors is that it reminds us as practitioners how difficult it is to implement and maintain health behavior plans. At times, it is easy to lose perspective regarding the difficulty associated with maintaining long-term behavior change programs. By adopting the same sets of rules we expect of our patients, we come to appreciate their struggles to find the time or make the effort to engage in behavior change more fully.

ACQUISITION OF REFLECTIVE PRACTICE
COMPETENCIES IN CLINICAL HEALTH PSYCHOLOGY

Congruent with the foundational competencies associated with professionalism (see Chapter 4), competencies in reflective practice, self-assessment, and self-care are expected to be acquired early in the sequence in training. Hopefully, if we do a decent job of selecting trainees admitted into doctoral training programs, the critical thinking skills associated with reflective practice will be at least partially developed during the undergraduate years. Self-assessment skills—and the criteria to be used to conduct the self-assessment—will need to be developed through the formative and summative feedback students get as they progress through graduate training. The level of feedback that occurs during undergraduate training is rarely adequate to foster the development of solid self-assessment skills. As an example, students are typically not given specific enough feedback regarding their written and oral work during their undergraduate years for them to truly gain an accurate appraisal of their own relative strengths and weaknesses. Consequently, it is essential that graduate faculty deliver accurate feedback regarding each student's specific strengths and weaknesses so that he or she can acquire these important self-assessment skills. Faculty members who provide only negative criticism or uniformly positive commentary are not doing students any favors as students work toward establishing competence in self-assessment.

Self-care skills require attention throughout both undergraduate and graduate training and the years as professional clinical health psychologists that follow. Depending upon one's history of engaging in health behaviors, patterns of acquiring and maintaining appropriate health care behaviors will vary. Students who chose to smoke cigarettes earlier in life will struggle with altering that health behavior as they emerge as young clinical health psychology professionals. Obviously, students who have never smoked or used tobacco products will have no problem adhering to that specific health behavior. Adopting and maintaining appropriate health behaviors will fluctuate throughout one's life, both during graduate training and the years thereafter. Maintaining regular exercise behaviors may be fairly easy to do early in life, but it may become more challenging while aging or following physical injury. Similarly, efforts to engage in adhering to a healthy diet may fluctuate throughout one's professional life, and even during annual holidays and other celebratory events.

Skills in reflective practice, self-assessment, and self-care are critical foundational competencies that influence the daily practice of clinical health psychologists. This cluster of competencies pertains to both our professional and personal lives, and as such, reminds us that becoming competent clinical health psychologists requires sacrificing some of the freedoms nonprofessionals enjoy. By attending to the development of these competencies early in training, they provide the bedrock upon which functional competencies of scholarship, education, and the practice of clinical health psychology are built.

SIX

Scientific Knowledge and Methods
of Clinical Health Psychology

As mentioned in Chapter 2, the practice of psychology stands out among professions through its firm foundation upon the recognized scientific discipline of psychology. Among all of the psychological specialty areas of practice, clinical health psychologists are unique in that the majority of us assume positions in health sciences centers, public health agencies, and other health care–related facilities. As such, we come into regular contact with individuals comprising numerous related health care professions, including but not limited to physicians, nurses, social workers, pharmacists, and occupational and physical therapists. The vast majority of these other health care professionals are trained in evidence-based practice, but none are trained as scientists. Noting the exceptions of physicians with MD/PhD credentials and doctoral-trained nurses and social workers, clinical health psychologists stand alone in the health care arena as team members trained as scientists. Although this unique attribute of our profession makes it challenging at times for members of other professions to understand the role of clinical health psychologists in the health care environment, it is the hallmark distinctive credential of our profession since the days of the Arden House Conference. Without this attribute, clinical health psychology becomes indistinguishable from the other mental health professionals (e.g., social workers; nurse practitioners; counselors) that practice in health care environments.

The Competency Benchmarks Work Group (Fouad et al., 2009) outlined three specific foundational competencies under the general heading of scientific knowledge and methods: scientific mindedness, knowledge of the scientific foundation of psychology, and knowledge of the scientific foundation (evidence base) for psychological practice. Regarding foundational competencies for clinical health psychologists, we have added one additional competency area to this domain: knowledge of the scientific foundation of other health-related disciplines. We will consider each of these areas with reference to the current standards of competence for professional practice in clinical health psychology.

SCIENTIFIC MINDEDNESS

There are various ways of knowing. Scientific knowing involves generating hypotheses, developing appropriate methods of controlled observations to test hypotheses, adhering to systematic collection of data, and restricting conclusions to those that were adequately tested empirically. This approach stands in direct contrast to other ways of knowing, including intuition, faith, and adopting beliefs based upon one's life experiences. As the professional practice of a scientific discipline, the foundation of clinical health psychology lies in adherence to scientific forms of knowing, or scientific mindedness. Engaging in practices based on other forms of knowing may be of interest to health care providers and patients, but this has no place in the professional practice of clinical health psychology.

Every patient clinical health psychologists evaluate or treat or every clinical situation they encounter should be approached scientifically. That is, observations are made and data are gathered in a structured way (often through formal psychological assessments), hypotheses are generated and tested, and interventions are selected and tested based upon empirical evidence and solid theoretical considerations. Ongoing observations either confirm or refute clinical hypotheses, and modifications are made to interventions based upon these observations. In sum, scientific mindedness is a necessary ingredient to fundamental clinical competence. Individuals who base their practice on other ways of knowing would do best to pursue careers in other occupations.

SCIENTIFIC FOUNDATION OF PSYCHOLOGY

As described in Chapter 2, the Arden House participants outlined the fundamental knowledge bases for both the science of health psychology and the profession of clinical health psychology (see Table 2.1). In creating this model curriculum, the influence of the biopsychosocial model is easily detected. Both knowledge and skill-based competencies across the biological, psychological, and social realms are required for any psychologist training to become a clinical health psychologist. Attesting to the longevity of the curriculum recommendations made at Arden House, the most recent enumeration of competencies in scientific knowledge and methods for the practice of clinical health psychology (see Table 6.1) still resembles the table devised 30 years earlier. The first four competency areas (items 1–4 in Table 6.1) correspond with the biological, psychological, and social bases of health and disease domains articulated at Arden House. Note that the biopsychosocial model extends these knowledge bases from focusing primarily on psychological factors into knowledge bases associated with health and disease from a range of scientific disciplines for those acquiring competencies in clinical health psychology. Upon careful review of the behavioral anchors listed for each of the four competencies distinctive to clinical health psychology, one detects numerous sources of knowledge-based competence not typically covered in most professional psychology training programs. For example, understanding the normal values associated with various clinical laboratory tests or having an awareness of the classes of medications used for treating common medical problems and their side effects is rarely taught in professional psychology training programs. Similarly, understanding health disparities associated with limited access to health care for several common medical conditions is not uniformly taught in professional psychology training programs.

Because the focus of research by clinical health psychologists is on physical diseases, disorders, or disabilities rather than psychiatric or behavioral disorders, the required knowledge base of research findings is much broader in clinical health psychology than those typically acquired in the traditional professional psychology training programs in clinical, counseling, or school psychology. Each of the specific competency areas defined by participants at Tempe focuses on a specific literature base found in journals, books, or related resources that extend beyond the literatures covered in traditional professional psychology course work. In most cases, this requires extensive reading in literatures outside of psychology. In this regard, clinical health psychologists-in-training spend as much time reading medical journals as they do reading psychology journals. This creates an extra challenge for these students, particularly if their library collections are constructed separately for health sciences holdings and traditional scientific holdings (and they often are). Fortunately, with the availability of electronic databases, these physical limitations do not pose as much of a challenge as there was in the past.

TABLE 6.1 **Competencies and Behavioral Anchors in Scientific Knowledge and Methods Unique to Clinical Health Psychology**

1. **Knowledge of pathophysiology of disease and biomedical treatments specific to medical specialty or environment in which the practice will occur[a]**
   - Understands a range of medical conditions, their treatments, and biomedical measures used to evaluate them (e.g., HbA1C)
   - Recognizes names and appropriate dosages of medications for commonly occurring medical and psychological/behavioral conditions (e.g., diabetes, hypertension, depression) and their common side effects
2. **Knowledge of the pathways and reciprocal interactions among psychosocial (cognitive/affective/behavioral) and biological phenomena as they relate to health promotion, illness prevention, and disease progression[a]**
   - Articulates understanding of health belief models and attitudes regarding help seeking that influence health and illness
   - Demonstrates knowledge of cognitive, affective, and behavioral factors that mediate and/or moderate disease processes, reactions to diagnoses, and processing of health information
3. **Knowledge of life span developmental and social-environmental factors associated with health behavior, illness, and disease[a]**
   - Demonstrates knowledge of social developmental factors in the etiology of health conditions and behaviors (e.g., obesity, smoking)
   - Demonstrates awareness of geographic factors that influence health disparities and outcomes
4. **Knowledge of the interactions among population and contextual variations (e.g., age, gender, ethnicity, culture, religion, etc.) and the impact on health behavior and health outcomes[a]**
   - Demonstrates knowledge of health disparities across diverse populations
   - Demonstrates knowledge of the influence of diversity on the assessment and treatment of various health conditions (e.g., hypertension, diabetes)
5. **Knowledge of the scientific foundations and research methods of other health disciplines (e.g., epidemiology, biostatistics)[a]**
   - Demonstrates knowledge of epidemiological research methods
   - Demonstrates knowledge of the sensitivity and specificity of medical diagnostic tests
6. **Knowledge of relevant scientific literatures as they bear on health care and the ability to conceptualize and generate new issues, concerns, and questions based on that knowledge[a]**
   - Utilizes health information technology to search medical literature (e.g., Cochrane, Medline, Up-to-Date)
   - Demonstrates an understanding of how to translate research findings into clinical practice

[a]Adapted from Competencies in Clinical Health Psychology. France et al. (2008, pp. 577–578).

EVIDENCE-BASED PRACTICE OF PSYCHOLOGY

In addition to the broad and general requirements currently listed in the APA's accreditation guidelines and principles, students who pursue training in any area of professional psychology, including clinical health psychology, are exposed to the evidence base supporting the practice of psychology. These include some key domains of knowledge that date back to years prior to the Arden House Conference, including ethical and legal issues, as well as both exposure to and experience in psychological assessment, intervention, and consultation.

An important facet of training in the evidence-based practice of psychology is the importance of an organized set of practical learning experiences called practicum. In this regard, there is general acknowledgment that training in the knowledge of this domain would be incomplete without some experiential learning on "how to do" them. Although the specific skill-based competencies in the areas of assessment, intervention, and consultation are addressed in greater detail in later chapters of this book, it is important to mention here that training in these areas integrates knowledge-based content with skill acquisition from the beginning of training and throughout graduate and postgraduate training. To borrow a metaphor from sports, one can read a lot of books on how to hit a golf ball and learn about the aerodynamics of how golf balls travel through the air, but competence in golfing never really occurs until one experiences driving a straight shot or putting the ball into the cup on the green.

Given the importance of experiential learning in professional psychology (as well as other health disciplines), training is extremely labor intensive. Training often starts with direct behavioral observation where periods of supervision can require more time than the duration of applied activities being supervised. It would not be unusual, for example, for a beginning trainee to spend hours preparing for his or her first clinical interview, another hour or two going over the tape of the interview, and another hour or more receiving feedback from his or her clinical supervisor. Just like a surgeon would not hand a medical student a scalpel and ask him or her to conduct a biopsy without the surgeon being present, beginning-level trainees in clinical health psychology are supervised very closely with extensive use of tape review and feedback. It probably goes without saying that this type of supervision would be virtually impossible to conduct using online teaching methods. Consistent with our colleagues in the other health professions (e.g., medicine), clinical health psychologists must receive the bulk of their training in their work directly with patients in a face-to-face context. In this regard, while one could envision creating an online course aimed at covering knowledge of the biological bases of behavior, it would be another story altogether to create an online course that presumably covered acquisition of skills in conducting psychological assessment other than as a model or demonstration.

SCIENTIFIC KNOWLEDGE OF RELATED HEALTH CARE DISCIPLINES

Clinical health psychologists almost always work in health environments among a cadre of other health professionals, including but not limited to physicians, nurses, dentists, public health officials, occupational and physical therapists, and pharmacists. Because of this unique attribute, it is essential for clinical health psychologists to learn to "speak the languages" of these other professions and acquire competency in the basic scientific knowledge of other health care professions (see competency items 5 and 6 in Table 6.1). This is not an easy task, however, because most clinical health psychologists are educated alongside other clinical health psychologists or other professional psychologists. Speaking about reinforcement contingencies, diagnostic axes, or T-scores would be easily understood by our peers in professional psychology but likely misunderstood or not adequately comprehended by members of an interdisciplinary treatment team in the medical environment. Similarly, psychologists often do not understand the language used by members of other health disciplines. An obvious remedy for this situation is for clinical health psychologists-in-training to take elective courses in some of these other disciplines. Although not often easily carried out due to the numerous required courses in most accredited doctoral training programs in professional psychology, opportunities to interact with trainees in other disciplines are critical learning experiences for budding clinical health psychologists. Table 6.2 lists several examples of courses doctoral students pursuing training in clinical health psychology might consider in improving their interdisciplinary vocabulary.

Employing the biopsychosocial model as a guide, the traditional training programs in professional psychology concentrate heavily on the psychological domain. In contrast, although courses in biological and social aspects of behavior are commonly required, much less emphasis is placed upon them. To remedy the limited competency development in these two areas for clinical health psychology trainees, course work should be prioritized in these two domains. It does little to promote competency development to enroll in a public health course in mental health law or a pharmacy course in psychopharmacology. Instead, trainees should aim to add diversity to their knowledge base by enrolling in courses that expose them to the actual biological or social bases of the related discipline. Although epidemiology and biostatistics are mentioned as specific examples in item 5, there are other disciplines that could also be named, like genomics, bioinformatics, medical technology, and bioengineering. The exact composition

TABLE 6.2 **Examples of Courses in Other Health-Related Disciplines That Complement Training in Clinical Health Psychology**

Basic pharmacology
Biostatistics
Community health
Epidemiology
Health policy
Health promotion
Health services and outcomes
Human anatomy
Human physiology
International and global health
Psychophysiology
Public health

of the specific knowledge base to be acquired depends upon the nature of the clinical health psychologist's program of research, the types of patient problems he or she encounters frequently in daily practice, and his or her eventual career goals. For research projects examining the physiological mechanisms through which stress exerts its negative effects on symptoms of fibromyalgia or lupus, an understanding of human physiology would be critical. For research projects examining physical barriers to access to health care in rural communities, a working knowledge of epidemiology and public health are more important. The take-home point here is that clinical health psychologists need to "speak the language" of related health care disciplines. As such, transcripts of most clinical health psychologists show evidence of their exposure to non–psychology course work taught by members of other health care disciplines.

Although taking courses in related disciplines is an obvious strategy for assuring knowledge competence in this domain, this approach falls short of integrating these bodies of knowledge. Optimally, a truly integrative approach involves instruction from faculty with expertise in more than one domain of knowledge. Imagine, for example, taking a course that focused on diabetes care cotaught by a physiologist who studied how cellular receptivity to insulin is altered by obesity, a psychologist who studied the relation between exercise and blood glucose levels in diabetic patients, and a community health educator who studied how environmental factors impede effective diabetic screening programs. Alternatively, enrolling in a course taught by an instructor with credentials in more than one scientific discipline would also permit this sort of integration. For example, taking a course from a clinical health psychologist who also obtained a degree in behavioral genetics would promote the development of this type of integrated knowledge. Of course, these types of courses are not commonly seen in the academic environment, but there is reason to believe that they will increase as more and more young trainees obtain dual credentials and engage in this important integrative teaching. Unfortunately, the traditional departmental structure of academic settings typically prevents the creative thinking required to offer these types of educational experiences. Teaching assignments are often restricted by departmental boundaries (e.g., psychology faculty are not assigned to teach courses in the biology department and vice versa). These boundaries appear to be more permeable in health science center environments, where coinstruction of courses is more common and units are becoming increasingly identified through centers of excellence rather than traditional academic departments.

ACQUISITION OF SCIENTIFIC FOUNDATION
COMPETENCIES IN CLINICAL HEALTH PSYCHOLOGY

As a core competence, scientific mindedness should be infused throughout training, from the earliest moments of doctoral instruction and the extensive undergraduate course work that preceded it, through the internship and postdoctoral periods of training, to the continuing educational opportunities that are needed to keep abreast of new developments in the field throughout professional careers. As clinical health psychologists function throughout their careers, they stay in touch with the scientific knowledge base of their practice by reading the empirical literature and attending professional meetings in their areas of expertise as well as in areas of developing competence. Professional psychologists who fail to engage in these activities risk losing touch with the foundation of their practice, which presents both ethical and legal challenges for them. Hopefully, academic training programs instill these values in emerging clinical health psychologists early in training, so that these values are translated into good professional habits of staying in touch with the literature and scientific base of their practice.

Although both the original Boulder model of professional training in psychology and the Arden House proceedings recommended completing training in the breadth of the science of psychology before exposing students to the foundational courses for professional practice and the practical experiences associated with them, training is not typically accomplished in this order. As more and more practical training is being done during the doctoral training years, it has become more important to expose students to knowledge of the evidence base for professional practice during the first few years of doctoral training in order to place students on practicum earlier in their plans of study. Consequently, course work covering the breadth of the science of psychology may occur concurrently with the acquisition of clinical skills rather than prior to their development. Although this sequence of training deviates from the original scientist-practitioner model of training, it is the compromise most doctoral programs have made to assure that their trainees obtain the requisite practical experiences to compete successfully for internship placements in an increasingly competitive market.

Knowledge of scientific principles of related disciplines presents a challenge to the budding clinical health psychologist. How to fit additional courses and related experiences into an already jam-packed doctoral plan of study is no easy task. At best, the few elective courses afforded to the student will need to be reserved for these types of courses. At worst, it may take a student an extra year to complete these additional courses during the doctoral training years. Some doctoral programs are beginning to take advantage of other disciplinary programs offered at their universities and offering joint degree programs, in particular those granting master's degrees in public health.

Given the importance of acquiring knowledge of related scientific disciplines, it probably goes without saying that applicants to training programs in clinical health psychology look a bit different from applicants to traditional professional psychology training programs. Rather than evaluating files solely on psychology course work at the undergraduate level, successful applicants to doctoral programs in clinical health psychology are likely to possess undergraduate courses in a range of health-related disciplines. Selecting students that already have some knowledge of related disciplines will facilitate exposure to these other fields during graduate training and guarantee that students possess interdisciplinary language skills.

Although internship experiences build upon the scientific knowledge competencies established during doctoral training, there is rarely time during the internship year to devote to taking formal courses in clinical health psychology or related health care disciplines. The internship year, after all, is dedicated to the development of hands-on applied clinical health psychology skills. In this regard, acquisition of the foundational scientific competencies is typically accomplished before the internship year.

Depending upon the time in life when one becomes interested in clinical health psychology, not all trainees may have acquired the necessary interdisciplinary knowledge bases upon completion of the internship and receipt of the doctoral degree. For these individuals, a postdoctoral fellowship is a necessity. Many postdoctoral training programs are housed in interdisciplinary health care settings where opportunities abound for filling in the gaps in knowledge bases as well as experiential training opportunities.

Like the other foundational competencies, competency in scientific knowledge and methods is essential to the daily practice of professional clinical health psychologists. By selecting trainees committed to the scientific foundations of clinical health psychology and devising efficient ways to assure exposure to knowledge in related health care disciplines, doctoral programs shape these fundamental competencies early in training so that they are well in place prior to competing for internships and postdoctoral fellowships.

SEVEN

Relationships Within and Across Disciplines

Historically, the focus of the "relationship" competencies has been on the ability of the psychologist to form a working alliance that then facilitates the ability of the patient to make therapeutic progress. These have been labeled many things, from therapist factors to clinical skills. For purposes of this discussion, we acknowledge the importance of these relationship variables, but we will not address them directly. That is because these skills are so basic to the conduct of any type of clinical work that the required competencies in developing relationships are not unique or specific to the work of a clinical health psychologist. Thus, for this major area, we will focus on those aspects of relationships that are unique to the clinical health setting and not describe general relationship skills.

Almost by definition, anyone working in the area of clinical health psychology must establish professional relationships with a range of health care providers from other disciplines. For example, in working with a patient's poorly controlled diabetes, clinical health psychologists may interact with physicians who prescribe medications aimed at controlling blood glucose levels, nutritionists who advise the patient regarding dietary alterations needed to control blood sugar, nurses who teach the patient how to engage in daily monitoring of blood glucose, and exercise physiologists for developing and implementing effective exercise regimens. It is quite common for patients with behavioral health problems associated with medical conditions like diabetes to be referred to clinical health psychologists for assistance with improving adherence to dietary/exercise/medication treatment plans prescribed by their physicians as well as assess for any concurrent psychological disorders that would complicate treatment. Almost all of the training of other health care professionals is conducted in hospitals, clinics, and other health care agencies where interdisciplinary patient care is the norm. Therefore, it should come as no surprise that an important step in establishing a successful practice in clinical health psychology is developing relationships with a network of health care providers to either work with on interdisciplinary treatment teams or from whom referrals can be generated. With the knowledge of addressing a broad range of behavioral health issues in addition to treating traditional mental health problems in hand, clinical health psychologists are highly desirable members of these professional networks, particularly because they often practice in the immediate health care setting. It is quite obvious that the ability to develop relationships with a range of other health care professionals and to communicate with them regularly is fundamental to being a professional psychologist, and even more critical for being a competent clinical health psychologist.

In recent years, the ability to conduct both clinical work and research with professionals from other disciplines has been called many things—interdisciplinary, multidisciplinary, team science, interprofessional—each with a slightly nuanced difference in definition. What is common among all of these definitions, however, is the principle that each discipline cannot function in its own silo of expertise and, to borrow a term from primary school educators, must learn to "play well with others." To optimize health care for all patients and improve the overall functioning of the health care system, individuals from all health professions need to work cooperatively and collaboratively with each other. Thus, in addition to the important relationship competencies mentioned earlier, clinical health psychologists must possess knowledge of interdisciplinary functioning as well as the critical interprofessional skills.

The Competency Benchmarks Work Group (Fouad et al., 2009) addressed the ability to work with others in a number of places, some of which are covered in other areas of this volume (e.g., consultation). Most obvious, however, are the relationships competencies, including (a) the ability to develop and maintain interpersonal relationships, (b) the affective skills needed to manage difficult communications, and (c) the expressive skills to communicate clearly and effectively with others in both written and verbal ways. Additionally, the Work Group articulated four foundational interdisciplinary systems competencies: (a) understanding the contributions of other professions; (b) functioning within an interdisciplinary context; (c) understanding the impact of interdisciplinary collaboration on outcomes; and (d) the ability to form working relationships with other professionals. Both relationships and interdisciplinary systems competencies were considered foundational competencies by the Competency Benchmarks Work Group upon which the knowledge and skills required for daily functioning of all psychologists, including clinical health psychologists, were based. Suffice it to say that without these important foundational competencies, the effective practice of clinical health psychology would not be possible. Virtually all clinical health psychologists, whether clinical or research oriented, are likely to work closely with members of other health professions, and this is bound to increase in the future. Fortunately, because all other health professions have been involved in training their students in interdisciplinary settings for years, there is much we can learn from their efforts.

TRAINING IN INTERDISCIPLINARY PRACTICE
IN THE HEALTH PROFESSIONS

Within the health and health care industry, significant work in the area of interdisciplinary education and practice has been conducted by the many interdisciplinary groups involved in defining and promulgating integrated health care. Chief among these is the work being done by the Interprofessional Education Collaborative (IPEC). The IPEC represents the cooperation of representatives from a number of health care fields, including the American Association of Colleges of Nursing (AACN), the American Association of Colleges of Pharmacy (AACP), the Association of American Medical Colleges (AAMC), the American Association of Colleges of Osteopathic Medicine (AACOM), the American Dental Education Association (ADEA), and the Association of Schools of Public Health (ASPH). Funding from the Macy Foundation enabled the AAMC to launch an interprofessional education portal in support of these activities (https://www.mededportal.org/ipe/, downloaded May 30, 2013). The American Psychological Association (APA), the Physician Assistant Education Association (PAEA), and the American Physical Therapy Association (APTA) are now full members of this collaboration. In developing a description of these interprofessional competencies, IPEC required that the competencies be:

- Patient/family centered;
- Community/population oriented;
- Relationship focused;
- Process oriented;

- Linked to learning activities, educational strategies, and behavioral assessments that are developmentally appropriate for the learner;
- Able to be integrated across the learning continuum;
- Sensitive to the systems context/applicable across practice settings;
- Applicable across professions;
- Stated in language common and meaningful across the professions; and
- Outcome driven. (Interprofessional Education Collaborative Expert Panel, 2011, p. 2)

With these principles in mind, IPEC identified four domains of interprofessional competence: (a) values/ethics, (b) roles/responsibilities, (c) interprofessional communication, and (d) teams and teamwork. Not surprisingly, the IPEC Expert Panel's domains corresponded quite nicely with the interdisciplinary systems competencies outlined by the Benchmarks Work Group.

INTERPROFESSIONAL RELATIONSHIPS
COMPETENCIES IN CLINICAL HEALTH PSYCHOLOGY

Although the Competency Benchmarks Work Group identified the foundational relationships and interdisciplinary disciplinary systems competencies for all professional psychologists mentioned earlier, the most recent listing of professional competencies for the entry-level practice of clinical health psychology in these areas (see Table 7.1) merges these two areas into one—interprofessional relationships. In this respect, the listing of interprofessional relationships competencies distinctive to the practice of clinical health psychology parallels the work of the IPEC and reflects contemporary thought in defining these competencies. The unique interprofessional competencies in clinical health psychology are described in the sections that follow using the four domains of interprofessional competence defined by the IPEC.

Values/Ethics

Although more general issues of ethics will be described in Chapter 9, there are specific ethical issues to consider related to developing positive interprofessional relationships. To these ends, the IPEC described this domain as different disciplines working together "to maintain a climate of mutual

TABLE 7.1 **Competencies and Behavioral Anchors in Interprofessional Relationships Unique to Clinical Health Psychology**

VALUES/ETHICS

1. **Values and appreciates the interprofessional team approach to care[a]**
   - Demonstrates understanding that care of patient is the responsibility of a team of professionals, not a single clinician
   - Recognizes, respects, and supports activities of other members of the health care team
2. **Encouragement of behavior that demonstrates appropriate respect for the professional autonomy of other health care professionals[b]**
   - Models use of effective interpersonal strategies among treatment team members
   - Treats members of the treatment team from other disciplines with respect

---

INTERPROFESSIONAL ROLES/RESPONSIBILITIES

3. **Knowledge of strengths and potential pitfalls of role relationships that characterize interdisciplinary collaborative activities (e.g., research, education, clinical care, administration)[b]**
   - Accurately assesses the knowledge and skills of other disciplines
   - Aware of skills and competencies of other health service professionals (e.g., physicians, nurses, social workers) who (wish to) do research in health care settings
   - Able to identify successful collaborators for conducting interdisciplinary research
4. **Knowledge and appreciation of the role and primary responsibilities of other health care professionals (e.g., physicians, nurses, social workers) in providing care both in general and specific medical settings[b]**
   - Demonstrates knowledge of curricula of other health provider professions
   - Demonstrates awareness of and appreciation for the unique knowledge base, skill sets, roles in the health care team, and limitations and boundaries of the professions that function within an interdisciplinary health care team
5. **Able to access, evaluate, and utilize information from other health care providers, including use of methods that include new and emerging health technologies (e.g., EHR)[b]**
   - Reads, comprehends, and integrates information from members of other health care disciplines contained in the electronic health record
   - Comprehends the results of medical tests posted in the EHR (e.g., blood tests, radiology reports)

INTERPROFESSIONAL COMMUNICATION

6. **Development of facilitative and collaborative relationships with professionals from a variety of health care disciplines, including medicine, nursing, physical therapy, social work, etc.[b]**
   - Engages other health care professionals appropriately (e.g., nutritionist) in the care of an adolescent with morbid obesity
   - Assists a physician in informing a cancer patient of results indicating poor treatment outcome
7. **Ability to interact with fellow health care professionals in ways that facilitate improved treatment implementation based on the unique contributions that clinical health psychology can make in the health care setting[b]**
   - Rounds with interdisciplinary treatment teams and offers services when warranted
   - Volunteers to assist other team members in interacting with difficult or challenging patients

- Collaborates effectively in an interdisciplinary team meeting to plan the care of a patient with comorbid schizophrenia and diabetes[a]
- Coassesses a child's adherence to a treatment regimen for asthma with the pediatrician and the respiratory therapist[a]

8. Communication that cultivates mutual understanding regarding problems among individuals from diverse disciplines, including those that involve research and patient care[b]
- Verbally conveys important findings to other members of the interdisciplinary treatment teams
- Writes clear, concise electronic health records (EHR) notes focused on referral problem, frequency, duration, acute or long-term, functional impairment, and short specific recommendations

---

TEAM AND TEAMWORK

---

9. Ability to assess team dynamics and coach teams to improve functioning[a]
- Monitors team functioning and assists team members to better understand their interpersonal and communication styles, when appropriate
- Identifies when team is malfunctioning and uses psychological skills to address

10. Implementation of empirically supported health promotion, prevention, treatment, and rehabilitation in the context of the interdisciplinary team[b]
- Works with members of other health care disciplines to develop empirically supported interventions
- Integrates empirically supported behavioral interventions within the overall treatment plans of the interdisciplinary team

---

[a] Adapted from Competencies for Psychology Practice in Primary Care. Interorganizational Workgroup on Competencies for Primary Care Psychology Practice (2013, pp. 29–30).
[b] Adapted from Competencies in Clinical Health Psychology. France et al. (2008, pp. 577–579).

respect and shared values" (2011, p. 19). The specific competencies in the area of values/ethics enumerated by the IPEC boiled down to items 1 and 2 of the areas of interprofessional relationships competency depicted in Table 7.1. The first area of competency pertains to valuing an interprofessional approach to patient care. Obviously, in order to function on interdisciplinary treatment teams, one must view the various contributions of members of other health professions as valuable rather than with either suspicion or as unhelpful. Accordingly, this value system promotes respect for individuals from other health professions and an appreciation for the contributions they make to the health care team. Thus, the second interprofessional relationship competency in the area of values/ethics, treating members from other health professions with respect, builds upon the first.

Roles/Responsibilities

IPEC's general competency statement about knowledge of role and responsibilities is as follows: "Use the knowledge of one's own role and those of other professions to appropriately assess and address the healthcare needs of the patients and populations served" (IPEC Expert Panel, 2011, p. 21). Three specific competencies in the area of roles/responsibilities are depicted in Table 7.1 based upon the competencies articulated by the IPEC. The first competency is gaining an understanding of the knowledge and skills of members of other health professions. The second competency is related—an understanding of how members from each health profession contribute to providing patient care in health settings. In the fast-paced medical environment that uses a team approach, it is all too easy for tasks to fall between the cracks, and knowing which health care provider is handling specific tasks can help assure that tasks are completed correctly and on time. In the Benchmarks document, these competency areas are listed under "Knowledge of the shared and distinctive contributions of other professions." In this regard, competencies associated with items 3 and 4 in Table 7.1 are knowledge-based competencies.

Critical to being able to work as a clinical health psychologist is knowing and understanding the roles, specialties, and relative contributions of each member of the health care team. These include not only physicians but also, nurses, occupational therapists, physical therapists, clergy members, dieticians, and social workers, for example. Regardless of the presenting problem, many members of functional health care teams believe that dealing with "psychosocial" issues falls well within the purview of their discipline. Being aware of the unique contributions each field can make to the care of an individual patient is critical. For example, recent changes in the medical education curriculum have put increased emphasis on the development of interpersonal and relationship-building skills. This does not mean, however, the physicians are being trained to supplant or subsume the jobs of psychologists. Similarly, nurses have long been trained in issues such as quality of life, emotional reactions to illness, family responses to illness, and other psychosocial aspects of care. However, nurses do not do what clinical health psychologists do, nor might nurses respond the same way to reports of psychosocial issues. Knowing what each discipline does—and equally important what it does not do (i.e., the limits of its practice)—is crucial.

Some of the knowledge of roles and responsibilities of other health professions comes through experience with members of other health professions. Unfortunately, the IPEC Expert Panel (2011) noted that training for interdisciplinary practice has lagged far behind calls for and implementation of changes to how health care is delivered. Although traditional universities may provide education and training to individuals from numerous other health professions, rarely do professional psychology programs encourage students to take these classes, and even more rarely are such classes required. In contrast, medicine, nursing, dentistry, pharmacy, public health, and osteopathic medicine all have begun to include interprofessional education and training as part of their discipline's core competencies, and some professions have even added this requirement to their accreditation standards (IPEC, 2011). For clinical health psychologists, this may mean that the ability to acquire knowledge of the roles and attributes of a broad range of health care disciplines may not be readily available during doctoral training. Internships and postdoctoral fellowships completed in medical centers, however, do provide an opportunity for clinical health psychologists to obtain some of these educational experiences. In these settings, didactic training (including medical rounds) is often conducted with trainees from all specialties on a given rotation. Grand rounds typically includes representatives from many fields, and, particularly in larger medical centers, various seminars and other educational activities comprised of trainees across various disciplines typically abound. Trainees interested in clinical health psychology will have to actively seek out these opportunities, however, as they may not be part of the typical psychology-specific training curriculum.

A major reason that training in knowledge of the roles and responsibilities of various disciplines is so critical is that, not only is it important to know what an individual from another discipline does, it also is important to know and understand the worldviews, values, and beliefs that often form the basis of the discipline. In Chapter 4, identity as a psychologist was listed as one of the foundational competencies of our profession. Just as one of the basic competencies of being a psychologist is "thinking like a psychologist," other medical/helping fields inculcate their students and practitioners in the same way, so that each practitioner typically is trained to "think like" others in his or her discipline. Knowledge of these aspects is often more difficult to obtain, because (a) it requires exposure to members from another discipline in an array of situations, observing how they handle a range of topics and possible problem areas and circumstances, and (b) interacting with more than just one or two practitioners of the other discipline is needed in order to begin to see patterns or themes of their ways of conceptualizing and approaching patient problems. It is in this area that some of the work in interdisciplinary education and training in integrated primary care settings has made tremendous strides.

The final competency area pertaining to roles and responsibilities is the ability to understand and use information provided by other health care professionals to improve patient care (see item 5 in Table 7.1). The advantage of the electronic health record (EHR) is that it provides a common location for all members of an interdisciplinary treatment team to record their contributions to the care of the patient. However, the EHR does little good if members of the team do not read one another's notes and integrate information across disciplines to inform future contributions to the patient's care. In this regard, clinical health psychologists need to read and comprehend the progress notes and communications of providers from other health professions. To do so, this requires that clinical health psychologists become familiar with the terminology of other health professions and the meaning of their assessments for informing monitoring of treatment.

Interprofessional Communication

Although emerging and developing technologies (e.g., EHRs, patients being able to log in to their health care system to view test results) have greatly increased our ability to communicate within and across disciplines and professions, in health care as in other relationships, we often reach the point where technology alone is inadequate. Here we must rely on the ability to actually communicate with others. In the third area of interprofessional relationship competencies, the IPEC emphasizes that communications be "responsive and responsible" (2011, p. 23). To this end, the IPEC focused on choosing effective communication strategies that avoid discipline-specific jargon and terminology. In contrast to the knowledge-based competencies associated with the roles/responsibilities area of interprofessionalism, competencies in the area of interprofessional communication are skill based. As seen in Table 7.1, the skills for developing productive ongoing professional relationships with members of other health professions are highlighted in item 6 and the utility for these communications to facilitate improved patient care is highlighted in item 7. These two areas of competency relate closely to those listed under "Functioning in multidisciplinary and interdisciplinary contexts" in the Benchmarks document (Fouad et al., 2009, p. S16). Both of these competencies require that the clinical health psychologist communicates knowledge and opinions clearly and in a respectful manner so that problems and decisions about health care are made from an understanding that reflects the shared view of the health care team. Included is engagement in active listening and the ability to encourage everyone on the health care team to share ideas and opinions.

Rounding with the treatment team is an important part of developing effective interprofessional communication skills for clinical health psychologists who work in hospital settings. There is no better way to give timely, instructive, and helpful suggestions to members of the health care team than to participate in these activities that serve both patient care and educational goals. Rounding, which typically occurs in the mornings in most hospital settings, involves visiting all patients individually for whom the treatment team is responsible and assessing the status of the problem being treated, an active discussion among members of the team involved in their care, and developing plans for immediate treatment as well as for the eventual discharge from the facility. Rounds also serve an educational function, in that students from various health professions participate in them and are expected to acquire clinical knowledge of the various diseases and medical problems being treated. In this venue, clinical health psychologists play an important supporting role, keeping their eyes open for pertinent behavioral health issues that are sure to arise and volunteering their services for assisting the team with difficult or challenging behavioral problems confronting the team (e.g., patient adherence to the treatment plan; abuse of pain medications; disrespect of team member; family conflict, etc.). Sometimes these problems manifest in communication issues within the treatment team, and here again the clinical health psychologist can often facilitate discussion and refocus the issues back on the patient; this is discussed in more detail later. By assisting the treatment team with these sorts of patient or team problems, positive and productive interprofessional relationships are formed and the team very quickly notices when the clinical health psychologist is not present on rounds on a given day. Needless to say, clinical health psychologists who contribute very little during rounds are missing valuable professional opportunities.

Conflict inevitably occurs in the health care setting, just as it does in any other work or family environment where people function in close proximity with one another. When such conflict occurs, it is important to recognize the contribution of one's own unique viewpoint, including one's prior experience, culture, power, and role within the hierarchy of the health care team, to less-than-optimal functioning within the setting. Given the critical questioning and listening skills that clinical psychologists possess, they are uniquely positioned to assist in resolving these conflicts when they do occur.

The final competency area pertaining to interprofessional communication is the ability to communicate clearly to patients, families, and other health care professionals involved in the provision of care (see item 8 in Table 7.1). This is particularly important in the context of fast-paced medical care. Patients and members of other health professions tend to be somewhat familiar with the role of traditional psychological practice, but what clinical health psychologists do is less clear to them. For example, it may be difficult for patients to understand why, when they are presenting with a medical problem such as pain, asthma, or diabetes, they would be asked to see a psychologist; often, in these situations, a common response is, "I'm not crazy, I'm in pain!" Other health care providers, who may have been trained to adopt more traditional views of psychology, also may wonder what place a clinical health psychologist has on the medical treatment team. Being able to describe what the clinical health psychologist does, verbally, through progress notes, and through the actual work with patients and their families, provides evidence of the value of clinical health psychology to the health care team (and to the patient).

Team and Teamwork

Teamwork represents the final major competency domain recommended by IPEC. The overall competency statement provides an excellent overview of what interprofessional care is all about: "Apply relationship-building values and the principles of team dynamics to perform effectively in different team roles to plan and deliver patient-/population-centered care that is safe, timely, efficient, effective, and equitable" (IPEC, 2011, p. 25). The two remaining interdisciplinary systems competencies from the Competency Benchmarks Work Group (Fouad et al., 2009), understanding how participation in interdisciplinary collaboration enhances outcomes and developing respectful and productive relationships with individuals from other professions, overlap considerably with the team and teamwork competencies outlined by IPEC. As depicted in item 9 in Table 7.1, clinical health psychologists possess the competency to assess team functioning and reflect on functioning of individual team members as well as overall team functioning. Then, based upon a careful analysis of team functioning, clinical health psychologists possess the competencies to use this information to optimize team functioning in situations where team members are in conflict with one another or styles of communication among team members do not facilitate optimal patient care.

The final area of competency in the area of Team and Teamwork involves the leadership attributes of clinical health psychologists that support collaboration with interdisciplinary teams in developing evidence-based intervention and prevention programs. Based upon their considerable knowledge of research design and critical appraisal skills for evaluating the scientific literature, clinical health psychologists become natural leaders for the development, evaluation, supervision, and dissemination of efforts to evaluate the services provided by the treatment team for behavioral and/or medical problems. As health care outcomes become increasingly important to evaluate under the auspices of the Affordable Care Act, the ability for clinical health psychologists to lead efforts at evaluating treatment outcomes and conduct quality improvement efforts will position them as leaders for this type of interprofessional activity.

ACQUISITION OF INTERPROFESSIONAL RELATIONSHIPS COMPETENCIES IN CLINICAL HEALTH PSYCHOLOGY

Whether focusing on the work of the Competency Benchmarks Work Group, the IPEC, or the ongoing work of the Council of Clinical Health Psychology Training Programs, it is evident that building and sustaining interprofessional relationships are foundational competencies needed for entry into practice as a clinical health psychologist. In contrast to many of the foundational competencies already presented in previous chapters in this book (e.g., professionalism, reflective practice), interprofessional relationships competencies are typically not in place at the time of admission into doctoral training programs. This is not to say that trainees lack relationship competencies at the time they commence graduate study; in fact, many have exceptional interpersonal skills that are commonly evaluated and verified during interviews as part of the admissions process. However, upon entry into doctoral programs, they typically know very little about other health professions, the type of training conducted in other health professions, and almost none have received any exposure to working with members of other health professionals in a health care setting or as part of a health care team.

In contrast to other students in professional health care training programs who are increasingly exposed to instructors from other professions or scientific backgrounds, graduate students in clinical health psychology are rarely exposed to instruction from members of other health professions during their doctoral training. Additionally, information about the other health professions with whom they will interact throughout their professional lives is notably absent in professional training programs in psychology. This is unfortunate, as it postpones the development of these important interprofessional relationships competencies until later in their training. On the positive side, many students are exposed to members of various health professions as they begin practicum placements at hospitals or clinics where members of these professions are employed. And, certainly, during the internship year, most students are exposed to members of other health professions at some time. However, these practical experiences do not assure exposure to every health profession with which students will work in their eventual occupational settings. We would argue that all of professional psychology, including clinical health psychology, has to do a better job of assuring that these important foundational competencies are obtained prior to entering professional practice.

Perhaps the most formal method of obtaining interprofessional competencies is to take courses within other health profession's curricula, and perhaps the pursuit of a second health care credential (e.g., nursing, physician, geneticist, or dietician). The trend to pursue acquisition of interprofessional competencies in this manner is becoming increasingly popular among clinical health psychologists. Some are pursuing master's degrees in public health, while others pursue training as nurses or physician's assistants in order to acquire the credentials to treat a broader range of presenting problems. In some training programs, members of other health professions teach portions of courses in psychology departments, and these efforts certainly increase students' exposure to these health professions. To the extent that these sorts of experiences can be built directly into training programs without requiring additional coursework or experiences, students will benefit greatly by more rapidly acquiring the interprofessional competencies they will need to practice.

Taken together, interprofessional relationships competencies involve working and playing well with others, skills that most psychologists hopefully learned in elementary school. But it is much more than that. At its core, it has to be recognized that in the very near future, few psychologists will function as independent practitioners, seeing patients in their own private offices without regard for and without communicating with other members of the patient's health care team. While clinical health psychology has, for the most part, been somewhat ahead of other professional psychology health service providers in recognizing this fact, much of this has been self-taught. In other words, few models exist for how to educate students, early career professionals, and even individuals who need to retool their practices to better reflect the changing health care environment in the areas of interprofessional relationships competencies. What is clear, however, is that clinical health psychologists of the future must make sure that their training includes direct experience in an array of health care settings, working cooperatively with members from the full range of health professions. Learning to respect and appreciate the contributions of everyone on the health care team is an essential competency for all clinical health psychologists. Learning the language used by other health care providers is equally important, as many will struggle with learning these languages, and "translation" among professional terminologies will be needed.

One of the most problematic aspects of working with individuals from other health care fields is that few view the contributions made by clinical health psychologists as unique. For example, few individuals in any health care profession acknowledge that they lack adequate skills for exhibiting empathy, understanding, and/or providing emotional support and comfort to patients and their families. Many view the primary work of psychologists as providing a cathartic environment for the patient, and if that is all psychologists do, then the argument that most health care providers (and, in fact bartenders and hairdressers as well) can provide similar services is well taken. Consequently, it is important that clinical health psychologists and clinical health psychologists-in-training take the time to identify their unique expertise in relationship building and maintaining that they bring this expertise to the health care team. Many have talked about the need to articulate the "value added" of doctoral-level training of psychologists to health care, and if we do not do so, we will likely find ourselves being excluded from the health care team. The ability to ask empirically verifiable questions and to translate those questions into research projects and program evaluation efforts that can be of value to the entire health care team is one unique attribute of clinical health psychology. Another is the ability to modify interventions that have been demonstrated to be effective for one illness or disease for use in an unusual or unique presentation of a similar or related disease; again, the importance of being able to involve the entire treatment team in the modification, and to utilize the skills and abilities of everyone on the team, is pivotal.

In summary, the ability to work with others on the health care team and develop ongoing productive relationships with them is a foundational competency in clinical health psychology. It is hard to imagine being able to treat the wide range of problems, diseases, and diagnoses that enter into the clinical health psychologist's office without being able to work closely and collaboratively with others in health care settings.

EIGHT

Individual and Cultural Diversity in Clinical Health Psychology

There is no doubt that the country and world are becoming more ethnically and culturally diverse (e.g., Perez & Luquis, 2008). We can get from country to country in a matter of hours, and oceans no longer represent the barriers to traveling abroad that they once did. Estimates now indicate that non-Hispanic Caucasians will no longer be the majority ethnic-racial class in the United States by 2043 (United States Census Bureaus, 2012). Given the range of individual and cultural diversity that exists in our communities wherever we live, all psychologists, including clinical health psychologists, need to possess competencies to work with a broad range of patients presenting with a wide range of health problems. It is important to note that, particularly in the area of health psychology, "minority" and "culturally diverse" populations do not refer solely to individuals grouped by ethnicity and race. Rather, diversity in health care includes people with disabilities as well as any individual who may be treated differently because of factors such as age, socioeconomic status, language differences, or sexual orientation.

Clinical psychology doctoral programs (where the vast majority of health psychology training programs are housed) have had to become more deliberate in ensuring students obtain training about culture, diversity, and other special issues that arise when working with diverse populations. In contrast, because they are often housed in Colleges of Education, and because schools are often the first place where issues of diversity come to be recognized, counseling and school psychology programs have long addressed these issues. Assuring competence in dealing with all aspects of diversity has become a fundamental part of course work and related experiences required to meet American Psychological Association Commission on Accreditation guidelines for training in professional psychology (2007). In addition, because some diseases are increasing in prevalence as our population ages, training must include a life span perspective in order to ensure that clinical health psychologists are appropriately responsive to the health issues of an aging population.

Research in health psychology and behavioral medicine has increasingly begun to address issues of diversity. That these issues have become important is evidenced not only by the inclusion of articles that cover these topics in mainstream journals (e.g., *Health Psychology, Journal of Behavioral Medicine, American Journal of Public Health, Annals of Behavioral Medicine*) but also by the emergence of journals devoted specifically to these topics (e.g., *Journal of Healthcare for the Poor and Underserved, Ethnicity and Disease, Social Science and Medicine*). The National Institutes of Health now requires both grant applicants and recipients in annual reports to provide specific data on the ethnicity and gender of individuals who participate in clinical and health research; investigators who do not include diverse populations (or who fail to adequately explain why these populations are not included, if appropriate) will not be funded or re-funded. Numerous journals now have special issues devoted to ethnicity/health disparities (e.g., *Journal of Behavioral Medicine*, 2009, 32[1]) or routinely include special sections or articles devoted to these topics (e.g., *American Journal of Public Health*). In addition, numerous books and chapters have been published that focus on culture/ethnicity, health, and illness. Health psychologists have played a fundamental role in conducting and reporting the results of health research that impacts diverse groups, beginning with efforts to prevent the spread of HIV/AIDS among men who have sex with men in the 1980s. Since then this research has expanded to include the full array of chronic and acute illnesses that differentially affect various groups. As evidence of the field's emphasis on this topic, the flagship journal of Division 38 (Health Psychology) of the American Psychological Association, *Health Psychology*, has begun a recurring special section on health disparities. This special section occurs two or three times a year; focuses on specific, preidentified themes related to health disparities; and consists of three or four thematically related empirical articles. Additional evidence that health psychology research is increasingly focused on issues of diversity can be found in the field's responsiveness to the emerging health problems associated with aging, which reflects the changing needs of society. More research related to geriatric/aging populations is being conducted. This also has been manifested in increased interest in care-giver research, a problem that is becoming more salient as the population ages, and is a place where health psychology can contribute information and data to assist in meeting population needs.

Because research has begun to focus on issues related to cultural and individual diversity, so has clinical treatment, such that investigators have begun to pay particular attention to issues of cultural context, language differences, educational level, cultural literacy, and individual differences. For example, Dr. Beverly Thorn has written a book that describes treatment methods for chronic pain (Thorn, 2004); she then prepared a literacy-adapted manual that supplemented the original materials and made it available to practitioners free of charge (http://psychology.ua.edu/people/faculty/bthorn/documents/IntroductiontoManualw.doc).

HEALTH DISPARITIES RESEARCH

One reason developing competencies in diversity is so critical in the specialty area of clinical health psychology pertains to what has come to be known as health disparities. Health disparities are differences in the incidence, prevalence, access, treatment, morbidity, and mortality of illness, disease, and symptoms associated with belonging to one group versus another (Truman et al., 2011). The problem has been recognized for quite a while. Over two decades ago, in 1993, the National Institutes of Health established the Office of Research on Minority Health (ORMH); this became the National Center on Minority Health and Health Disparities, whose mission was to promote minority health and lead, coordinate, support, and assess the NIH effort to reduce and, ultimately, to eliminate health disparities. To do so, the Center funded initiatives designed both to impact health disparities themselves and to produce a new generation of underrepresented researchers. Nonetheless, these disparities, and the negative consequences that go along with them, have persisted; in fact, one of the changes that was included as part of the 2010 Patient Protection and Affordable Care Act (Public Law 111-148) was to redesignate NCMHD as its own Institute, the National Institute on Minority Health and Health Disparities (NIMHHD). In 2002, the Institute of Medicine (IOM) produced a milestone report that brought these issues more clearly to the attention of the greater medical and the health-related research communities (Smedley, Stith, & Nelson, 2003). The IOM report identified a number of sources for these health disparities and concluded that, while some of these sources may be related to the way health care was administered in the United States, other causes appeared to be related to aspects of the clinical encounter itself.

One characteristic that makes disparities in the area of health uniquely challenging is that the direction of the differences in health care and health care utilization is often hard to predict. While White, middle- and upper-class Americans may have better access to health care, it does not ensure that their health is uniformly superior. For example, Landrine and Klonoff (2004) provided evidence that, for those members of ethnic communities who move to the United States, acculturation may make some health or lifestyle behaviors (e.g., eating a healthy diet, exercising, smoking) better or worse depending on the ethnicity and/or gender of the group in question. Similarly, studies of low birth weight in infants demonstrate that Mexican mothers in Mexico give birth to healthier and larger babies than Mexican mothers in the United States; this is true even if the Mexican mothers recently emigrated to the United States (e.g., Hessol & Fuentes-Afflick, 2012). Although poverty and the resultant inability to access medical care when it is needed clearly negatively impact health and illness, these are not the only factors. For example, even in the United States, there are clear gender differences in smoking rates among Whites (Ward et al., 2002). In order for a clinical health psychologist to function competently in the health care setting, he or she must be able to access information about and understand the epidemiological implications of these disparities. Because health disparities are ubiquitous and so well recognized in the health field, any discipline, including psychology, seeking to deal with health-related issues must address issues of diversity during training and the years beyond.

The Competency Benchmarks Work Group (Fouad et al., 2009) identified four domains of competency pertaining to individual and cultural diversity. The first three competencies involved the recognition of self, others, and the interaction between self and others as cultural beings in all of the daily activities of a professional psychologist. The final area of competency in individual and cultural diversity identified by the Benchmarks Work Group involves the application of this awareness and development of skills in using appropriate strategies for assessing and treating patients that are sensitive to individual difference characteristics. This area of competency also involves using culturally relevant "best practices." Thus, all entry-level professional psychologists should have knowledge of the literature on individual and cultural diversity, skills in implementing culturally relevant practices, and attitudes valuing cultural diversity that serve as foundational professional competencies.

TABLE 8.1 **Competencies and Behavioral Anchors in Individual and Cultural Diversity Unique to Clinical Health Psychology**

1. **Knowledge of self and others as cultural beings in health care settings, including knowledge of health disparities across a number of different diversity-related characteristics**[a]
   - Knowledge of the diversity of health belief models and attitudes toward health and wellness held by diverse patients and health care providers[c]
   - Knowledge of the distribution of diseases and health-related behaviors in diverse populations adjusted to account for local differences in illness incidence and prevalence (e.g., high rates of specific kinds of cancers in agricultural communities)
   - Demonstrates knowledge of factors that influence health care and access to health care (e.g., developmental, cultural, socioeconomic, religious, sexual orientation)
2. **Application of knowledge of the relations between social and cultural factors and the development of health problems to patient care, including access to health care**[a]
   - Collaborates with relevant others, including linguistic, visual, and hearing interpreters that may be required to provide appropriate services[c]
   - Incorporates local population-based information and research in the provision of health care services[c]
   - Modifies interventions for behavioral health change that are sensitive to a variety of social and cultural factors
   - Uses culturally sensitive measures and procedures when conducting research, evaluation, or quality improvement projects
   - Provides supervision that takes into account individual and cultural differences of both consumers and other members of the health care team[b]

---

[a]Adapted from Competencies for Psychology Practice in Primary Care. Interorganizational Workgroup on Competencies for Primary Care Psychology Practice (2013, pp. 24–25).
[b]Adapted from Competencies in Clinical Health Psychology. France et al. (2008, p. 579).
[c]Adapted from Health Service Psychology Education Collaborative (2013).

Recognizing the importance of considering individual and cultural differences when assessing health behaviors and access to health care, the latest list of competencies in clinical health psychology includes two additional competencies in the area of individual and cultural diversity (see Table 8.1). The former pertains to knowledge of issues of diversity within the context of the health care environment (including the impact of diversity on health belief models and factors related to health disparities) and the latter pertains to application of one's knowledge in this area to daily practice.

KNOWLEDGE OF DIVERSITY ON HEALTH BELIEF MODELS

Because of the importance of health to cultures, ethnic groups, and sociodemographic groups (e.g., individuals of differing sexual orientations, ages, disability status), most groups have their own set of group-specific health beliefs. Some of these are health belief systems that derive from different cultures or religions (e.g., traditional Chinese medicine, Ayurvedic medicine). The importance of these approaches to medical treatment is evidenced by the fact that, in 1998, the National Institutes of Health established the National Center for Complementary and Alternative Medicine (NCCAM, http://nccam.nih.gov/). The name of the Center refers to the two different ways individuals use these approaches; "complementary" refers to using a nonmainstream approach in combination with more traditional, Western medicine, while "alternative" refers to the use of these approaches in lieu of traditional Western medicine. According to their Web site (http://nccam.nih.gov/health/whatiscam, accessed August 11, 2013), nearly 40% of the population uses one or more health care approaches developed outside of mainstream Western medicine; thus, these methods are not limited to a relatively small number of individuals. The Center divides complementary and alternative practices into two major groups, "natural products" and "mind and body practices." Natural products include vitamins and minerals, herbs, and probiotics, and are often sold as dietary supplements. Mind and body practices range from acupuncture, spinal manipulation, and massage, to meditation, relaxation techniques, tai chi, and yoga. Health psychologists often use relaxation and other meditation techniques and may not realize that these fall generally into complementary medical interventions. However, it is important to know about the other types of treatments patients might be using, to ask about these in initial evaluations, and to make sure that whatever adjunct treatments a patient is using are communicated to the medical team in order to ensure that these do not negatively impact other treatments. Barnes, Bloom, and Nahin (2008), for example, reported on the relative decrease in the use of St. John's wort between 2002 and 2007 following reports of harmful herb–drug interactions with antidepressants, some seizure medications, birth control pills, and warfarin. Patients often do not see the use of these products as something that needs to be described to their medical providers, and so it is important that clinical health psychologists are aware of them and assess their use during evaluations.

A clear example of the importance of being able to understand the belief systems of another culture is evident in the book *The Spirit Catches You and You Fall Down: A Hmong Child, Her American Doctors, and the Collision of Two Cultures* (Fadiman, 2012). Originally released in 1997, this book provides a detailed account of the tragic life of Lia Lee, a young girl from Laos who was diagnosed with a seizure disorder at a very young age. When the diagnosis was first made, there were no Hmong interpreters working at the hospital, and as a result the parents of the then infant did not provide the medical treatment as prescribed. In the parents' home culture, what the American doctors saw as epilepsy, the Hmong saw as *qaug dab peg*, the spirit catches you and you fall down. An array of folk remedies, often in combination with some of the Western medicine and treatments being prescribed, were tried by the parents in an effort to coax what they believed to be her wandering soul back into her body. The miscommunication between the family and the well-intentioned medical staff, members of the community who tried to help, and various social service agencies persisted for about 4 years, during which the child was actually put into foster care for a year because the parents were not following the medical regimen. As a result of this miscommunication, at around age 4 Lia lost all higher brain functioning and lapsed into a persistent vegetative state. Although the original book stopped at this point, a more recent paperback edition included an afterword that provided follow-up information about the effects on the family of caring for this seriously ill child. Although it was not known when the newer version was published, Lia remained in that same persistent vegetative state until her death almost 26 years later at age 30. While having an interpreter, working with the parents' beliefs system, and trying to integrate Western treatment into what the parents felt they were compelled to do to save their child might not have resulted in a different outcome, it most certainly would have increased the likelihood of having everyone working together for the benefit of this child. As one reads the book, it becomes increasingly clear how even the best of intentions can easily go awry when there is neither communication nor understanding among various cultural, racial, or other types of diverse groups.

Kleinman and his colleagues (Kleinman, Eisenberg, & Good, 1978) identified eight questions that they recommend asking any patient from a culture other than that of the health care provider. Their recommendations include the following:

> Clinicians need to be persistent in order to show patients that their ideas are of genuine interest and importance for clinical management. [1] What do you think has caused your problem? [2] Why do you think it started when it did? [3] What do you think your sickness does to you? How does it work? [4] How severe is your sickness? Will it have a short or long course? [5] What kind of treatment do you think you should receive? Several other questions will elicit the patient's therapeutic goals and the psychosocial and cultural meaning of his illness, if these issues have not already been incorporated into his answers: [6] What are the most important

results you hope to receive from this treatment? [7] What are the chief problems your sickness has caused for you? [8] What do you fear most about your sickness? (p. 256)

The goal of these questions is to allow the clinician to put the person's illness in the context of the person's understanding of the illness.

Health beliefs and health practices may or may not change when one moves from one country to another. It is particularly important to assess these factors among those who have recently immigrated into a new country. As noted earlier, there is abundant evidence that moving to the United States has dramatic effects on health and health-related behaviors. However, the direction of those changes and the degree to which changes may be positive or negative vary by ethnicity and country of origin. For some countries, for example, where a diet including large amounts of fruits and vegetables is commonplace, the goal may be to encourage recent immigrants to continue with what would be their indigenous healthier lifestyle. In other instances, where tobacco use is common, the goal may be to help people reduce smoking rates. In sum, knowledge of how individual and cultural diversity influence a patient's health beliefs, health practices, and beliefs about health care is an essential competency for any clinical health psychologist.

KNOWLEDGE OF HEALTH DISPARITIES

At the current time, there is no a priori reason to believe race or ethnicity alone actually accounts for variance in health outcomes across groups. Trying to identify biological differences among identifiable demographic groups (e.g., ethnicity, race) has been a focus of medical research in the United States since the earliest attempts to provide a rationale for slavery (Kawachi, Daniels, & Robinson, 2005). However, the number of illnesses where clear genetic links have been established (e.g., Tay-Sachs disease or sickle-cell anemia) are small (Adler & Rehkopf, 2008), and the bulk of the work derived from these efforts has been devoted to developing ways to decrease risk among genetically susceptible groups by reducing the environmental conditions that trigger the disease (Kawachi et al., 2005). In the absence of biological underpinnings of illness and disease, clinical health psychologists focus on the biopsychosocial aspects that may be contributing to behaviors associated with the disease and social factors that influence its occurrence and treatment.

While the range of illnesses, health behaviors, and interventions for which disparities have been documented is beyond the scope of this volume (and in fact would be volumes unto itself), it is important for clinical health psychologists to be cognizant of the crucial role health disparities play. Specific examples of research documenting disparities for two of the topics clinical health psychologists are often called upon to deal with, tobacco and diet, are shown in Tables 8.2 and 8.3. It is important that clinical health psychologists know, understand, and recognize issues that may be related to disparities in their practice. This necessitates more of an epidemiological approach to diagnosis and treatment than psychologists typically obtain in their doctoral training. It requires that one read the disease or organ-specific journals related to his or her practice and regularly search the literature for evidence or data that suggest new or emerging findings related to disparities. Because the concept of disparities

TABLE 8.2 **Articles Related to Diversity and Its Role in Use of Tobacco and Tobacco Cessation**

Blosnich, J., Jarrett, T., & Horn, K. (2010). Disparities in smoking and acute respiratory illnesses among sexual minority young adults. *Lung, 188*(5), 401–407. PMID: 20496074

Freedman, K. S., Nelson, N. M., & Feldman, L. L. (2012). Smoking initiation among young adults in the United States and Canada, 1998-2010: A systematic review. *Preventing Chronic Disease,* 9:E05. Epub 2011 Dec 15.

Hatzenbuehler, M. L., Wieringa, N. F., & Keyes, K. M. (2011). Community-level determinants of tobacco use disparities in lesbian, gay, and bisexual youth: Results from a population-based study. *Archives of Pediatrics and Adolescent Medicine, 165,* 527–532, doi:10.1001/archpediatrics.2011.64.

Kendzor, D. E., Businelle, M. S., Costello, T. J., Castro, Y., Reitzel, L. R., Cofta-Woerpel, L. M., Li, Y., Mazas, C. A., Vidrine, J. I., Cinciripini, P. M., Greisinger, A. J., & Wetter, D. W. (2010). Financial strain and smoking cessation among racially/ethnically diverse smokers. *American Journal of Public Health, 100,* 702–706. PMID: 20167886

Margerison-Zilko, C., & Cubbin, C. (2013). Socioeconomic disparities in tobacco-related health outcomes across racial/ ethnic groups in the United States: National health interview survey 2010. *Nicotine and Tobacco Research, 15*(6), 1161–1165. doi:10.1093/ntr/nts256.

Mukherjea, A., & Modayil, M.V. (2013). Culturally specific tobacco use and South Asians in the United States: A review of the literature and promising strategies for intervention. *Health Promotion Practice, 14*(5 Suppl), 48S–60S. doi:10.1177/1524839913485585

Paula, C. A., Cox, L. S., Garrett, S., Suarez, N., Sandt, H., Mendoza, I., & Ellerbeck, E. F. (2010). Tobacco use and interest in smoking cessation among Latinos attending community health fairs. *Journal of Immigrant and Minority Health, 13,* 719–724. doi:10.1007/s10903-010-9404-y

Rath, J. M., Villanti, A. C., Rubenstein, R. A., & Vallone, D. M. (2013). Tobacco use by sexual identity among young adults in the United States. *Nicotine and Tobacco Research, 15,* 1822–1831. doi:10.1093/ntr/ntt062

Stahre, M., Okuyemi, K. S., Joseph, A. M., & Fu, S. S. (2010). Racial/ethnic differences in menthol cigarette smoking, population quit ratios and utilization of evidence-based tobacco cessation treatments. *Addiction, 105* (Suppl 1), 75–83. doi:10.1111/j.1360-0443.2010.03200.x

Trinidad, D. R., Pérez-Stable, E. J., Messer, K., White, M. M., & Pierce, J. P. (2010). Menthol cigarettes and smoking cessation among racial/ethnic groups in the United States. *Addiction, 105 (Suppl 1),* 84–94. doi:10.1111/j.1360-0443.2010.03187.x

Vargas, B. A., Chen, J., Rodriguez, H. P., Rizzo, J. A., & Ortega, A. N. (2010). Use of preventive care services among Latino subgroups. *American Journal of Preventive Medicine, 38,* 609–610.

TABLE 8.3 **Articles Related to Diversity and Its Role in Diet and Exercise**

August, K. J., & Sorkin, D. H. (2010). Racial/ethnic disparities in exercise and dietary behaviors of middle-aged and older adults. *Journal of General Internal Medicine, 26,* 245–250. doi:10.1007/s11606-010-1514-7

Castro, F. G., Shaibi, G. Q., & Boehm-Smith, E. (2009). Ecodevelopmental contexts for preventing type 2 diabetes in Latino and other racial/ethnic minority populations. *Journal of Behavioral Medicine, 32*(1), 89–105. doi:10.1007/s10865-008-9194-z.

Carroll-Scott, A., Gilstad-Hayden, K., Rosenthal, L., Peters, S. M., McCaslin, C., Joyce, R., & Ickovics, J. R. (2013). Disentangling neighborhood contextual associations with child body mass index, diet, and physical activity: The role of built, socioeconomic, and social environments. *Social Science and Medicine,* pii: S0277-9536(13)00214-1. doi:10.1016/j.socscimed.2013.04.003.

Grigsby-Toussaint, D. S., Zenk, S. N., Odoms-Young, A., Ruggiero, L., & Moise, I. (2010). Availability of commonly consumed and culturally specific fruits and vegetables in African-American and Latino neighborhoods. *Journal of the American Dietetic Association, 110*(5), 746–752. PMID: 20430136

Hollar, D., Lombardo, M., Lopez-Mitnik, G., Hollar, T. L., Almon, M., Agatston, A. S., & Messiah, S. E. (2010). Effective multi-level, multi-sector, school-based obesity prevention programming improves weight, blood pressure, and academic performance, especially among low-income, minority children. *Journal of Health Care for the Poor and Underserved, 21*(2 Suppl), 93–108. PMID: 20453379

Kirkpatrick, S. I., Dodd, K. W., Reedy, J., & Krebs-Smith, S. M. (2012). Income and race/ethnicity are associated with adherence to food-based dietary guidance among US adults and children. *Journal of the Academy of Nutrition and Dietetics, 112,* 624–635.

McCloskey, J., & Flenniken, D. (2010). Overcoming cultural barriers to diabetes control: A qualitative study of southwestern New Mexico Hispanics. *Journal of Cultural Diversity, 17*(3), 110–115. PMID: 20860336

O'Hea, E. L., Moon, S., Grothe, K. B., Boudreaux, E., Bodenlos, J. S., Wallston, K., & Brantley, P. J. (2009). Interaction of locus of control, self-efficacy, and outcome expectancy in relation to HbA1c in medically underserved individuals with type 2 diabetes. *Journal of Behavioral Medicine, 32*(1), 106–117. doi:10.1007/s10865-008-9188-x

Walker, E. A., Stevens, K. A., & Persaud, S. (2010). Promoting diabetes self-management among African Americans: An educational intervention. *Journal of Health Care for the Poor and Underserved, 21*(3 Suppl), 169–186. PMID: 20675953

Wang, Y., Jahns, L., Tussing-Humphreys, L., Xie, B., Rockett, H., Liang, H., & Johnson, L. (2010). Dietary intake patterns of low-income urban African-American adolescents. *Journal of the American Dietetic Association, 110*(9), 1340–1345. PMID: 20800126

Zamora, D., Gordon-Larsen, P., Jacobs, D. R., Jr., & Popkin, B. M. (2010). Diet quality and weight gain among black and white young adults: The Coronary Artery Risk Development in Young Adults (CARDIA) Study (1985–2005). *American Journal of Clinical Nutrition, 92*(4), 784–793. PMID: 20685947

in health care is multifaceted, it is important to consider that disparities may be involved any time a patient presents with characteristics that are outside the bounds of patients more typically seen in that setting.

DISCRIMINATION IN HEALTH CARE

While discussions of diversity or disparities often touch upon the experience and impact of discrimination, nowhere is this more problematic than in health care. There is a growing body of evidence that suggests that individuals may be treated differently based on their ethnic, racial, or other characteristics. As noted earlier, the 2002 IOM report was among the first to identify discrimination on a wide-scale basis (Smedley, Stith, & Nelson, 2002). Klonoff (2009) briefly reviewed the literature in the years since the 2002 report and identified differences in such wide-ranging actions and procedures as how an appendectomy was performed (i.e., open versus laproscopically) to how much pain medication was given to a child with a broken arm in the emergency room. While some of these differences no doubt reflect differences in the quality of the hospitals where people receive their care and issues related to health insurance and access to care, some of these results remained robust even when controlling for insurance or location of care (i.e., all *Kaiser* patients, using records from the Veteran's Administration). MacIntosh, Desai, Lewis, Jones, and Nunez-Smith (2013) used data from the 2004 Behavioral Risk Factor Surveillance System "Reactions to Race" module to categorize participants into one of three self-identified/socially identified racial groups: minority/minority, minority/White, or White/White. Those who were socially identified as minorities were more likely to report discrimination than those who were socially identified as White; this discrimination was evident in influenza and pneumococcal vaccination, with those socially identified as minority having significantly lower vaccination rates. A study in Ontario, Canada, found that women with intellectual and developmental disabilities were twice as likely *not* to be screened for cervical cancer and 1.5 times as likely not to receive mammography than women without these disabilities (Cobigo et al., 2013).

One of the negative side effects of the experience of discrimination in health care is the development of conspiracy beliefs or medical mistrust as a consequence. We are only now becoming aware of the impact of this mistrust. For example, there are data to suggest that African American men believe that AIDS is a government conspiracy (e.g., Klonoff & Landrine, 1999); these and similar conspiracy beliefs have been shown to be related to risky sexual behavior (Bogart, Galvan, Wagner, & Klein, 2011) and to lower adherence to antiretroviral medication (Bogart, Wagner, Galvan, & Banks, 2010). Similarly, medical mistrust has been shown to decrease the likelihood of obtaining BRCA1/2 genetic testing in African American women at high risk for having this genetic mutation that increases the risk of breast and ovarian cancer (Sheppard, Mays, LaVeist, & Tercyak, 2013).

That there has been increased interest in the role of discrimination within the medical setting itself is evidenced by emerging literature in the area. Shavers and colleagues (2012) reviewed the literature on the effects of both interpersonal and institutional racism within health care settings. A total of 58 studies were reviewed, including perceived discrimination by both patients and providers. While the majority of studies showed that discrimination was associated with negative health outcomes, not all studies did. The authors concluded that there was a real need for innovative methodology, improved instruments, and better designed strategies to identify discrimination in health care settings, in part because of the way in which health care is delivered. Specifically, there may be system- or setting-level practices or actions that contribute to discrimination, and these may be confounded with issues related to insurance coverage as well.

As before, clinical health psychologists should remain vigilant for instances where discrimination—not only from the primary medical practitioner but from office staff, nursing staff, and others—may be occurring. Sometimes when patients do not adhere to the recommended regimen, it may be because they feel they were treated with less respect and courtesy than others around them. Patients often will not volunteer that they have been mistreated, so clinical health psychologists need to be very comfortable asking about it. However, if you ask, then there is an implied obligation to do something about it. You need to understand what the limits of your role are in the health care setting, and be very clear to the patients what you can and cannot do.

ACQUISITION OF COMPETENCIES IN INDIVIDUAL AND CULTURAL DIVERSITY IN CLINICAL HEALTH PSYCHOLOGY

Because of its importance to the field, some competency in dealing with cultural and individual diversity are requirements of any graduate training in professional psychology. The *Guidelines and Principles for Accreditation* (G&P, 2011) devote an entire domain to efforts to recruit and retain diverse faculty, staff, and trainees, and to how diversity is included in the educational experience. In addition, other domains (e.g., A, B, and E) ask specific questions related to diversity. Even though the G&P are currently being rewritten, diversity will remain an integral part of the required training for individuals in professional psychology. What that means is that education and training in cultural and individual differences and diversity should occur at all points in the sequence of training and must also be part of practitioners' lifelong continuing education experiences. For clinical health psychologists, foundational competencies such as these are initially acquired at the doctoral level; these are then further elaborated and enriched during the internship and postdoctoral residency. Experienced practitioners need to include regular updating in the area of diversity because of changing demographics and resulting observations of epidemiological patterns of diseases and behaviors. Professional psychology doctoral programs already must provide curricular materials and practica experiences that form the basis of trainees' abilities to integrate individual differences and diversity into courses, didactic experiences, clinical training, and research. These competencies and skills are further defined during internship, with postdoctoral residency programs providing the refinement of these competencies, allowing for the integration of issues of individual and cultural differences and diversity into clinical practice and research activities.

As noted earlier, training in areas related to diversity is part of the requirements of accredited doctoral, internship, and postdoctoral residency programs, and as a result all accredited programs must provide education and experience in this core area. However, the evaluation of student, intern, and trainee competence in this area is typically left to individual programs, and a range of methods are used to demonstrate and evaluate this competence. At the doctoral level these include the following: performance in classes that cover the topic; comprehensive/qualifying examination results; completion of scholarly work in the area; and supervisor ratings of work with diverse clients in practica. At the internship and postdoctoral levels, this evaluation includes supervisor ratings of work with patients and an assessment of the trainee's ability to integrate and apply knowledge about these topics to the clinical and research activities. It is important to note that evaluation of the understanding of individual and cultural differences is often integrated into other core evaluations as well, in part because it is considered central to the work of a clinical health psychologist.

NINE

Common Ethical and Legal Challenges in Clinical Health Psychology

One part of the definition of a profession is that it is self-regulating. As such, the members of every profession need to develop a set of guidelines through which they distinguish themselves from members of other professions as well as to identify rogue members of the profession who do not uphold the appropriate standards for professional conduct. In psychology, we have known this since 1958 when the first collection of Ethical Principles and Standards of Conduct for psychologists was written and distributed (American Psychological Association). The importance of ethical issues is highlighted in the fact that coverage of this content area is required in all accredited doctoral programs, internships, and postdoctoral residency programs, and it comprises more items on the Examination for Professional Practice of Psychology (EPPP) than any other content area.

Beginning clinical health psychologists are often surprised at the range of and frequency with which issues with ethical implications are raised in health care centers. While training in professional psychology prepares practitioners to deal with the legal and ethical implications of such things as child and elder abuse, domestic violence, and "duty to warn" others of potential for violent behavior, rarely does training cover issues that are routine in health care settings. These issues include topics such as making end-of-life decisions; providing expensive and invasive treatments to patients with a history of noncompliance with their usual and customary care; deciding whether a patient should or should not have surgery he or she desires; and issues that arise with organ donation. Clinical health psychologists are often called upon to "talk a patient into" a treatment he or she has decided against for a myriad of reasons. Because these kinds of ethical dilemmas often elicit strong emotional responses associated with consideration of moral, religious, worldview, or lifestyle reasons by the patient, the patient's family and friends, and the medical staff, these encounters can be particularly problematic. Unfortunately, the typical ethical training most psychologists receive does not prepare one for these types of encounters.

Research ethics is another area where prior training may not adequately prepare the clinical health psychologist. Researchers whose prior experience was with Institutional Review Boards (IRBs) affiliated with Colleges of Arts and Letters or Colleges of Sciences may find that medical IRBs operate using a very different worldview. While medical IRBs may see administering new pharmaceuticals or implementing new surgical techniques as routine, they often perceive asking questions about mental health concerns like depression or anxiety as involving more than minimal risk. Thus, even the experience of designing and conducting research in the health care setting involves knowledge of and experience with ethical principles from other health disciplines.

The Competency Benchmarks Work Group (Fouad et al., 2009) articulated three foundational competencies in the area of ethical legal standards and policy: (a) knowledge of ethical and legal standards and guidelines, (b) awareness and application of ethical decision making, and (c) ethical conduct. While the first competency area focuses on knowledge of our professional ethical code of conduct, the latter two competencies involve the application of this knowledge both in decision making and behavioral conduct. Participants at the Tempe Summit adopted these three foundational competencies for clinical health psychologists as well; however, they also recognized that there were some competencies in the area of ethical and legal standards that were uniquely associated with the practice of clinical health psychology. In particular, in contrast to functioning solely within the behavioral and mental health system, clinical health psychologists function in the broader health care system where they routinely interact with health professionals from other disciplines who possess ethical codes that vary in certain ways from the ethical codes of psychologists. Consequently, we need to be well prepared to respond appropriately when confronting situations in which our ethical principles are challenged by the differing ethical principles of other health care professionals and the broader health care system. Recognizing the importance of handling these situations gracefully, the latest list of competencies in clinical health psychology includes three additional competencies in the area of ethical standards and legal issues and policy (see Table 9.1).

TABLE 9.1 **Competencies and Behavioral Anchors in Ethical Standards and Legal Issues and Policy Unique to Clinical Health Psychology**

1. **Knowledge of ethical and legal ramifications of biopsychosocial assessment, intervention, and research/quality improvement strategies in addressing health conditions seen in health care settings[b]**
   - Develops close relationships with colleagues for ethical consultations and contacts risk management when necessary
   - Follows IRB regulations for conducting both research and quality improvement activities
   - Follows state laws related to abuse reporting, adolescent reproductive health, and determination of decision-making capacity[a]
2. **Identifies and addresses the distinctive ethical issues encountered in clinical health practice, where multiple ethical codes exist, particularly if these are in conflict with the ethical code of other members of the health care team[a]**
   - Demonstrates an understanding of the types of ethical dilemmas that occur in clinical health settings and how ethical codes of various professions guide behavior of colleagues from other professions
   - Demonstrates a commitment to ethical principles of psychologists with particular attention to dual relationship matters, confidentiality, informed consent, boundary issues, team functioning, and business practices of the health care environment
3. **Knowledge of policies that regulate the delivery of services in health care systems[a]**
   - Demonstrates familiarity with hospital/medical setting bylaws, credentialing, privileges, and staffing responsibilities
   - Demonstrates knowledge about standards set forth by national accrediting bodies

[a]Adapted from Competencies for Psychology Practice in Primary Care. Interorganizational Workgroup on Competencies for Primary Care Psychology Practice (2013, pp. 25–26).
[b]Adapted from Competencies in Clinical Health Psychology. France et al. (2008, pp. 577–578).

The first of these reflects competence in the legal and ethical issues unique to the health care setting. Many areas of health care provision have specific laws that govern practice. Examples include providing sexual education or reproductive and pregnancy health care to adolescents, dealing with various aspects of drug and alcohol abuse, and specific reporting requirements surrounding patients with seizures and their ability to drive automobiles. Clinical health psychologists who work in health care settings must be aware of the limits and allowances of their practice in the specialties or areas in which they see patients. Similarly, clinical health psychologists need to understand the role of ethics regarding research in their health care practice. As has been described elsewhere in this volume, clinical health psychologists are often called upon not only to do the more traditional kinds of research but also to develop and conduct program evaluation efforts and generate quality improvement indices and studies. There are both human subjects and setting implications associated with these sorts of tasks (e.g., what if you demonstrate that specific interventions are not effective within your population and/or setting), and clinical health psychologists not only need to carefully consider them but also need to be prepared to consult with other colleagues to determine the most appropriate actions.

The second competency involves the interface between the ethical and legal concerns of the clinical health psychologist and those of other members of the health care team. There are a number of aspects of this. The first involves knowing and understanding differences among the ethical standards of the various health professions. For example, individuals trained in the psychology tradition are often both surprised and shocked to find that during morning rounds patients are openly described and discussed, often in front of the patients and as if he or she or his or her family do not exist. While the clinical health psychologist might educate the treatment team about the negative implications of this type of discussion, and may be more circumspect when presenting psychological data regarding the patient in their presence, rounding with the treatment team is part of the health care culture and sometimes must be tolerated, even if not accepted. Similarly, some disciplines have different norms about things such as touching patients and involvement in what would be, in psychology, a dual relationship (e.g., performing hernia surgery on your realtor or your stockbroker). Two things are crucial to functioning ethnically in this context. The first is education about and the ability to consult with other disciplines in the health care team to ensure that the behavior of one or two individuals in your specific setting are within the ethical bounds of that discipline across other settings. The second is to be able to consult with other health psychologists in order to explore similarities and difference in working with members of the health care team. Although there is a good bit of overlap among the various ethical codes that health care professions possess, there are times when professional ethical principles may come into conflict. It is important for the team to have open discussions and an understanding of the ethical principles that will guide team behavior.

The current APA Ethical Guidelines (2002) provide some guidance in this regard; however, the standards of conduct stated in our code of ethics focuses more on communicating limits to psychological practice imposed by our ethical principles to members of the health care team and patients than how to balance our standards with those of other professions. It is not unheard of for these ethical issues to involve patients directly. For example, clinical health psychologists often receive requests from patients for recommendations regarding "better" medications or which medical procedure to select; here the limits of one's expertise and competence needs to be made clear because clinical health psychologists do not normally possess the competencies to answer these sorts of questions.

The final distinctive competency associated with clinical health psychology focuses on the knowledge of health care laws as they apply to one's practice. Many of these laws and legal statutes may be specific to the state and/or the agency in which one works. Some of them may reflect policies and practices about charting and recordkeeping. For example, what the clinical health psychologist may have learned in graduate school (e.g., to write long, detailed comprehensive notes that record all aspects of what the patient said to you) may not be so effective in health care settings that value concise notes and brevity. Similarly, many medical settings have specialized credentialing policies and procedures that all individuals on the medical staff must follow. It is the responsibility of the clinical health psychologist to make sure he or she is informed of these requirements and meets the standards for the facility in which he or she is working. Most health facilities require that providers undergo an extensive initial credentialing process in order to provide care within their facility as well as complete annual credentialing activities (e.g., training in exposure to blood-borne pathogens, physical examinations with TB testing, emergency procedure) to maintain their practices.

ACQUISITION OF COMPETENCIES IN ETHICAL AND LEGAL ISSUES IN CLINICAL HEALTH PSYCHOLOGY

Because of their importance in the education, training, and development of a professional psychologist, elements of basic ethical practice must be acquired relatively early in the sequence of training. Understanding the need to report some kind of abuse or to deal with homicidal or suicidal risk, for example, are typically acquired sufficiently early in one's training and the appropriate, legal, and ethical way to deal with these types of situations is taught early during training. Ethics are considered so fundamental, for example, that many states have mandatory ongoing coverage of topics pertinent to ethical practice as part of the continuing education requirements to maintain licensure. Letters of recommendation for internship typically cover the person's ability to engage in ethical practice, and as noted earlier, a large number of items on the EPPP exam cover the topic. Consequently, coverage of ethics is routinely reviewed by the Commission on Accreditation when programs seek initial or reaccreditation. Thus, the basic tenets of ethical practice should be well inculcated into a person as he or she begins professional work, even the initial practicum experiences the individual encounters in graduate school.

For many students, the early years of doctoral training do not afford them the exposure to health care settings that would allow them to explore and learn about the unique ethical and legal competencies of health psychology as well as related health care disciplines. That is because most mental health settings that serve as common practicum locations involve exposure to practitioners with similar training (e.g., social workers, counselors, applied behavior analysts), and the issues raised tend to have similar ethical guidelines across mental health fields. However, from the time clinical health psychology trainees begin to work in a health care setting, issues of ethics begin to be raised, particularly those involving exposure to different codes of ethics of other health professions. Internship and postdoctoral training should provide both knowledge-based and experiential training in these sorts of settings for clinical health psychologists in training. At this level, ethical issues should be openly discussed as they arise. Trainees need to be taught to discriminate when their own personal worldview is coloring the possible ethical decisions that they may be making. Regular ongoing consultation with peers, with others on the health care team, and even with medical setting clergy needs to be part of this experience so that trainees can begin to acquire these skills early in their career. Obviously, faculty should model active engagement in this process. This can be done in a number of ways. Most health care facilities have both an IRB and some kind of ethical review team that assists staff when ethical questions or concerns are raised. Faculty should be active participants in these activities, and they should encourage their trainees to sit in on and be exposed to the discussions that typically occur in these settings. Because of our extensive knowledge and skill in designing and conducting research, faculty are often invited to serve on these committees; rather than consider this type of activity as "busy work," it is a testament to our competencies and we should consider these types of appointments as another way to demonstrate them to our peers.

Faculty should take advantage of every opportunity to discuss ethical issues when trainees under their supervision encounter them. A regular part of clinical supervision should be reserved to address these ethical issues as they arise (see Chapter 14). Knowing how to behave when other members of the health care team accept gifts from a patient, how to respond to another team member who taps the trainee for advice on how to handle challenges of raising his or her child, or whether to share the details of a patient's divorce with the rest of the team when the trainee was asked to keep the information confidential all represent important conversations that should occur during supervision meetings.

Finally, because laws and policies are often in a state of flux (witness the changes that occurred to our profession when HIPAA was passed), clinical health psychologists must continue to remain abreast of policies and laws that are enacted that could affect their practice. Professional LISTSERVs represent one strategy for discussing these issues and being aware of them, as well as ongoing continuing education activities and opportunities. Maintaining lifelong learning in the areas of ethical and legal issues needs to be part of every clinical health psychologist's ongoing commitment to the field.

PART III

Functional Competencies in Clinical Health Psychology

TEN

Assessment in Clinical Health Psychology

Psychological assessment is a prominent activity that all professional psychologists, including clinical health psychologists, conduct on a regular basis. In fact, one could argue that with our knowledge of psychometric theory and training in both formal and less formal modes of assessment, professional psychologists stand out as members of the only health care discipline with credentials in assessing individual differences in intellectual-aptitude as well as personality-temperamental functioning. In this regard, we contribute uniquely to the health care system.

According to the Competency Benchmarks document (Fouad et al., 2009), competence in assessment is comprised of six domains: (a) measurement and psychometrics; (b) knowledge of evaluation methods; (c) application of methods; (d) diagnosis; (e) conceptualization and recommendations; and (f) communication of findings. These domains roughly parallel the process a professional psychologist takes when conducting a psychological evaluation. First, through extensive training in psychometric test construction, psychologists select appropriate methods for evaluation. They are aware of the strengths and limitations of the various assessment approaches and administer, score, and interpret test findings using strategies in which they have received training to administer competently. In many cases, the psychological assessment is aimed at arriving at a diagnosis that will inform the practitioner's conceptualization of the problem. In the final step of the process of conducting an assessment, recommendations are made and communicated effectively to the patient or the health care team. Elucidation of behavioral anchors associated with each of these steps of the assessment process can be found in the Competency Benchmarks document (Fouad et al., 2009, S16-18). Suffice it to say that these functional areas of competence are pertinent to all professional psychologists, including clinical health psychologists. However, because clinical health psychologists function primarily within health care environments that extend beyond those that only provide mental health care, there are some additional competencies required for clinical health psychologists who conduct psychological assessments in the broader health care arena. Using decades of literature focusing on clinical health psychology assessment, these unique competencies were reviewed by participants of the Tempe Summit of Education and Training in Clinical Health Psychology (France et al., 2008) and have been incorporated into the most recent listing of competencies in clinical health psychology.

ASSESSMENT COMPETENCIES AMONG
CLINICAL HEALTH PSYCHOLOGISTS

In fast-paced, multidisciplinary health care settings, clinical health psychologists are often called upon to use their expertise in psychological assessment to identify mental health issues that are potentially complicating provision of adequate medical care. For example, adherence to medical intervention in a diabetic patient may be compromised by presence of a major depressive episode. Or a patient presenting with symptoms of irritable bowel syndrome may have an underlying generalized anxiety disorder. Patients benefit greatly when health care professionals seek the expertise of clinical health psychologists when mental health diagnoses are suspected to be interfering with ongoing medical evaluations and interventions. Although these sorts of psychological evaluations are commonly done by clinical health psychologists, making a diagnosis of a major depressive disorder or generalized anxiety disorder is not a unique attribute of a clinical health psychologist. In fact, these diagnoses could be determined by almost any competent licensed psychologist. In this regard, participants at the Tempe Summit considered all of the functional competencies outlined in the Competency Benchmarks document (Fouad et al., 2009) and fairly quickly agreed that all of these broad and general competencies in assessment were also applicable to the field of clinical health psychology (France et al., 2008).

Using the extensive literature in clinical health psychology assessment as a guide (see Andrasik, Goodie, & Peterson, 2014; Rozensky, Sweet, & Tovian, 1997), Tempe Summit participants added several knowledge- and skill-based competencies to the list of assessment competencies required for the competent practice of clinical health psychology (France et al., 2008). The exact wording of these competencies has undergone some revision since they were first reported, lending credence to the premise that the initial list was considered a work in progress. The current list of assessment competencies unique to the practice of clinical health psychology is depicted in Table 10.1. Each of these additional competencies in the area of assessment will be considered in more detail in the following sections.

Knowledge-Based Competencies in Assessment

Using the biopsychosocial model as a guide, three domains of knowledge were included in this functional area of competence for the practice of clinical health psychology: knowledge of biological, psychological, and social-environmental methods of assessment that are used in health care settings. Given the multidisciplinary staffing of the health care environment, clinical health psychologists need to have a broader knowledge base of assessment strategies than professional psychologists trained in the traditional specialty areas of clinical, counseling, or school psychology. Most training in professional psychology focuses primarily on psychological assessment, with much lesser emphasis (if any) on biological and social-environmental methods of assessment. Furthermore, the assessment competencies outlined in the Competency Benchmarks document (Fouad et al., 2009) are focused on evaluating, diagnosing, and communicating treatment recommendations for a single patient rather than evaluating the biological composition of the patient or the broader environment in which the patient lives. These three knowledge-based competencies assure that clinical health psychologists are familiar with methods of assessment that operate across the full spectrum, from molecular levels (biologically based methods of assessment) to molar levels (environmental-systems methods of assessment) of assessment.

Let's consider biological methods of assessment first. Modern health care environments have clearly transcended the days when physicians relied almost exclusively on the results of a comprehensive history and physical examination to assess, diagnose, and treat common medical ailments. This is not to say, however, that physicians have given up listening to bodily functions and palpating various body tissues, but rather they have added countless new methods of diagnostic assessment tools. With technological advances, medical practitioners have access to a full array of laboratory tests (e.g., urinalysis, blood work, immunologic titers),

TABLE 10.1 **Competencies and Behavioral Anchors in Assessment Unique to Clinical Health Psychology**

KNOWLEDGE-BASED ASSESSMENT COMPETENCIES

---

1. **Knowledge and understanding of biological assessment strategies and their results used in health care settings[b]**
   - Recognizes names and appropriate dosages of medications for commonly occurring medical and psychological/behavioral conditions (e.g., diabetes, hypertension, depression)
   - Understands the meaning of biological assessment levels (e.g., blood pressure, A1Cs)
2. **Knowledge and understanding of psychological assessment strategies used in health care settings[b]**
   - Identifies assessment instruments that are optimal for use in specific health care settings (e.g., PHQ, Brief Symptom Inventory, SF-36, Millon)
   - Devises appropriate assessment strategies for which no validated measures exist
3. **Knowledge and understanding of social and environmental assessment strategies used in health care settings[b]**
   - Assesses social, cultural, financial, and familial background during initial interview and follow-up appointments
   - Considers broader assessments of environmental factors known to promote health (e.g., access to health care and health clubs)

SKILL-BASED ASSESSMENT COMPETENCIES

---

4. **Ability to evaluate the presenting problem and to select and administer empirically supported biopsychosocial assessments appropriate for the patient's physical illness, injury, or disability[b]**
   - Reviews electronic health record core behavioral risk measures to determine where to focus screenings[a]
   - Select and administer measures to include in routine appointments to identify common presenting problems (e.g., depression, anxiety, substance use disorders, sleep difficulties, disruptive behavior)[a]
   - Displays ability to identify instruments appropriate for medical patients and consistent with use in medical settings (with norms appropriate for patient demographics)
5. **Ability to conduct a comprehensive biopsychosocial interview and evaluate objective biological and psychosocial findings related to physical health or illness, injury, or disability[b]**
   - Conducts mental status interview independently
   - Assesses how the patient's physical condition (e.g., body mass index, HbA1c, out-of-range lab values), thoughts, emotions, behaviors, habits, interpersonal relationships, and environment influence the identified problem and functioning[a]
6. **Ability to assess biopsychosocial and behavioral risk factors for the development of physical illness, injury, or disability[b]**
   - Evaluate tobacco and substance use using validated protocols
   - Identifies existing exercise programs
   - Evaluates social support system
7. **Ability to assess environmental factors that facilitate or inhibit patient knowledge, values, attitudes, and/or behaviors affecting health functioning and health care utilization[b]**
   - Interviews patient about socioeconomic/financial stressors/social support/geographic local/transportation issues that impact access to health care

8. Ability to assess biopsychosocial factors affecting adherence to recommendations for medical and psychological care[b]
- Identifies barriers that could potentially impact adherence (transportation, finances, insurance coverage)

9. Ability to assess the biopsychosocial impact of medical procedures (including screening, diagnostic, and intervention/prevention procedures)[b]
- Conducts suitability of transplant evaluations
- Conducts gastric bypass surgery candidacy evaluations
- Evaluates suitability of spinal cord stimulator candidates

10. Ability to solicit input of significant others in the assessment process as indicated[a]
- Obtains information from caregivers (e.g., for children, elderly, those with chronic illness) in the assessment process
- Seeks feedback from a couple simultaneously about how they can work together to ensure compliance with a postoperative bariatric surgery lifestyle

11. Ability to communicate the results of assessments to both professional and lay audiences in the health care setting[b]
- Writes clear and concise consultation reports/chart notes free of psychological jargon
- Communicates professionally with other health service providers
- Communicates with patients free of psychological jargon

---

[a]Adapted from Competencies for Psychology Practice in Primary Care. Interorganizational Workgroup on Competencies for Primary Care Psychology Practice (2013, pp. 36–39).
[b]Adapted from Competencies in Clinical Health Psychology. France et al. (2008, p. 577).

specimen assays (e.g., biopsies), evaluations of genetic composition, and various scopes (e.g., endoscopy, colonoscopy) and scans (e.g., magnetic resonance imaging, X-ray scans). Although clinical health psychologists will never be called upon to conduct these evaluations or interpret their results, they should possess knowledge of the reasons these biological methods of assessment are used and what the results will reveal. For example, clinical health psychologists working with patients with essential hypertension should understand how blood pressure is properly assessed, the range of what is considered "normal" and "abnormal" blood pressure, and what the resulting values from such an assessment mean. Likewise, for clinical health psychologists working with patients diagnosed with diabetes, it is essential to know the normal values associated with blood glucose and glycated hemoglobin (HbA1c) levels, and how to use these values in monitoring adherence to treatment aimed at regulating blood glucose levels or following specific dietary recommendations. In contrast to our peers in the traditional professional psychology areas, it is clear that clinical health psychologists need to understand and use information from biological assessment methods conducted by professionals in other health care disciplines.

Comprehensive knowledge of all biological assessment strategies would require extensive course work in medicine or other health-related disciplines, an aspect of training unlikely to be achieved by most trainees in clinical health psychology. However, clinical health psychologists should know enough about a range of basic medical tests and a good bit about the tests used with the most frequent medical problems they encounter in their practice. Clinical health psychologists often develop subspecialties within clinical health, typically corresponding to the medical specialties with which they work on a day-to-day basis; their biological knowledge is often specific to that medical specialty. For instance, clinical health psychologists who work in obstetrics and gynecology clinics need to know a good bit about methods to determine pregnancy, nutritional standards given to pregnant women, what happens during amniocentesis, how to interpret blood tests administered to examine Rh factor compatibility between parent and child, what anesthetic options are available during labor and delivery (including what the relative risks and benefits of each might be), and how use of various substances may influence fetal development. Clinical health psychologists who rarely work with pregnant patients may not need this depth of knowledge in these areas.

Familiarity with terminology most commonly employed with medical diagnostic tools is part of the knowledge-based assessment competency for clinical health psychologists. For example, in making medical diagnoses, the sensitivity and specificity of measurement strategies and diagnostic methods are always reported, as well as indices of positive and negative predictive value. These terms are critical when binary decisions, like making a diagnosis versus not being diagnosed, are made based upon measurement values from a given test. Because most psychological assessment strategies purport to measure constructs that are theoretically normally distributed, lesser emphasis is placed upon binary decision making commonly employed in the medical environment in most professional psychology training programs. Thus, indices of sensitivity and specificity represent indices of measurement validity for a given diagnostic test, and an important component of the clinical health psychologist's knowledge in this assessment domain, and may differentiate the clinical health psychologist from his or her more traditional psychologist colleagues.

Knowledge of psychological assessment strategies is a hallmark area of competence for all professional psychologists. However, most assessment competencies acquired in training focus primarily on deriving psychiatric diagnoses and making recommendations regarding provision of mental health care. Because the domain of health is so much broader than mental health, clinical health psychologists need to develop additional competencies in creating and using psychological assessment strategies beyond those that tap into the assessment of mental health constructs. It is well known, for example, that psychological factors influence the experience of pain, and a multitude of psychological assessment tools have been developed to assist in the assessment of both acute episodes of pain and chronic pain conditions (e.g., Turk & Melzack, 2001). Measuring adherence to medical recommendations or treatment plans represents another area where knowledge of psychological assessment has facilitated the construction of relevant assessment devices (e.g., Quittner, Modi, Lemanek, Ievers-Landis, & Rapoff, 2008). Development and use of these instruments is based upon a sound background in psychometric theory and psychological assessment, knowledge bases that all professional psychologists should have. Self-report measures of health behaviors (e.g., Centers for Disease Control and Prevention, 2006), stress (e.g., Cohen, Kessler, & Underwood Gordon, 1997), and coping (e.g., Penwell, Larkin, & Goodie, 2014) represent additional psychological assessment tools that are widely used in health care environments and that extend the assessment repertoire of the clinical health psychologist beyond the measurement of mental health constructs.

In addition to possessing a solid knowledge base of biological and psychological assessment strategies, clinical health psychologists need to have a basic understanding of methods of assessment of social-environmental influences on health, including those used in community health education, public health, and health policy. Using a systems approach, this knowledge base of assessment methods extends beyond the individual patient and taps into environmental influences on health and/or treatment. Founding their assessments on the biopsychosocial model, clinical health psychologists are well aware that these are important factors that impact health outcomes. Belar and Deardorff (2009) provide a helpful rubric for considering family, health care system, and sociocultural contextual factors when conducting a clinical health psychology assessment. Family factors include consideration of characteristics of the home, feelings and expectations of family members, and reinforcement of health or illness behaviors provided by the family. Factors associated with the health care system include availability of health care, provider's knowledge and attitudes toward the patient and his or her treatment, and communication competencies of the provider. Broader sociocultural factors must also be evaluated, including exposure to health hazards or terrorism, sentiment about and understanding of the culture to the patient's illness, the possible role health disparities play, the quantity and quality of the social network, and federal and local laws regulating the health care system. Understanding the environmental context within which the symptomatic patient presents involves acquiring assessment competencies that go beyond the typical assessment strategies most professional psychologists are exposed to during training. In this regard, clinical health psychologists need to extend their knowledge of assessment by learning from their peers in these interdisciplinary health care settings who have explicit training in other methods of assessing the social-environmental milieu (e.g., public health researchers).

Skill-Based Competencies in Assessment

The biopsychosocial model also provides the foundation for eight skill-based assessment competencies distinctly associated with the practice of clinical health psychology. The term "biopsychosocial" is actually used in defining five of these skill-based competencies. Essentially, these competencies assume development of the benchmark competencies in assessment (see Fouad et al., 2009) and fundamental knowledge-based competencies pertinent to the assessment of clinical health conditions outlined in the previous section. These skill-based competencies then reflect the application of the fundamental knowledge of assessment within the health care environment.

Selection and administration of empirically supported tools for conducting clinical health psychology assessments is positioned first among the skill-based assessment competencies (see item 4 in Table 10.1). This area of competence is similar to those described by the Competency Benchmarks Work Group (Fouad et al., 2009), except that it is uniquely focused on the patient's "physical" illness, injury, or disability instead of his or her mental illness or behavioral disorder. Very frequently, patients evaluated by clinical health psychologists are not seeking care for mental health services, so the approach taken to evaluate them is quite different than assessment strategies used in traditional mental health treatment settings. In this regard, most patients presenting for treatments of "physical" ailments would see very little need for completing a personality assessment (à la the MMPI or Rorschach) or a full intellectual evaluation. Although effective rationales for employing these extensive assessment strategies can be generated for patients seeking help for mental health problems, it is more challenging to come up with a rationale that would be acceptable to most patients presenting with physical health problems. Recognizing the difficulty in providing a rationale for extensive psychological testing and the challenges in implementing such an approach in a fast-paced health care setting, clinical health psychologists have tended to use briefer assessment tools, including self-report screening instruments that often contain fewer than 10 items.

Foremost among the clinical health psychologist's tools is the comprehensive biopsychosocial interview, which is highlighted in the second skill-based competency on the list (item 5 in Table 10.1). Using this approach, patients in medical or related health care settings become easily engaged in the evaluation and provide the information needed to complete the assessment. Opting to use a traditional psychiatric interview often results in less engagement from the patient, who is left wondering how such an evaluation will enhance his or her medical care at best, and resistant to treatment or irritable at worst.

The next four skill-based competencies distinctly associated with clinical health psychology assessment are focused on specific types of assessment commonly employed in the health care arena. Due to the frequency of their occurrence, they are perceived as areas of competence required of all clinical health psychologists. The first competency area in this cluster of four (item 6 in Table 10.1) pertains to assessing risk factors for onset of physical illnesses, injuries, or disabilities. Using this approach, clinical health psychologists draw upon their knowledge of epidemiological research to understand the potential for future health-related problems in patients with whom they are evaluating. In this regard, the clinical health psychologist has an eye toward the future when conducting evaluations of patients in health care environments. In fact, many of the assessments we conduct are specifically aimed at predicting whether there is any future risk for medical or psychological complications or iatrogenic illnesses (e.g., bariatric surgery evaluations, evaluations of transplant candidates, etc.), or what needs to be done to decrease the likelihood of complications or illness in the future (e.g., preventive health care). In particular, our knowledge of psychological and behavioral risk factors for numerous medical conditions is highly regarded. It is well known, for example, that depression is a risk factor for myocardial infarctions, both among healthy samples and patients already diagnosed with cardiac disease (Rozansky, Blumenthal, & Kaplan, 1999), and we are uniquely positioned in the health care environment to conduct evaluations specifically addressing this risk factor. It goes without saying that an evaluation of psychological or behavioral risk factors would likely influence the outcomes of interventions prescribed and inform the delivery of preventative services.

The second area in this cluster of skill-based competencies (item 7 in Table 10.1) focuses on our ability to evaluate knowledge, values, and attitudes of patients and their families that will assist in health care delivery. The question of whether patients have the requisite knowledge and cognitive functioning to engage in appropriate medical decision making falls into this category. Teams of medical providers are often at a loss when evaluating how influential these factors are when patients and their families make decisions about medical assessments and interventions. Countless medical tests and procedures are conducted without patients or their families fully comprehending the potential outcomes and associated medical risks. Although situations like this typically are not concerning to the health care team when the patient or medical guardian agrees with the recommendations of the team, they become problematic when the patient or guardian makes a medical decision that differs from the recommended course of action by the health care team. In these cases, it calls into question the patient's (or the family's) ability to make appropriate decisions regarding medical care. Again, it is the domain of the clinical health psychologist to assist the health care teams in navigating these situations, even when the outcome of the decision-making process may not be consistent with the immediate recommendations of the health care team.

Assessment of adherence to recommendations to medical and psychological care is specifically addressed in the third area of this cluster of skill-based competencies (item 8 in Table 10.1). Although health care providers, including professional psychologists, like to believe that patients will follow treatment recommendations and engage in prescribed behaviors consistently, we are all aware that this is not the case. Patients with essential hypertension do not take their medications, patients with diabetes do not follow the prescribed diet, patients with asthma fail to use their inhalers properly, and patients referred for specialty care frequently fail to make those appointments. In fact, it could probably be argued that nonadherence is the norm of medical care. Based upon the biopsychosocial model, clinical health psychologists are uniquely positioned to evaluate adherence to treatment recommendations and to assist health care providers in optimizing treatment outcomes for their patients.

The fourth specific competence in this cluster of skill-based competencies for clinical health psychologists involves assessing how various medical procedures affect patients undergoing them (item 9 in Table 10.1). The modern health care environment contains an array of assessment and intervention procedures that can be stressful and overwhelming to many patients. Consider waiting for results of a blood test to confirm the diagnosis of a sexually transmitted disease, undergoing confinement in a magnetic resonance imaging scanner, or holding still during a bone marrow aspiration. In all cases, these procedures—and the results that come from them—can evoke strong emotional reactions among patients. Given that clinical health psychologists practice in health care settings, they are often called upon (correctly or incorrectly) to evaluate, moderate, and even from time to time to ameliorate these reactions when they occur. As such, clinical health psychologists need to use their extensive training in assessment to approach these situations when they arise to comprehend the underlying reasons for these reactions that may be amenable to modification by the treatment team (i.e., alternative methods for obtaining the same result that produce lesser emotional reactions could be adopted). In other cases, the emotional reaction might be considered entirely normal, despite the objections of members of the medical team who insist it is an overreaction. For example, it is not uncommon for clinical health psychologists to be referred to evaluate newly diagnosed cancer patients for depression by members of the health care team because of the patient's prolonged crying. In many of these cases, the crying is an understandable reaction to receiving the news that one has cancer and no other symptoms of depression are apparent.

The next skill-based competency in assessment (item 10 in Table 10.1) pertains to the ability to cointerview a patient and family member (frequently a spouse). Unlike many traditional encounters in mental health care settings where the patient and provider meet confidentially, it is the norm in health care settings like medical hospitals for patients to be evaluated in the presence of a family member. Although it is certainly the purview of the psychologist to request some time alone with the patient and excuse the family member, there is often good reason to assess the patient in the presence of a family member. If the patient is suffering from a condition where he or she is confused or delirious, information from the family member may likely be more accurate than information obtained from the patient. Also, interviewing a patient in the presence of a family member can provide the evaluator with the opportunity to assess the quality of the interaction that is present in this relationship. Sources of agreement as well as disagreement between the patient and family member can provide important clues to the clinical health psychologist's assessment of the patient's social network.

The final skill-based competency in clinical health psychology in the area of assessment focuses on another benchmark competency in assessment, namely communication of findings (item 11 in Table 10.1). The key distinction between the general professional psychologist and the clinical health psychology specialist is the ability to communicate with other relevant health care professionals. Whereas a generalist needs to communicate effectively by writing a comprehensive report and going over it with the patient, the clinical health psychologist is almost always communicating findings to another health care provider or a treatment team. This requires a different set of skills, foremost of which is the ability to speak succinctly and be heard. The fast-paced health care environment will not tolerate the five-page integrative reporting format learned in graduate school. Communication has to be quick and to the point and progress notes should adapt to the SOAP (Subjective, Objective, Assessment, Plan) format used in many medical settings. In this regard, the participants at the Tempe Summit believed it represented a unique area of competence in the area of assessment among clinical health psychologists.

ACQUISITION OF ASSESSMENT COMPETENCIES IN CLINICAL HEALTH PSYCHOLOGY

In contrast to the foundational competencies presented in Section 2 of this book, specific functional competencies almost always can be divided easily into knowledge-based and skill-based types. The area of assessment is no exception to this general rule. Adopting the general rubric outlined by Nash and Larkin (2012), knowledge-based competencies are typically acquired before their associated skill-based competencies. This makes intuitive sense and is generally how training is conducted in professional psychology; doctoral training carries the bulk of the responsibility in developing knowledge-based competencies, and internship and postdoctoral training focuses more on training of skill-based competencies. With respect to training in assessment competencies, professional psychologists-in-training enroll in course work in psychometric theory and psychological and behavioral assessment early on during graduate training. Almost always, these courses rely on a textbook and a collection of theoretical and empirical articles, and methods of assessment tap into knowledge attainment of material read and presented in class. Following this extensive didactic learning experience, students in professional psychology training programs eventually learn to conduct a variety of these assessments in clinical applied settings with real patients seeking care. In some cases, these practical assessment experiences are conducted within training clinics operated by the programs themselves, and in other cases, they are conducted at community clinics willing to work with trainees in closely supervised settings. In today's academic environment, these early skill-based learning experiences occur during the doctoral training years, and they prepare students for more intermediate and advanced skill acquisition that occurs during their internship experiences.

Although one could argue that internship programs do not typically conduct formal knowledge-based competency development in assessment, many interns acquire entirely new assessment competencies during their internship year. It is not uncommon for trainees with no exposure to neuropsychological assessment, for example, to complete a rotation in that specialty area while on internship. To accomplish this, faculty members in internship programs, by default, find themselves teaching knowledge-based competencies using fairly didactic methods for these trainees. In this regard, it is better to think of the internship year as a time to fill in the gaps of assessment competence that were not taught during doctoral training than to view it solely as a time to engage in skill-based learning.

The same sequence from knowledge-based to skill-based competency attainment applies to the specialized list of competencies outlined for clinical health psychologists in this chapter. In contrast to the functional competencies of assessment described by the Benchmark Competencies Workgroup (Fouad et al., 2009), there is no reason to believe that doctoral students beginning their internships and trainees graduating from their programs to assume careers in professional psychology possess any of these specialized assessment competencies in clinical health psychology. Courses that teach the knowledge-based competencies in clinical health psychology assessment and subsequent practical experiences that provide opportunities for skill-based competency development are not required in accredited doctoral or internship programs. Therefore, only students who elect to expose themselves to the content of clinical health psychology assessment during their doctoral training years and the internship that follows would possess elements of these specialized competencies. Fortunately, there are several doctoral programs with devoted tracks, areas of concentration, or major emphasis areas in clinical health psychology (Larkin, 2009) and a multitude of internship programs that have major rotations in health care environments that provide opportunities for students with interests in becoming competent clinical health psychologists. For students who are unable to take advantage of these opportunities during their doctoral and internship years, a range of postdoctoral programs exist that are geared toward filling in the gaps in knowledge-based competencies as well as experiential training opportunities in the area of clinical health psychology assessment.

Assessment using the biopsychosocial model is part of the daily practice of professional clinical health psychologists. Exposure to this area of competence spans the entire training sequence, from doctoral programs where initial knowledge-based elements of assessment are typically acquired to the internships and postdoctoral fellowships beyond that traditionally concentrate on skill-based competency acquisition. Using this developmental sequence, trainees that emerge from these programs possess the requisite competencies for conducting assessments within the health care system by evaluating the spectrum of biological, psychological, and socio-environmental factors related to physical illnesses, injuries, and disabilities that are seen in these settings.

ELEVEN

Intervention in Clinical Health Psychology

Professional psychology blossomed following World War II when rank-
ing members of the military forces in the United States recognized the
need for clinical services for veterans suffering from various psychological conditions associated with their time in battle and the transition
home afterward. Recognized as experts in psychological assessment (see
Chapter 10), the military community welcomed professional psychologists into their relatively new roles as care providers and created a multitude of positions in a significant number of Veterans Administration
hospitals and clinics across the United States. Since this time, intervention has been a prominent activity that all professional psychologists,
including clinical health psychologists, conduct on a regular basis.
Consequently, all training programs in professional psychology include
a healthy dose of both knowledge-based and skill-based learning experiences in intervention, with the most recent efforts focused on the
use of evidence-based therapeutic techniques (Goodheart, Kazdin, &
Sternberg, 2006).

It should be stated up front that competency of intervention is inextricably connected to competency in assessment. Because intervention is
always based on a solid understanding of the case, it does not have a prayer
of being successful if accompanied by an inadequate initial assessment.
Furthermore, the ongoing therapeutic process requires continual assessment so the care provider knows whether the intervention is working,
including when to modify the treatment plan when it is not working as
planned. From this perspective, our success in acquiring competence in
intervention is dependent upon our competence in assessment.

The Competency Benchmarks document (Fouad et al., 2009) outlines competence in intervention across five domains: (a) knowledge of interventions; (b) intervention planning; (c) skills; (d) intervention implementation; and (e) progress evaluation. Despite the popular media portrayals of interventions being one-session, in-your-face altercations, professional psychologists recognize that interventions occur over time and involve a somewhat typical process of establishing a therapeutic alliance, evaluating the problem and arriving at a coherent case formulation, devising a treatment plan, implementing the intervention, and terminating treatment when data suggest the therapeutic goals have been achieved (Kanfer & Schefft, 1988). The general domains outlined by the Benchmark Competency Workgroup were associated with these recognized steps in the process of therapy. The first area of competence focuses on the basic knowledge of the scientific and theoretical bases for psychological interventions. Here, we draw heavily upon our knowledge of the evidence-based practice of psychology. As a scientific discipline, we need to know which therapies work for which conditions under which circumstances as well as those that do not. Using the evidence base as a foundation, coupled with the results from the initial assessment, the problem is conceptualized and a treatment plan devised to address the problematic behaviors with which the patient presented. This process of case formulation or conceptualization reflects the second area of intervention competence. The third and fourth competency areas in intervention represent skill-based competencies in developing therapeutic relationships (skills) and implementing successful behavior change interventions (intervention implementation), with the former focusing more on relationship-building skills and the latter focusing more on skills in implementing specific intervention strategies. The final benchmark competency listed in the area of intervention focuses upon the ability to systematically gather data throughout the therapeutic process for purposes of evaluating treatment outcomes and informing practitioners when modifications to the treatment plan need to be made. Behavioral anchors associated with each of these intervention competencies can be found in the Competency Benchmarks document (Fouad et al., 2009, pp. S18–S19). Like assessment, the functional areas of competence in intervention are important for all professional psychologists. It is true that some professional psychologists may spend their entire careers only performing psychological assessments and never conducting interventions (some forensic psychologists and neuropsychologists come to mind here). However, because these individuals often make treatment recommendations as part of their evaluative work, knowledge of potential interventions and some understanding of how they work are critical for making plausible recommendations. In this regard, intervention was considered an essential functional competency of all professional psychologists by the Benchmark Competency Workgroup.

It probably goes without saying, but because clinical health psychologists function within health care environments that extend beyond those that only provide mental health care, some additional competencies in intervention for clinical health psychologists have been identified. These unique competencies were reviewed and considered at the Tempe Summit of Education and Training in Clinical Health Psychology (France et al., 2008) and are described in the following section in their current form.

INTERVENTION COMPETENCIES AMONG
CLINICAL HEALTH PSYCHOLOGISTS

Many referrals in multidisciplinary health care settings might resemble requests for professional consultation (see Chapter 12), but hidden in the referral question care providers often can detect questions such as "Can you do anything with this patient? He is driving me crazy!" In cases like these, clinical health psychologists are called upon to intervene and assist the health care team in providing better health care to the identified patient. Common antecedents for this type of referral include patients who refuse a medical procedure, patients who monopolize valuable time in the clinic, patients who fail to comply with treatment recommendations, and patients who erupt into crying spells (or other displays of intense emotion) during medical visits. Providing intervention in these cases not only addresses the patient's psychological needs but also promotes more positive relationships between the patient and the medical team regarding treatment of the medical condition. Implementing a successful intervention in such cases produces a win-win situation in which the patient's emotional state improves *and* the members of the patient's medical team no longer feel inept in addressing the patient's medical needs.

In this regard, participants at the Tempe Summit considered all of the functional competencies pertaining to the area of intervention outlined in the Competency Benchmarks document (Fouad et al., 2009) and agreed that all of these broad and general competencies in intervention also were applicable to the field of clinical health psychology (France et al., 2008). Through careful consideration of the literature on interventions in clinical health psychology settings, Tempe Summit participants added several intervention competencies required for the practice of clinical health psychology

TABLE 11.1 **Competencies and Behavioral Anchors in Intervention Unique to Clinical Health Psychology**

1. **Ability to access, evaluate, and utilize information in designing and implementing treatment, health promotion, and prevention interventions using new and emerging health technologies[b]**
   - Uses technology to deliver health care and health promotion programs (e.g., Web-based protocols for smoking cessation or relaxation)[a]
   - Encourages use of patient portal of the electronic health record to be involved in the patient's care[a]
2. **Implementation of individual- or family-level evidence-based treatment interventions to treat health- and mental health-related issues[b]**
   - Uses evidence-based intervention and prevention programs to improve individual and systems functioning in areas beyond provision of mental health services (e.g., improved sleep, decreased autonomic arousal, decreased pain, improved exercise and nutrition)[a]
   - Focuses interventions on patient self-care, symptom reduction, and functional improvement (e.g., deep breathing, relaxation, cognitive disputation, sleep hygiene, self-management)[a]
3. **Implementation of evidence-based interventions for individuals and populations along a continuum from acute clinical need to subclinical problems to prevention and wellness[b]**
   - Implements evidence-based health promotion programs
   - Focuses outcomes on pertinent behavioral risk factors (e.g., smoking cessation, colon screening, seat belt use)
4. **Ability to evaluate, select, and administer appropriate assessments for the purpose of monitoring and evaluating the process and outcomes of treatment and rehabilitative services[b]**
   - With the patient's input, identifies appropriate measures of treatment outcome for the presenting problem
   - Develops monitoring systems that assess both the benefits and risks associated with treatment
   - Works collaboratively with health care team to perform ongoing assessment of fluctuations in presenting problem and of emerging problems (e.g., use of Patient Health Questionnaire 9 to screen for depression annually)

[a]Adapted from Competencies for Psychology Practice in Primary Care. Interorganizational Workgroup on Competencies for Primary Care Psychology Practice (2013, pp. 39–42).
[b]Adapted from Competencies in Clinical Health Psychology. France et al. (2008, p. 577).

(France et al., 2008). Like the additional competencies in assessment, the exact wording and the organization of these competencies have undergone some revision since they were first reported. These additional competencies distinctive to the practice of clinical health psychology are shown in Table 11.1 and described in more detail in the text that follows.

Knowledge-Based Competencies in Intervention

All knowledge-based intervention competencies unique to clinical health psychology are based on a complete understanding of the biopsychosocial treatment approach. In a nutshell, this approach to intervention extends beyond identifying treatment goals aimed at solely improving psychological functioning and, instead, requires developing treatment goals that target biological, psychological, and socio-environmental functioning. In a sense, by eschewing the mind-body dichotomy belief systems that continue to differentiate mental from physical health, the biopsychosocial treatment approach reflects a more holistic treatment approach. As a result, the goals of such an approach extend far beyond the elimination of symptoms or disease management to the realm of wellness and health promotion. Whereas traditional interventions in professional psychology and psychiatry are aimed at relief from emotional or behavioral symptoms (e.g., elimination of panic attacks, reduction in depressed affect, reducing social avoidance), goals of the biopsychosocial approach to treatment might extend into biological domains (e.g., improvement in blood glucose regulation; reduction in frequency of migraines; increased adherence to medical recommendations) or social-environmental domains (e.g., altering availability of fattening foods in the house; family interventions aimed at improving adherence).

Although initially clustered under intervention competencies, the knowledge competencies essential for conducting intervention in clinical health psychology (e.g., understanding of medical diseases and their treatments, knowledge of how psychological factors affect how the patient presents to the health care team and how these factors influence the delivery of appropriate health care services) are now considered foundational scientific competencies (see Chapter 6). Armed with this scientific knowledge base, the most appropriate interventions can be selected and timed well to coincide with the ongoing medical treatment. For example, there are very effective psychological treatments for panic disorder that involve training in a variety of anxiety management skills accompanied by exposure to anxiety-eliciting stimuli. Using this approach, patients with panic attacks who visit emergency rooms frequently claiming they are dying or going crazy are eventually discouraged from going to emergency rooms while experiencing sensations of panic. There is solid theoretical and empirical support for this approach (see Craske & Barlow, 2008). Let's consider a minor variation to this clinical presentation: Would it matter if this patient with a diagnosed panic disorder was also diagnosed with cardiac disease? Would the patient's medical provider endorse a treatment plan discouraging visits to emergency departments upon symptom onset? It is this sort of situation that clinical health psychologists encounter regularly. It is easy to see, then, why a fundamental knowledge of the pathology of a range of physical diseases and their accompanying biomedical treatments is an essential area of competence for the clinical health psychologist.

Clinical health psychologists need to be aware that the primary purpose for seeking care for the patients they see is not typically to receive mental health care. Our patients do not come to the health care facility to be seen by a clinical health psychology specialist, but rather they are typically seeking help for a medical problem they are experiencing. However, we possess knowledge of a body of scientific literature that is very important in the health care environment. Most of the reasons people end up with the diseases and injuries that result in seeking medical care are related to behavioral choices they make in their lives (e.g., smoking, not eating properly, not wearing seatbelts, failure to use sunscreen, leading sedentary lives), and as experts in the science of behavior, we are the professionals best positioned to assist in changing these problematic behaviors that are associated with myriad of life-threatening medical conditions. Knowledge of the science of health psychology and how it applies to health behaviors is a critical competency for today's clinical health psychologists.

Skill-Based Competencies in Intervention

Conducting interventions within the health care environment looks quite a bit different than conducting interventions in psychiatric facilities, community mental health centers, or counseling centers. For the most part, there are no 50-minute hours and often no completely private place to meet. Patient contacts tend to be brief in duration and aimed at specific target behaviors. When seeing patients in a hospital setting, there are roommates and interruptions by other health care providers with which to contend. Because of these significant contextual differences in the nature of service delivery, four skill-based assessment competencies distinctly associated with the practice of clinical health psychology have been elucidated (see Table 11.1).

The first skill-based competency focuses on the ability of clinical health psychologists to make use of emerging health technologies. For the most part, health care systems rely on electronic medical records for documenting patient care, interdisciplinary communication, and access to Web-based programs for monitoring treatment adherence or delivery of health care services, including online weight loss or smoking cessation programs or relaxation training sites. The science of psychology has been instrumental in converting its repertoire of evidence-based interventions into Web-based service delivery systems or smartphone applications that have a broader reach to those in need, particularly those who have limited access to medical care. Clinical health psychologists who work in health sciences centers often provide behavioral health services to patients who are in the hospital but who live hours away from the facility and do not have the resources to travel back weekly to obtain follow-up services. In this regard, the typical course of treatment for even the briefest forms of therapy is not possible. Reliance on continued development and use of computer-based methods for delivering behavioral health care interventions was articulated as an essential competency at Tempe and continues to be an essential competency for practice in clinical health psychology today.

The next two skill-based intervention competencies cluster around implementing the evidence-based practice of clinical health psychology (items 2 and 3 in Table 11.1). Although evidence-based practice was acknowledged in the benchmark competencies document, participants at the Tempe Summit felt that it needed to be more explicitly stated. Evidence-based medicine (Evidence-Based Medicine Working Group, 1992; Sackett, 1996) and evidence-based practice in nursing (Craig & Smyth, 2007; Simon, 1999) were fully integrated into medical and nursing curricula before professional psychology hopped onto this bandwagon. However, because of clinical health psychology's regular affiliation with members of these other health care disciplines, the importance of evidence-based practice clearly needed to be a fundamental competency embedded within training programs. These two competencies pertain to specific applications of the evidence-based practice approach, one focusing on treatment and the other on health promotion and prevention programs. In a sense, the common reliance upon scientific evidence in guiding our treatment and prevention efforts permits members of the health care team to communicate easily with one another in optimizing patient care. This allows us to provide our nonpsychologist colleagues with evidence-based justifications and explanations for what we recommend.

The final skill-based intervention competency recognizes the overlap between competencies in assessment and intervention. Based upon the importance of monitoring progress during treatment outlined by the Benchmark Competencies Working Group (Fouad et al., 2009), this area of competence focuses on using the clinical health psychologist's skills in assessment to monitor overall progress of the patient undergoing medical treatment or rehabilitative services or participating in preventive interventions. For example, our skills in assessment permit us to monitor change in mental status or emotional state throughout a medical treatment course. For relatively short courses of treatment (e.g., a 10-day course of antibiotic for an intervention), such assessments are rarely needed. However, for relatively longer courses of treatment accompanied by extensive rehabilitation, like that seen with patients recovering from stroke, undergoing blood or marrow transplants, and prolonged courses of chemotherapy, our capability in assisting health care treatment teams in monitoring the progress of patients is essential. This competency area positions the clinical health psychologist as an evaluator of treatment outcomes broadly defined, and not solely interventions being provided by the psychologist.

One interesting feature to note regarding specific competencies in intervention among clinical health psychologists is that no specific interventions are uniquely associated with clinical health psychology. In general, interventions within clinical health psychology involve applying what we already know about behavior change, both theoretically and empirically, from several decades of intervention work conducted since professional psychologists first started treating returning veterans following World War II. Consequently, what is unique about the practice of clinical health psychology is not the nature of the behavior change strategies selected, but that they are applied with patients with primary medical rather than psychiatric diagnoses. Of the intervention strategies commonly used by clinical health psychologists that were outlined at the Arden House Conference (Tulkin, 1987) and more recently (Belar & Deardorff, 2009), almost all resemble lists of interventions commonly taught in current clinical and counseling psychology training programs (e.g., relaxation training, contingency management, desensitization, cognitive restructuring). The distinctive quality of interventions conducted by clinical health psychologists relates to the sorts of problems the behavior change programs are designed to address and the unique skills involved in implementing them with patients who do not see themselves as having "psychological problems." For example, relaxation training is aimed at lowering blood pressure or frequency of migraine headaches instead of treating generalized anxiety disorders or phobias. The goal of a contingency management program is to alter the reinforcement family members provide for pain behaviors emitted by patients with chronic pain conditions instead of reinforcement of aggressive behaviors in children with conduct disturbances.

Hypnosis and biofeedback stand out as intervention strategies employed more frequently by clinical health psychologists than traditional clinical or counseling psychologists. Although hypnosis was originally employed by psychoanalysts to tap into unconscious phenomena, it is rarely used in contemporary mental health care settings for these purposes. However, hypnosis has found a place in the clinical health psychologist's armamentarium for treating patients experiencing chronic pain or undergoing acutely painful medical procedures (Accardi & Milling, 2009; Patterson, 2010). In contrast, from their inception as viable interventions, biofeedback strategies have targeted a range of medical conditions (see Schwartz & Beatty, 1977). Although biofeedback has been employed with central nervous system activity (e.g., Sokhadze, Cannon, & Trudeau, 2008), the predominant systems modified via biofeedback are those innervated by the autonomic and somatic nervous systems in the periphery, the same systems thought to mediate the association between stress and numerous physical diseases. Despite their common applications in medical settings, not all clinical health psychologists employ hypnosis or biofeedback interventions, and the competent practice of clinical health psychology does not require specialized knowledge and skill in using these forms of intervention.

ACQUISITION OF INTERVENTION COMPETENCIES IN CLINICAL HEALTH PSYCHOLOGY

Like the functional competencies in assessment, the functional competencies in intervention associated with the practice of clinical health psychology can be categorized into knowledge-based and skill-based types. Acquisition of these competencies follows the same sequence described previously for assessment (see Chapter 10), with knowledge-based competencies being learned before skill-based competencies. In general, the knowledge-based competencies are introduced in doctoral training programs, and the skill-based competencies are acquired later on during internship and postdoctoral training experiences. Acquisition of the knowledge-based areas of competence might require course work offered outside traditional training programs in professional psychology. In particular, mastering knowledge of the pathophysiology of diseases and associated biomedical treatments is likely to require course work in departments of physiology or pharmacology.

Once the knowledge-based competencies in intervention have been acquired, clinical health psychologists-in-training can begin practicing their skill-based counterparts in closely supervised practicum experiences in health system settings. This often begins during doctoral training, but it is most certainly dependent upon the program's access to health care facilities with clinical supervisors who are devoted to educating the next generation of health care providers. Skill-based competencies continue to develop throughout graduate school and internship years until they reach the intermediate to advanced levels required for granting of the doctoral degree. Like assessment competencies, the internship year is not typically the trainee's first experience with direct contact in providing interventions to medical patients. Rather, it is a time to fill in the gaps of patient experiences to assure that the trainee possesses a breadth of intervention experiences across a range of patients coping with a variety of medical and health-related problems.

It is possible that some trainees will not have gained the critical knowledge-based competencies in intervention prior to applying for and obtaining an internship placement. This could happen for several reasons, including being a student who discovers clinical health psychology later in training, being a practicing professional who desires respecializing in clinical health psychology, or being enrolled in a doctoral training program that has limited resources to offer this sort of fundamental training. In these cases, postdoctoral training programs are essential. Internship programs often consider creative ways to provide the deficient knowledge-based competencies within their training environments, like permitting interns to attend educational events (e.g., grand rounds) in other departments.

There is a range of postdoctoral training opportunities available for trainees with interests in clinical health psychology. Some focus primarily on research training, some on clinical health psychology service provision, and some provide a combination of research and service activities. Although it is important for all clinical health psychologists to have the specific competencies in intervention described in this chapter, it must be acknowledged that not all will conduct interventions as part of their professional lives. In these cases, as long as the functional competencies in clinical health psychology intervention have been acquired, there is no reason to seek additional training in this area. That said, there is a growing need for the types of services clinical health psychologists provide (e.g., integrative behavioral health care), and the desire to be prepared to accept these positions will likely increase the popularity and availability of postdoctoral training experiences providing training in the area of intervention.

Like competence in assessment, exposure to intervention competencies spans the entire training sequence, from the knowledge-based components during doctoral training years to the skill-based applications of that knowledge during the internships and postdoctoral fellowships that follow. By taking advantage of these training opportunities, the next generation of clinical health psychologists will graduate with a substantial array of intervention tools that will position them well for practicing in integrative behavioral care settings as well as other health care environments.

TWELVE

Consultation in Clinical Health Psychology

Given the exponential rate at which new information is being acquired within psychology as well as related scientific disciplines, even the most devout journal consumers will find themselves quickly out of date with respect to maintaining the full range of skills needed to practice competently as professional psychologists. Thankfully, the professional practice of psychology touts consultation as a core functional competency through which we operate within a larger community of psychologists to assure we have easy access to knowledge and skills in areas where we do not regularly practice. In this regard, we are not expected to have a comprehensive knowledge base concerning every possible situation that might be encountered in health care settings, but rather we know how to access this information should we need it. Clinical health psychologists primarily treating cancer patients to improve their pain regulation strategies might find it necessary to assist one of their patients to quit smoking. Or clinical health psychologists who primarily work with patients in weight reduction programs might encounter patients from time to time experiencing emotional distress associated with receiving medical diagnoses with which the psychologist may be less familiar (e.g., AIDS, stroke). When these situations arise, all professional psychologists, clinical health psychologists included, resort to seeking professional consultation to assure their patients receive state-of-the-art care. To assure a community of competent providers, we need to recognize that consultation is a two-way street. We seek consultation when needed but also are willing to serve as consultants for peers requesting information pertaining to knowledge and skills in which we profess competence or expertise.

The Competency Benchmarks Work Group (Fouad et al., 2009) outlined four domains of competence in consultation: (a) understanding the role of consultant; (b) addressing the referral question; (c) communicating results of the assessment; and (d) applying methods of consultation. The first area of competence draws upon the knowledge of how being a consultant differs from other roles in which professional psychologists engage, like being a therapist, supervisor, or teacher. The most important consideration regarding patient care with respect to this competency is the understanding that consultants do not assume patient care responsibilities. Rather, they make recommendations to referring health care providers or systems of care and let them choose to implement them or not. Knowledge in how to conduct an effective needs assessment in response to the referral question and how to communicate the results of this assessment constitutes the second and third competency domains in the area of consultation. The final area of competence listed in the area of consultation focuses upon the application of knowledge to conducting consultations. Behavioral anchors associated with each of these consultation competencies are provided in more detail in the Competency Benchmarks document (Fouad et al., 2009, p. S20).

It is important to note that consultation competence was defined by Rodolfa et al. (2005) and the Benchmark Competency Work Group (Fouad et al., 2009) as "the ability to provide expert guidance or professional assistance in response to a client's needs or goals" (p. 351). Because these efforts promoted standards of competence in professional psychology, it is understandable that the description and behavioral anchors associated with this area of competence have been interpreted primarily in the context of patient or client care. However, using this context, it is important to recognize that the "client" could be a specialized practitioner, health care team, hospital administration board, school, or work setting. In brief, knowledge and skills in consultation are not confined to situations involving direct patient care, and in fact most often are not. Indeed, professional psychologists have been called upon to lend their expertise in consulting on research projects, for developing and evaluating training programs, and for program evaluation efforts in workplace, school, and governmental settings; recently they were involved in redesigning the MCAT exam. Across these various types of consultation settings, Wallace and Hall (1996) outlined a common sequence of the consultative process, including entering into the role of the consultant, conducting a needs assessment, establishing realistic consultative goals, devising a plan that addresses these goals, guiding implementation of the plan (if accepted), and of course, devising a strategy for evaluating program effectiveness and terminating the consultation arrangement. The stages of the consultation process described by Wallace and Hall parallel the specific competencies described by the Benchmark Competency Work Group quite nicely, although in a somewhat more detailed manner.

Although consultation is a necessary competency for all professional psychologists, it is not uniquely our domain. Even psychologists who are not health service providers (e.g., behavior neuroscientists, experimental psychologists, industrial organizational psychologists) are often called upon as research and educational consultants, and as such, many possess the same competencies in consultation as those who receive training in professional psychology training programs. For example, health psychologists without clinical training (termed "health psychology scientists" at the Arden House Conference) also offer consultation on research, educational efforts, and policy changes that relate to health and wellness occurring in work, school, or community environments. In contrast, clinical health psychologists uniquely possess consultation competencies for a range of situations involving direct patient care and programs of patient care that occur in health care settings.

Because the clinical health psychologist's area of special expertise is based on the biopsychosocial model of health and wellness, we are most likely to be identified as consultants for questions pertaining to the impact of stress and other psychosocial factors on health in patient care settings. However, because of our unique attributes as both scientists and as practitioners, we are also often called upon as consultants in research design and data analysis by our peers in the health care environment who received lesser or no training in research as part of their professional development. As noted in Chapter 2, training in most other health care disciplines involves far less exposure to research design and statistics than training as psychologists, and training in none of these other disciplines requires completion of empirical theses or dissertations. Based upon our distinctive competencies in both clinical practice and research within health care environments, some additional competencies in consultation for clinical health psychologists were identified by participants at the Tempe Summit of Education and Training in Clinical Health Psychology (France et al., 2008). Description of these distinctive competencies continues to evolve, and they remain in the latest rendition of the list of clinical health psychology specialty competencies.

CONSULTATION COMPETENCIES AMONG
CLINICAL HEALTH PSYCHOLOGISTS

Consultation is a critical part of practice within the modern health care arena. Like psychology, no medical or health care provider possesses expertise in all organ systems, diseases, procedures, or interventions. In this regard, professionals with specific sets of expertise are consulted to assist health care teams in the provision of optimal care. Cardiologists are brought in to lend their expertise in cases where chest pain of uncertain origin is a predominant component of the symptom presentation; ear, nose and throat (ENT) specialists are sought to assist in the diagnosis and treatment of prolonged sinus pain and swelling; and palliative care teams are consulted when end-of-life decisions are being considered by patients and their families. In this regard, it is advantageous for hospitals to have access to clinical health psychologists to consult on cases where psychological factors overlap with medical diseases, disorders, and disabilities.

Although there is an extensive history of consultation-liaison activities within the field of psychiatry, historically this involved providing traditional psychological or psychiatric care to someone who happened to be occupying a medical bed. Consulting for purposes of managing the stress of being diagnosed with a medical illness, to assist patients undergoing extensive medical testing, and to alter behavioral risk factors for disease is of more recent origin. Consultation among clinical health psychologists is quite different from the sorts of professional activities performed by consultation-liaison psychiatrists. Psychiatric consultation would be an appropriate action if the medical team needed help in confirming a diagnosis of depression in a cardiac patient and desired assistance in prescribing an antidepressant with the fewest cardiac side effects, or if they desired consultation for the appropriate course of action for dealing with a patient with schizophrenia who had lapsed into a psychotic episode while in the hospital for treating an infectious disease. In contrast, traditional psychiatric consultation would not be an optimal approach for making recommendations for patients who desire to manage their pain nonpharmacologically, quit smoking, acquire appropriate stress management techniques for coping with an upcoming medical procedure, or increase adherence to the prescribed treatment. These cases would be better served through consultation with a clinical health psychologist.

Like the competencies in both assessment and intervention, participants of the Tempe Summit examined all of the functional competencies pertaining to the area of consultation outlined in the Competency Benchmarks document (Fouad et al., 2009) and agreed that all of these

TABLE 12.1 **Competencies and Behavioral Anchors in Consultation Unique to Clinical Health Psychology**

KNOWLEDGE-BASED CONSULTATION COMPETENCY
1. **Knowledge of own and others' professional roles and expectations within the context of intradisciplinary and interdisciplinary consultation in the health care setting**[a]
• Recognizes the difference between consultation and supervision in the health care setting
• Understands the importance of a timely response to medical consultation

SKILL-BASED CONSULTATION COMPETENCIES
2. **Conceptualization of referral questions that bear on human behavior (including an understanding of the client's, other provider's, or health system's role)**[a]
• Conducts a thorough review of the health record of the referred patient
• Responds directly to the initial consultation question
3. **Translation and communication of relevant scientific findings as they bear on the health care consultation/liaison questions**[a]
• Communicates clear recommendations to the referral source
• Writes a succinct consultation note on the electronic health record in jargon-free language
4. **Ability to work with professionals from other disciplines to increase the likelihood of appropriate early referral for consultation with clinical health psychologists as opposed to "last resort" referrals**[a]
• Develops relationships with potential referral agents educating them regarding your professional competencies
• Rounds with health care teams to proactively recruit referrals before the problems become more challenging (e.g., learning pain control strategies before medical procedures)

[a]Adapted from Revised Competencies in Clinical Health Psychology. Masters, France, & Thorn (2009, p. 196).

broad and general competencies in consultation were applicable to clinical health psychology (France et al., 2008). Following deliberations at the Tempe Summit and subsequent revisions of the competencies initially articulated there, one additional knowledge-based and three additional skill-based competencies in consultation were added (see Table 12.1). These competencies in the area of consultation distinctive to the practice of clinical health psychology will be considered next.

Knowledge-Based Competency in Consultation

Because clinical health psychologists are most often called upon as consultants in health care facilities like hospitals and clinics, the knowledge-based competencies in consultation unique to clinical health psychology center on functioning in these types of environments. The additional knowledge-based competency in consultation pertains to understanding the professional role of engaging in consultation within the context of the health care setting. In this regard, specialized competencies in consultation in the health care environment are required of all clinical health psychologists, while other types of consultative experience are more or less optional. Although it may be desirable for clinical health psychologists to function as consultants for research projects in other settings, within schools, within work environments, or in community-based participatory research settings, these locations do not constitute the unique domain of the clinical health psychologist and are not considered core competencies for all clinical health psychologists. Broad models of psychological consultation, like the one proposed by Wallace and Hall (1996), apply to a range of consultative environments. Consulting within the health care environment stands out as the primary domain (or one might say "turf") of the clinical health psychologist, and as such, all clinical health psychologists need to demonstrate competence in this area.

The health care environment is unique in many regards, and consultants in these settings need to be aware of many of its idiosyncrasies. Unlike many other settings, consultation is such a frequent occurrence in health care environments that most facilities have developed and implemented rules and procedures regarding who can perform consultations, how they should occur, and what type of documentation is required. Essential to the competent consultant is an awareness of the rules and regulations that operate in these environments. Foremost among these rules and regulations is adherence to the credentialing process health care institutions go through to determine which providers are qualified to serve as consultants. With rare exceptions, these rules and regulations were not devised by psychologists, and at times they may not be all that friendly to psychologists. As such, it is important for those conducting consultations in health care settings to gain an understanding of the scientific literature on medical consultation to assure that their consultations provide the health care team with the information they desire.

Skill-Based Competencies in Consultation

Consultations in the broader health care environment are somewhat different than conducting consultations in psychiatric facilities. All other professionals working in psychiatric facilities are familiar with the multiaxial diagnostic system employed in the earlier versions of the *Diagnostic and Statistical Manual of Mental Disorders* and the entire range of terminology unique to working with patients with psychiatric disorders, including phrases like "the patient exhibits Cluster B traits," "has a GAF score of 65," or "has a 4-9 profile on the MMPI." Because members of other health care professions regard psychiatric terminology as a foreign language, it behooves clinical health psychological consultants to employ very little technical jargon in their consultation notes and conversations with members of the health care teams. As with all consultations, the best ones result in a concise consultation note that specifically addresses the referral question. Consultation notes are not the place to try and impress other members of the health care team with the sophistication of one's case conceptualization or the elegance of one's prose.

The first skill-based consultation competency unique to clinical health psychology focuses on the process of shaping the referral questions into meaningful professional communications between the clinical health psychologist and members of the health care team requesting the consultation. Unless the health care provider or team has an extensive history of working with clinical health psychology consultants, it is sometimes difficult for them to understand when behavioral health consultations should be requested and how the referral questions should be phrased. For example, it is not uncommon for clinical health psychologists to be consulted to answer a referral question such as "Is this patient depressed?" Certainly, the team desires more than a "yes" or "no" response in the consultation note (although some have been tempted to try this approach!). In instances like these, the clinical health psychologist consultant needs to discern how much more information is desirable. Options to consider include providing information about how the diagnosis of depression might complicate the patient's medical treatment, what treatment options might be recommended (e.g., cognitive-behavioral therapy, behavioral activation, antidepressant medication), and who is available to perform these interventions should the team choose to pursue them. Using this approach, the clinical health psychologist rephrases the referral question so that a meaningful result can be communicated to the consulting health care team. This may require additional communication with the individual or team requesting the consultation in order to ensure that the question being answered is indeed the question being asked.

Although the first skill-based competency focuses on discernment of the referral question, the next skill-based competency pertains to the artful communication of findings to the health care team. Both written and verbal communication skills are important here, as the clinical health psychology consultant should competently write a brief report that all other members of the health care team can decipher *and* verbally report key findings to critical members of the health care team. Given the fast pace of the health care environment and numerous pieces of data being collected and recorded on patients' medical charts, written consultation notes can become easily buried among other less important components of the medical record. Thus, it is always important to verbally relay any key features of the report to the physician (or whichever health professional) in charge of the health care team; whenever possible, these data also should be provided to nursing and other staff working with the patient and physician. Both written and verbal forms of communication take into account the consultant's knowledge of the various health care professionals comprising the health care team and his or her capacity for explaining findings using terminology they would understand.

The final skill-based competency in consultation among clinical health psychologists pertains to the skills in developing productive working relationships with members of the interdisciplinary health care team. To operate competently in this domain, it is best if clinical health psychologists acquire at least a working knowledge about how members of other health care disciplines are trained and the nature of their daily work assignments (see Chapter 7). On any health care team, the day-to-day, hands-on tasks involved with patient care are carried out by allied health professionals, and failure to recognize this fact will certainly interfere with a successful consultation. In this regard, it is essential that productive working relationships be developed with all disciplines functioning regularly on the team. Developing productive working relationships with physicians, nurses, and social workers is a must on any health care team, but establishing relationships with other professionals can also be crucial, including physical and occupational therapists, various health care technicians, massage therapists, nutritionists, dentists, and chaplains. Through development of these interdisciplinary relationships, clinical health psychologists then educate others about the types of clinical services they can provide, and as a result, appropriate referrals and requests for consultation often increase.

Consultation-liaison psychiatrists draw a distinction between consultation activities and liaison activities. While the former focuses on addressing a direct request from the health care team pertaining to a specific patient, the latter focuses on becoming an involved member of the health care team. In brief, consultants come when called, but liaisons are present even when their services are not needed. Engagement in liaison activities (e.g., rounding with a medical team; attending grand rounds in another department; attending staff meetings) can be used to alter the frequency with which one is consulted. For example, while rounding with a medical team, a clinical health psychologist might suggest that a behavioral health consultation would be appropriate for a patient encountering difficulties in regulating pain. Had the clinical health psychologist not been on rounds, it is unlikely that need for such a consultation would have been identified. In this regard, rounding with the team is rarely a poor use of a clinical health psychologist's time, and it almost always results in improved relationships with other members of the health care team.

ACQUISITION OF CONSULTATION COMPETENCIES IN CLINICAL HEALTH PSYCHOLOGY

Unlike the functional competencies in assessment and intervention, competence in consultation arrives a bit later in the sequence in training. After all, the purpose of consultation is to seek expertise to address a patient problem beyond the competencies of the health care team. To solicit consultation by a graduate student or psychology intern would not result in the desired outcome due to their early stages of competency development. Professional consultation works best when it operates professional to professional. This creates a complication then for acquiring competencies in consultation during training as it is challenging to acquire skills in consultation when one is never consulted. About the best one could expect is to gain the knowledge-based competencies in consultation during doctoral training years and/or internship, accompanied by direct observations of faculty members conducting consultations effectively. In some cases, upper-level graduate students or psychology interns may earn the respect needed in a specific area of interest that could result in conducting consultations (under supervision of course). For example, throughout graduate study, a student might have acquired a special competency for evaluating sleep problems in older adults and have even conducted original empirical work examining methods for best assessing these individuals. In a health care facility devoid of these services (e.g., nursing home), it would only be natural for the graduate student to be asked to consult on cases of older adults presenting with sleep disturbances under the supervision of a mentor. For others, however, acquisition of the skill-based competencies in consultation may need to wait until postdoctoral training experiences, where most trainees possess a few areas in which they are now qualified to serve as consultants.

Although trainees may need to wait until they achieve competence in a certain area before they fully acquire competencies in consultation, they can practice liaison activities earlier in training. In fact, rounding with medical treatment teams is an excellent strategy for exposing young clinical health psychologists-in-training to the importance of interdisciplinary functioning in the modern health care environment. By working with members of other health professions early during training, the clinical health psychology trainee's comfort level in interacting with members from other health care professions grows *and* it simultaneously shapes members of other health care discipline's comfort with clinical healthy psychology. Optimally, this would be done conjointly with a more experienced clinical health psychologist, so the trainee would have the opportunity to participate in all aspects of the consultation process, from rounding with the treatment team to sitting in on the consultation interviews as appropriate; this would allow the trainee, then, not only to model what was done but to discuss questions or issues that arise with the more experienced health psychologist. The future practice of clinical health psychology will certainly be enhanced by this type of mutual training of students in health care environments.

Some clinical health psychologists enter the specialty area later in life, some even completing formal respecialization programs in clinical health psychology. Establishing competencies in clinical health psychology consultation is likely a bit easier for these individuals. Because of their longer careers as professional psychologists, it is likely that they have established several areas of expertise and have consulted from time to time during their practice; as such, the translation of professional consultation skills from their previous professional practice area to professional consultation in clinical health psychology is likely to occur more rapidly.

Specialized competencies in consultation increase throughout the training sequence, from a primary focus on the knowledge-based components during doctoral and internship training years to the skill-based components that occur primarily during postdoctoral fellowships. Deliberative encouragement of liaison activities for clinical health psychology students early in training bodes well for the subsequent development of their competencies as consultants, particularly as the members of the allied health professions recognize and seek the expertise of clinical health psychology consultants in their future careers.

THIRTEEN

Research Competencies in
Clinical Health Psychology

Based upon the foundational competencies of scientific mindedness (see Chapter 6) and an appreciation for evidence-based practice of psychology, clinical health psychologists read and conduct research on topics closely associated with health, health policy, and provision of health-related services. The assessments we conduct and the interventions we carry out are selected based upon their empirical support and cases are approached scientifically. That is to say, systematic data collection is highly valued even in purely applied roles, so that clinical health psychologists aim to show evidence that our assessments are accurate and that our interventions work.

Two approaches for conducting research in the health care environment are commonly observed among clinical health psychologists: the Translational Health Program of Research Model (see Khoury et al., 2007) and the Practice-based Clinical Research Model. The Translational Health Program of Research Model involves the systematic investigation of hypotheses that inform the scientific understanding of specific health conditions, but it may not relate immediately to the patients we see in our clinical roles. For example, studies on the influence of stress on blood glucose regulation are important for gaining a better understanding of the underlying physiological mechanisms responsible for this stress-disease linkage. Diabetic patients who volunteer for research projects in which blood glucose levels are measured under conditions of stress will likely not benefit personally from their participation; yet these research projects easily translate into knowledge that informs development of improved methods for evaluating stress reactivity among patients with diabetes mellitus or stress management interventions that assist in regulating levels of blood glucose among these patients. It is not essential for clinical health psychologists conducting this type of research to use samples of patients that come from their own clinical practices. They could collaborate with health care professionals for purely research purposes and gain access to appropriate samples of patients through these research connections. In fact, to conduct research to examine the stress–blood glucose regulation link does not require the use of clinical samples at all. It is entirely possible to carry out studies of stress and blood glucose regulation on samples of animals, assuming the clinical health psychologist has appropriate credentials for directing empirical work in animal laboratory facilities or access to collaborators with these credentials. Although this type of program of research focuses primarily on discovering basic disease mechanisms, the purpose of this type of research is to "translate" findings from the bench (laboratory) studies to the bedside (clinic/hospital) and from patients to the broader community at large (e.g., Khoury et al., 2007).

In contrast to the Translational Health Program of Research Model, the Practice-based Clinical Research Model involves designing empirical questions around the types of assessments and interventions used in one's daily practice as a clinical health psychologist. For example, a clinical health psychologist might receive a few referrals each week to conduct psychological evaluations for obese patients being referred for bariatric surgeries. Rather than simply conducting the evaluations and writing up reports, the clinical health psychologist might use the results of the presurgery screenings to test empirical questions regarding whether psychological factors predict weight loss or emotional outcomes that follow surgery. In this regard, the clinical health psychologist develops a program of research surrounding a common element of his or her clinical practice, and as such, the program of research becomes fully integrated with one's clinical practice.

Both the Translational Health and Practice-based Clinical Research Models depict viable ways in which clinical health psychologists carry out programs of research in health care environments. In contrast to independent research projects commonly seen in traditional academic departments, programs of research in health care environments are largely determined by the availability of interdisciplinary collaboration. One can have the world's best hypothesis and the most innovative methods for assessing it, but the project will fizzle out without the right type of collaboration. Access to certain types of patients, animal care facilities, and health care instrumentation (e.g., imaging devices, laboratory tests) is not possible without the right collaboration. Recalling that clinical health psychologists do not as a rule own or operate health care centers, the types of research projects clinical health psychologists pursue are often more closely linked to the interests of potential collaborators and availability of facilities than devising their own research agenda. If one is fortunate enough to collaborate with a scientist who is located within the health care facility where the clinical health psychologist works, the partnership can result in an extensive program of research that resembles those commonly seen in traditional academic science departments, where faculty members typically have more control over the direction of their programs of research. However, should the collaborator retire or move to another facility, maintaining one's program of research becomes much more challenging. Due to these circumstances, conducting research in a health care facility requires some adaptability on the part of the clinical health psychologist. And as a consequence, research endeavors of clinical health psychologists may appear a bit less programmatic than psychologists who work in traditional academic departments. Their curriculum vitae may show publications and presentations across a broader range of topics addressed or clinical populations serving as participants due to the need to rely on available collaborators.

Both descriptions of the functional competencies in research by Rodolfa et al. (2005) and the Benchmark Competency Work Group (Fouad et al., 2009) focused on the importance of research among all professional psychologists, including clinical health psychologists. Rodolfa et al. defined the competency area as "the generation of research that contributes to the professional knowledge base and/or evaluates the effectiveness of various professional activities" (p. 351). The key word in the definition of this area of competence is "generation." In contrast to other health-related disciplines, professional psychologists are trained to "do" research, not merely to consume it (Larkin, 2014). As mentioned in Chapter 2, there are many health-related professions that train providers to read and comprehend research and use research to inform their clinical practice, but very few professions train providers to "do" research. We are one of the few.

The Competency Benchmarks Work Group (Fouad et al., 2009) outlined two domains of competency in research for all professional psychologists: (a) having a scientific approach to knowledge generation; and (b) applying the scientific method to practice. Based upon the foundational competency of scientific mindedness (Chapter 6), the first area of competency involves conducting research that spans the bench-to-bedside-to-community continuum using research methods and data analytic techniques to address empirical questions confidently. In contrast, the second area of competence in research according to the Competency Benchmarks Work Group involves applying this scientific approach to clinical practice, including assessing treatment outcomes empirically and conducting program evaluations. Behavioral anchors associated with each of these generic research competencies are provided in more detail in the Competency Benchmarks document (Fouad et al., 2009, p. S21).

Competency in conducting research is not unique to professional psychology. In fact, it could easily be argued that all graduate programs in the discipline of psychology aim to train competencies in research (e.g., experimental psychology, developmental psychology, behavioral neuroscience, etc.), as do all graduate programs in the sciences. To the extent that professional psychology aligns itself with the same goals as our underlying core scientific discipline, like those we share in conducting research competently, the field will benefit. Fractionation of the field almost always occurs when the importance of research is de-emphasized. This is considerably important in clinical health psychology, where there is a long and vibrant relationship between clinical health psychology and health (nonclinical) psychology, dating back to the Arden House conference (1983). Adopting this perspective, the first domain of research competence elucidated by the Competency Benchmarks Work Group reflects a goal for all psychologists, while the second domain of research competence is primarily aimed at those who professionally apply the science of psychology.

Because clinical health psychologists (and our health psychologist colleagues) conduct research in health care settings, there are several unique research competencies that we share that enable us to carry out empirical efforts successfully in this setting. As noted previously, we possess a certain amount of prestige in the health care environment due to our extensive training in research design and statistics, and we should not overlook the importance of this position. Due to our distinctive competencies in research, participants at the Tempe Summit of Education and Training in Clinical Health Psychology (France et al., 2008) elucidated several unique research competencies acquired by all clinical health psychologists. Although these competencies have been revised over the years since the Tempe Summit, most are still recognized and described in the following section.

RESEARCH COMPETENCIES AMONG
CLINICAL HEALTH PSYCHOLOGISTS

Provision of high-quality patient care probably ranks as the top priority in mission statements of most health sciences centers around the world, but involvement in medical research ranks a close second. It is not all that surprising, then, that funding for these institutions is largely based upon payment for patient services (mostly through third-party reimbursement) *and* obtaining external research funding. The extent that a health sciences center succeeds fiscally in these two areas largely determines whether the institution survives. Given the importance of clinical health psychology both in terms of provision of high-quality patient care and development of grant-supported programs of research, it is not surprising that many health sciences centers have created positions for clinical health psychologists. Additionally, because they come at a lower cost than their MD/PhD peers, the cost/benefit ratio can be kept fairly low for institutions desiring the unique constellation of competencies that clinical health psychologists possess.

As with the previous functional competency areas, participants of the Tempe Summit examined the two functional research competencies from the Competency Benchmarks document (Fouad et al., 2009) and agreed that both were applicable to clinical health psychology (France et al., 2008). However, due to the unique research environment in which clinical health psychologists conduct the majority of their empirical work, several additional skill-based competencies in research were added (see Table 13.1). Before examining the specific areas of competency outlined, it is important to note that research skills of the clinical health psychologist reflect the multilevel and interdisciplinary nature of our profession. In contrast to the oftentimes single levels of analysis employed in basic programs of research (e.g., cellular, organ system, psychological, social-environmental), the biopsychosocial model that drives our field encourages us to examine research questions that stretch beyond single levels of analysis. As such, it is not unusual to see clinical health psychologists involved in data collection efforts that cut across a full range of biological, psychological, and social-environmental domains. Additionally, as mentioned earlier, these empirical efforts are conducted in health care environments, in which collaboration with researchers from other health care disciplines is all but guaranteed.

Based upon the breadth of knowledge across a range of health care disciplines and a comprehension of how to conduct interdisciplinary research, clinical health psychologists are well equipped to conduct research projects in health care settings. The first two skill-based research competencies (items 1 and 2 in Table 13.1) focus on the ability to apply our training in research design and data analysis to research questions that arise in health care settings. For the most part, the application of our research skills in this setting does not present a serious challenge. After all, most research

TABLE 13.1 **Competencies and Behavioral Anchors in Research/Evaluation Unique to Clinical Health Psychology**

---

1. **Application of diverse methodologies to scientifically examine psychosocial and biological processes as they relate to health promotion, illness prevention, and disease progression**[b]
   - Use scientific literature on weight management and developmental psychology to design research project on teenage obesity
   - Use the scientific literature to design and evaluate a population-sensitive health promotion program
   - Demonstrates knowledge of human subject protection issues when writing institutional review board protocols in health care settings
2. **Selection, application, and interpretation of quantitative and qualitative data analytic strategies that are best suited to the diverse research questions and levels of analysis characteristic of health psychology**[b]
   - Uses survival analysis to evaluate the impact of an intervention
   - Conducts a meta-analysis of intervention programs containing both health and behavioral outcomes
3. **Formulation and implementation of health-related research using interdisciplinary research teams**[b]
   - Completes a successful institutional review board submission for interdisciplinary health research
   - Leads an interdisciplinary research team
   - Translates issues presented by professionals from other disciplines into testable research questions and devises appropriate methods for investigation
4. **Accurate and efficient communication of research findings in ways that can be understood by fellow psychologists, professionals from other disciplines, and lay audiences**[b]
   - Presents scientific papers/posters on topics pertinent to clinical health psychology at national conferences
   - Writes scientifically informed pieces for a local newspaper
   - Publishes empirical work pertinent to the practice of clinical health psychology
5. **Use of research skills to evaluate the effectiveness and quality of clinical health psychology services within health care settings, including participation in quality improvement efforts**[b]
   - Participates in implementing diagnostic screening guidelines and evaluating program outcomes
   - Provided in-service training on research methodology to members of health care team for purposes of program evaluation
   - Demonstrates the ability to participate in the formal evaluation and assessment of standards for being a National Committee for Quality Assurance (NCQA)-certified Patient Centered Medical Home (PCMH)[a]
   - Uses informatics and other technology-based methods to obtain information to track patient outcomes for purposes of program evaluation (e.g., Web-based tracking systems of safety, patient satisfaction, and quality of care)[a]

---

[a]Adapted from Competencies for Psychology Practice in Primary Care. Interorganizational Workgroup on Competencies for Primary Care Psychology Practice (2013, pp. 15–17).

[b]Adapted from Competencies in Clinical Health Psychology. Masters, France, & Thorn (2009, pp. 197–198).

design and data analysis skills are initially acquired through course work using examples and data sets that we did not generate. Early training in research involves translating this fundamental knowledge acquired in course work into successful thesis and dissertation projects. In this manner, all professional psychologists are expected and trained to apply research competencies in new and different settings. With respect to clinical health psychology, this process results in translating these skills into addressing research questions that arise within the health care setting.

On any given day functioning in a health care environment, dozens of excellent and testable research questions arise, including such questions as "Will intervention X work for patient A?," "Is the patient improving as a result of the intervention?," or "Will the presence of a specific individual difference variable impact treatment outcome?" Clearly, the dilemma for the clinical health psychologist is *not* coming up with testable research questions; rather, the challenge is in recognizing which questions would be of interest to the broader community of clinical health psychologists and would be possible to test in the immediate health care setting. Using this approach, clinical health psychologists view patients they see for purposes of assessment, intervention, or consultation as potential sources of data to test research questions, and consequently, devise systematic methods for collecting data from them that can inform local questions regarding patient care and clinical outcomes as well as more distal questions that inform the broader field of health psychology.

The next two skill-based competencies in research unique to the profession of clinical health psychology (items 3 and 4 in Table 13.1) refer to skills in communicating with members of other health care disciplines. As noted earlier, because the type of research conducted by clinical health psychologists is almost always collaborative in nature, it goes without saying that we should understand the strengths and limitations of these research endeavors. Unlike other competency areas, acquiring competency in implementing interdisciplinary research can rarely be done through extensive reading and course work in other health-related professional areas. Rather, these skills are typically acquired experientially. Books and journals describing best practices in doing interdisciplinary research are few in nature. Recognizing the importance of training in this area of competence, the National Institutes of Health launched the Interdisciplinary Research Program that aims to break down departmental barriers that impede interdisciplinary work and provide funding for institutions interested in training students to engage in these types of research projects (National Institutes of Health, 2010). Provided that we conduct our interactions with collaborating scientists from other disciplines skillfully and listen to the testable questions they generate, the research projects that arise from them can be incredibly successful, primarily because the health care professional who derived the initial question will be highly committed to participating in the project. For example, curiosity regarding the influence of chemotherapy upon cognitive functioning among oncology team members can easily be transformed into a research project in which the clinical health psychologist conducts tests of cognitive functioning on patients at designated times during treatment. Because the team generated the research question, all are committed to supporting the data collection effort.

It should also be noted that the rules for authorship credit for research products arising from collaborations in health care settings are somewhat different from those in traditional academic departments. First, due to the interdisciplinary nature of the research being conducted, sole authorships are rarely observed. It is the nature (and one might say the purpose) of conducting interdisciplinary research to publish or present papers with multiple authors. Members of other professions may have different expectations regarding authorship credit, and these conversations must be handled carefully. Our ethical code (American Psychological Association, 2002) stipulates that we accept authorship credit for work in which we "substantially contributed." Most psychologists differentiate among key personnel involved in conceptualizing and directing the research project whose participation warrants authorship credit and data coders, statistical consultants, and laboratory technicians whose participation in the project does not warrant credit. These distinctions may be less clear in health care settings, and clinical health psychologists who conduct empirical work in these settings need to be prepared to navigate these issues skillfully and with a degree of tact.

In contrast to the traditional areas of the professional practice of psychology, clinical health psychologists commonly share the results of their empirical work with a range of scientists who are not psychologists (item 4 in Table 13.1). These efforts include publishing in medical and other health discipline's journals, presenting papers at conferences attended by members of the broader health care community, and presenting results of empirical work at grand rounds or related continuing medical education events. As mentioned previously, because psychologists are trained both as scientists and practitioners, and the research we conduct translates easily to clinical practice, we are popular speakers for these venues. In a sense, it is members of the other health care disciplines that we aim to reach, even more than other clinical health psychologists. Data showing that reductions in headache frequency occur following a cognitive-behavioral intervention coupled with a medication (e.g., Holroyd et al., 2010) is of much greater interest among physicians who see these sorts of patients daily than audiences of clinical psychologists. And data showing that a biofeedback intervention improves severity of asthma symptoms and requires less medication (e.g., Lehrer et al., 2004) than placebo or waitlist control groups is of more interest to health care providers who work with patients with asthma than groups of clinical psychologists. As such, these types of papers are commonly published in medical journals, where they reach the intended audiences of health care professionals.

The final distinctive competency in research requires special consideration. In contrast to the other four competencies in this area, this final competency pertains to the skillful evaluation of health care services, including developing and implementing quality improvement assessments. Unlike other settings where behavioral health care is provided, health care facilities are required to engage in ongoing quality improvement efforts. In this regard, they continually gather data regarding treatment outcomes and patient satisfaction for almost all the health care services they provide. These efforts are only bound to increase as the cost-conscious Affordable Care Act shapes the health care system by reinforcing facilities that have the best outcomes. Obviously, equipped with their knowledge of sound research design, measurement validity, and systematic data collection, clinical health psychologists will emerge as the natural leaders of these quality assurance programs.

ACQUISITION OF RESEARCH COMPETENCIES
IN CLINICAL HEALTH PSYCHOLOGY

Significant competency in research is acquired during the doctoral training years for almost all clinical health psychologists. Certainly, courses in research design and data analyses during doctoral training provide the foundation upon which later research competencies are built. Completion of thesis and dissertation projects provides further opportunity to apply one's knowledge and skill in research competence, with the latter reflecting a fairly autonomous project devised and carried out by the trainee. Additionally, foundational knowledge of research from other health disciplines is often acquired during the doctoral training years, particularly for those students who express a commitment to clinical health psychology early in their academic training.

Although there are some exceptions, the predominant purpose of the clinical internship is to develop intermediate to advanced skills in the clinical/applied areas of competence. Due to the clinical foci of the internship year, further development of research competencies during this time of training is less prominent. However, when opportunities for research involvement occur during the internship year, they almost always involve data collection on patient populations. Furthermore, many involve functioning as part of interdisciplinary research teams, particularly among internships at health science center settings. As such, they provide excellent avenues for acquiring broader skills in research in the specialty area of clinical health psychology.

Most postdoctoral programs in clinical health psychology involve some combination of research and clinical service activities. Therefore, for students who completed their doctoral work in programs that had limited access to patients with medical diseases or disabilities, or who discovered an interest in clinical health psychology later in training, completion of the postdoctoral fellowship provides capstone training experiences for both research and clinical/applied competencies. In this regard, the postdoctoral fellowship rounds out the training, filling in the gaps in research competencies that were not acquired during earlier doctoral program and internship years.

It may have become obvious that some training institutions are better equipped to provide training in clinical health psychology research than others. Certainly, institutions with educational programs in health sciences (e.g., medicine, nursing, allied health professions) have an advantage over those without health sciences programs for providing access to course work that shapes the scientific competencies in research and experiences that foster development of the skill-based competencies in research. The location of the various programs can also complicate acquisition of these competencies, as health sciences programs of some universities are located on different campuses and even in different locations. There is definitely an advantage for a doctoral student to enroll in a public health, human physiology, or pharmacology course if he or she only needs to walk across the street to another building. Driving a hundred miles to another campus to attend the class would complicate and likely discourage these efforts.

In contrast to the other functional competencies considered up to this point (assessment, intervention, consultation), specialized competencies in research are typically shaped fairly early in the sequence of professional development. If students with interests in clinical health psychology conduct theses and dissertations in the area of clinical health psychology, they are well on their way to acquiring these competencies prior to earning their degree. The internship and postdoctoral years, then, can focus on developing opportunities for interdisciplinary research, a competency that most trainees do not achieve through conducting their theses and dissertations. Given the important linkage with the science of health psychology that has defined the specialty area since its inception, all clinical health psychologists acquire competencies in generating research rather than simply consuming existing science and in applying their skills to the evaluation of clinical practice, including programs of quality improvement.

FOURTEEN

Teaching and Supervision in Clinical Health Psychology

"See one, do one, teach one" is the standard sequence of professional competency development employed in medicine and several allied health care disciplines. Although one could argue with the simplicity of the model, it outlines the sequence of developing these competencies properly. In brief, we have no business teaching something we do not know how to do ourselves, and we probably should not attempt to do something we have never seen done before. That said, it is clear that development of teaching and supervision competencies occurs somewhat later in one's professional development, following acquisition of specific competencies in other domains of professional behavior.

Teaching occurs whenever one individual who possesses knowledge or skill on a given topic imparts these competencies to another individual or group of individuals who have yet to acquire the designated knowledge or skill. Most of us easily identify the educational efforts of an instructor teaching a course, a musician offering piano lessons, or a coach instructing a basketball player to shoot foul shots as teaching. These examples are congruent with our understanding of behaviors that constitute teaching, and those who engage in these instructional roles would acknowledge that they are, in fact, teaching. In contrast, not all professionals regard themselves as teachers or define teaching as part of their occupational functioning. For example, physicians or dentists who easily identify as health care providers may fail to acknowledge the important teaching roles they may play during their daily practice. Upon closer inspection, however, it becomes clear that competence in teaching is a standard for all professions;

that is, all professionals engage in teaching, even if they fail to recognize it. At the very least, it is the responsibility of members of any profession to "teach" others what one can and cannot do as a member of his or her profession. In particular, with the vast range of health professions comprising the modern health care arena, it is important for members of each health profession to educate others—patients as well as other health care providers—of the various functions associated with their profession. Unlike many occupations outside the health care environment (e.g., attorneys, plumbers, teachers, automobile mechanics), many people are unaware of the nature of the job responsibilities associated with each distinctive health care profession and possess a misunderstanding of their various roles. The common lack of differentiation by the public of the practices of psychology and psychiatry comes to mind as a common opportunity for health care providers to "teach" those seeking mental health care from our communities. Taking this broader perspective of teaching, then, teaching can be said to occur during each and every patient visit to a health care facility, as patients "learn" about the nature of their conditions, "understand" the treatments available, and "comprehend" what they can do to assist in managing their presenting symptoms. In this regard, new information is transmitted from the health care provider to the patient, the very foundation of most definitions of teaching. While not all health care professionals engage in formal modes of teaching, all are involved in the one-on-one teaching associated with good patient care.

There are many kinds of teaching, ranging from instruction in large lecture halls to individualized tutoring or apprenticeships. Although common elements of teaching and learning exist across larger and smaller sized venues, there are some important differences. When considering competencies in the area of teaching, some models lump all of these competencies into a single teaching domain, whereas others make distinctions between various teaching-related competencies, particularly placing special emphasis upon those associated with conducting clinical supervision. Rodolfa et al. (2005) considered teaching and supervision as a single area of competence when devising the cube model of competency development. In contrast, the Competency Benchmarks Work Group (Fouad et al., 2009) conceptualized teaching and supervision as two distinctive areas of competence. Teaching, according to the Competency Benchmarks Work Group, was "providing instruction, disseminating knowledge, and evaluating acquisition of knowledge and skill in professional psychology" (p. S23), whereas supervision was defined as the "training in the professional knowledge base and of evaluation of the effectiveness of various professional activities" (p. S21). Employing these definitions, teaching involves the facilitation of learning or instruction and assessing whether learning took place. Supervision, on the other hand, involves shaping the full range of professional aptitudes, skills, behaviors, and values. Using this distinction, it becomes clear that different competencies are required to teach someone to perform a card trick versus teaching someone to become a magician. Presumably, teaching is aimed at specific learning objectives and can be accomplished fairly quickly using a range of effective instructional methods, while supervision requires an extensive apprenticeship aimed at developing a broad array of competencies that are almost too numerous to list. One only has to look at the length of the list of behavioral anchors defined by the Benchmark Competency Work Group (see Fouad et al., 2009) as evidence of the numerous competencies required of an entry-level professional psychologist. Based upon the breadth and depth of competencies to be acquired during training in professional psychology, we rely heavily on supervision as the primary tool for shaping the behaviors that define our profession, and consequently, we agree that supervision competencies are worthy of special consideration.

The Competency Benchmarks Work Group (Fouad et al., 2009) outlined two domains of competence in teaching: (a) knowledge of teaching strategies and outcome assessments; and (b) skills in methods of teaching. The former domain focuses on demonstrating knowledge of theories of learning, various teaching strategies, making accommodations for teaching students with unique attributes, and assessing methods of teaching effectiveness. The latter domain focuses on the specific preparation and presentation skills required to teach effectively across multiple settings, as well as conducting accurate appraisals of whether learning objectives were met. As an example, by teaching an undergraduate course in psychology, a competent teacher would have knowledge of the literature pertaining to methods of teaching and student evaluation (knowledge-based competencies) as well as demonstrating effective methods of presenting course material in an interesting and informative way, coupled with fair methods for evaluating learning outcomes (skill-based competencies). Behavioral anchors associated with these two teaching competencies for all professional psychologists are provided in more detail in the Competency Benchmarks document (Fouad et al., 2009, p. S23).

In contrast to the relatively few specific competencies associated with teaching, the Competency Benchmarks Work Group (Fouad et al., 2009) outlined six domains of competence in supervision: (a) knowledge of the expectations regarding the role of supervision; (b) knowledge of the procedures and processes of supervision; (c) acquisition of basic skills required for supervising others; (d) awareness of aspects of the supervisory relationship that affect its quality; (e) participation in supervising others; and (f) awareness of ethical and legal issues associated with supervision. The first two domains of competence focus on knowledge-based competencies presumably acquired through reading the literature on models of supervision and how to implement these models into ongoing supervisory experiences. The third, fourth, and sixth domains of competence in supervision integrate various foundational competencies with competency in conducting supervision, with the third focusing on interpersonal skills (see Chapter 7) and reflective practice (see Chapter 5), the fourth focusing on sensitivity to individual and cultural diversity (see Chapter 8) and working in interdisciplinary settings (see Chapter 7), and the sixth focusing on consideration of ethical and legal issues that arise in supervisory relationships (see Chapter 9). Finally, the fifth domain of competence focuses on skill development of actually supervising the clinical work of less advanced trainees. Behavioral anchors associated with each of these supervision competencies are provided in more detail in the Competency Benchmarks document (Fouad et al., 2009, pp. S21–S23).

Like competency in conducting research, teaching and supervision competencies are not unique to professional psychology. Most graduates of programs in nonapplied areas of psychology (e.g., experimental psychology, behavioral neuroscience) also acquire competence in teaching and supervision (albeit not clinical supervision) during their graduate education. In many cases, greater attention to developing competencies in teaching might be paid among nonapplied psychology training programs, as these students are often funded via teaching assistantships and fellowships throughout graduate training. In this regard, students working toward degrees in either clinical health psychology or health psychology share common goals of acquiring competency in teaching. In contrast to the common goals of becoming competent teachers, providing supervision of clinical/applied activities (i.e., assessment, intervention, or clinical consultation) that directly influence patient care within the health care environment is the unique province of clinical health psychology. Although health psychology trainees acquire competence in supervising others in research or educational environments, they do not possess the clinical competencies required to conduct clinical supervision.

Like our research endeavors, clinical health psychologists (and our health psychologist colleagues) often teach or conduct supervision in health care settings. Unlike teaching experiences available in departments of psychology, however, teaching within health sciences centers typically involves addressing audiences comprised of learners without extensive backgrounds in psychology. Indeed, clinical health psychologists and health psychologists can find themselves lecturing to medical, pharmacy, public health, dental, or nursing students, in addition to supervising medical residents and fellows across a range of specialty areas. Because of the unique attributes of teaching that clinical health psychologists confront within health sciences center settings, several additional competencies in teaching and supervision were identified for entry-level clinical health psychologists by participants at the Tempe Summit (France et al., 2008; Masters et al., 2009; see Table 14.1). Like

TABLE 14.1 **Competencies and Behavioral Anchors in Education Unique to Clinical Health Psychology**

TEACHING

1. **Recognition of the range and type of students/trainees learning in health care settings, the potential skills they possess, and their necessary competencies[a]**
   - Demonstrates an awareness of the range of competencies of students in other disciplines and how they develop throughout their professional training
   - Understands the milestones in professional development of trainees in other health care professions
2. **Instruction in clinical health psychology to psychologists and psychology trainees[a]**
   - Writes educational objectives to support teaching programs
   - Models and reinforces behavior that appropriately respects the professional autonomy of other professions
   - Trains students to assert their professional autonomy and identity appropriately
3. **Instruction in clinical health psychology or methods and procedures for conducting health-related research to other health care professions (interprofessional education)[a]**
   - Create opportunities for interprofessional learning experiences
   - Collaborates with other interprofessional team members in the provision of clinical health education
   - Models effective interprofessional skills
   - Provide effective instruction in conducting health-related research across disciplines

SUPERVISION

1. **Supervision of clinical health psychology skills, conceptualizations, and interventions for psychologists, psychology trainees, and behavioral health providers from other health professions[a]**
   - Demonstrates knowledge of the literature on supervision and consultation-liaison in medical settings
   - Provides effective formative and summative feedback to trainees
   - Reviews documentation and monitors session outcomes of behavioral health providers
   - Listens to audio/video recording of sessions regularly
2. **Awareness of the conflicts between training and service in health care settings and negotiation for the optimal integration and reimbursement of these activities[a]**
   - Demonstrates an awareness that there are costs associated with supervision of trainees
   - Ability to negotiate an agreement that balances one's goals to generate clinical dollars and training students

[a]Adapted from Competencies in Clinical Health Psychology. France et al. (2008, p. 579).

the research competencies described in Chapter 13, the teaching and supervision competencies listed acknowledged the interdisciplinary environment of the health care environment within which clinical health psychologists function. Although not all clinical health psychologists practice within academic health sciences centers, many do. For those who practice in health care settings outside of academic medical center settings (e.g., pain clinics, rehabilitation hospitals, public health clinics, primary care facilities), teaching and supervision competencies are needed to engage in the instructional missions of these settings, as they often serve as externship placement sites for a range of health care professionals-in-training. As such, the additional competencies in teaching and supervision were considered essential for the entry-level practice of all clinical health psychologists. These distinctive competencies, although modified slightly over the past several years, are described in the following sections.

TEACHING COMPETENCIES AMONG CLINICAL HEALTH PSYCHOLOGISTS

The three additional teaching competencies that have been articulated for specialists in clinical health psychology are based on knowledge of the health care environment within which the instructional activity is occurring. The first competency in teaching requires the clinical health psychologist to gain knowledge of the types of students and other health care professionals comprising the learning environment as well as an understanding of their unique skills and competencies. Without this knowledge base, instructional efforts by clinical health psychologists are doomed from the onset. In contrast to teaching undergraduate students in departments of psychology, learners in the health care environment almost always have mastery of their specific content area that easily exceeds the clinical health psychologist's knowledge of that content area. For example, medical students know far more about human anatomy than most clinical health psychologists, and it would be fruitless for clinical health psychologists to attempt to teach them something about human anatomy. Similarly, pharmacy students know a lot more about drug action on various organ systems than most clinical health psychologists, and efforts to educate them further in pharmacology and toxicology would likely meet with failure. Thus, respecting the knowledge base of other disciplines is crucial to being successful as a clinical health psychologist. However, clinical health psychologists possess considerable expertise in understanding the principles of health behavior and can contribute meaningfully to the education of students from all other health professions, because all of them will eventually have careers where they interact with patients with various health conditions who engage in behaviors that either help or hinder resolution of their conditions. A solid piece of advice regarding teaching in health care settings is to stick to the area in which one possesses expertise, and for most clinical health psychologists that is an understanding of behavioral principles that influence health and health care.

Interestingly, problems often arise because our allied health and medical colleagues do not perceive that we have specialized or specific knowledge that demands the same respect in return. In fact, if one's colleagues believe all we are doing is "listening" and providing empathy, indeed these are skills that can easily be demonstrated by many disciplines. We must be able to demonstrate that the services and skills we provide are both unique and useful to the patient and the health care team. So being able to "teach" one's colleague what one does is a crucial skill in these types of environments.

The remaining two competencies in teaching focus on demonstration of effective skill in teaching, both with emerging clinical health psychology students or colleagues seeking specialty training (item 2 in Table 14.1) as well as students from other health care disciplines (item 3 in Table 14.1). Teaching courses or arranging didactic learning experiences for acquiring specialty area content, including those that focus on service provision and conducting health-related research, are highlighted as domains that clinical health psychologists can teach. Opportunities for formal teaching are largely dependent upon the health care institutions within which the clinical health psychologist works. In some settings, clinical health psychologists will be recruited to teach the principles of behavior to medical students, but in other settings, this content will be covered by a colleague in psychiatry or social work. The primary emphasis of these skill-based competencies is that clinical health psychologists need to be flexible and willing to engage in these teaching activities when asked to do so and when they are covering content within their area of expertise. In this regard, competent clinical health psychologists are good "utility infielders" who can be called upon to teach in a variety of venues and across the range of levels of training (i.e., undergraduate course work, graduate supervision, professional training, postdoctoral fellowship, continuing education programs, and/or departmental grand rounds).

As alluded to earlier, there is evidence that knowledge of behavioral health (i.e., psychology) is critical in the training of many other health care professions. Several allied health professions require completion of course work in the science of psychology (e.g., occupational therapy, nursing, physical therapy, social work), exposure to the behavioral sciences is required in various medical residencies (Accreditation Council for Graduate Medical Education, 2007), and exposure to behavioral dentistry is required in schools of dentistry (Commission on Dental Accreditation, 2010). Although often underrecognized, the role of understanding behavioral principles and predicting human behavior by any health care professional is critical in assessing and treating the range of complex diseases and disabilities seen in current health care environments. Recognizing that medical schools were not addressing these areas adequately, the Institute of Medicine (IOM) reviewed the curriculum standards a decade ago and recommended increased coverage of six domains pertinent to health behavior within medical education: (1) mechanisms associated with mind-body interactions; (2) principles of behavior change, (3) recognition of the influence of physician behavior, (4) training in physician–patient interactions, (5) social and cultural competence, and (6) knowledge of health policy and economics (Cuff & Vanselow, 2004, p. 10). To assure that physicians-in-training have been properly exposed to the behavioral sciences, the Medical College Admissions Test (MCAT) will soon include coverage of knowledge of the behavioral sciences. It is fairly easy to see how clinical health psychologists play important roles in assuring coverage of these important domains prior to and within the current medical education curriculum.

Instructional activities within any setting are difficult to devise without knowing the level of knowledge of the learners. In the structured sequence of an undergraduate psychology major, this can be easily accomplished by examining the content of the prerequisite course work for the course one is teaching. Within the health sciences educational environment, however, this task is far more complicated. For example, medical school classes are likely to be comprised of students with a broad range of knowledge of psychology, ranging from some who majored in psychology at the undergraduate level to those who have never had an introductory class in psychology. It has been our experience that a similar range of knowledge of psychology exists throughout medical education, even among psychiatry residents well into their postdoctoral periods of training. In this regard, competent teaching in these settings almost always requires gaining an understanding of the baseline levels of knowledge and/or skill of the learners. Painter and Lemkau (1992) provide some additional suggestions for teaching students from other health care disciplines, including using a considerable amount of clinical case material, emphasizing the scientific basis of psychology, and recognizing the competence levels of the learners.

Although not explicitly stated by participants at Tempe, there is a growing recognition of the value of integrative education in the area of behavioral health among health care professions (Carr, Emory, Errichetti, Bennett Johnson, & Reyes, 2007). Through this approach, coverage of the principles of behavioral health care is integrated into the curriculum with other core content, rather than segregating coverage of behavioral health content into a stand-alone class. This approach is entirely consistent with the mind-body approach we advocate and something clinical health psychologists can easily support. However, implementing such an approach requires clinical health psychologists to gain a greater understanding of the related course content outside the discipline of psychology. It would be impossible to integrate behavioral health content into a course without comprehending the material with which it is supposed to be integrated. Therefore, competence in teaching courses that integrate behavioral health content with relevant content from other health-related disciplines will require clinical health psychologists to acquire a fundamental understanding of the scientific foundations of these related disciplines, as described in Chapter 6. Indeed, calls for improving our medical knowledge have become more frequent as psychology identifies itself as a health care profession (Belar, 2008; Carr et al., 2007; HSPEC, 2013).

SUPERVISION COMPETENCIES IN CLINICAL HEALTH PSYCHOLOGY

Conducting supervision of behavioral health care provision within the health care setting requires two unique skill-based competencies above and beyond those articulated in the Competency Benchmarks document (Fouad et al., 2009). Because of the multidisciplinary nature of health care environments, competencies in supervising clinical health psychologists-in-training as well as trainees from other health care disciplines are required for entry-level practice. The learning objectives clearly differ based upon the audience of supervisees. For example, the goal of supervising clinical health psychologists-in-training is to assist them in achieving all of the competencies described in this book. In this regard, it would be appropriate to specify which competencies each supervisory experience aims to fulfill. Using this approach, trainees and their supervisors share a common goal of assuring that students are making adequate progress in achieving professional competencies in clinical health psychology in all of the relevant areas. In contrast, when supervising trainees from other health care disciplines, the instructional goals are typically elucidated by that discipline. For example, accreditation standards for various medical residencies by the Accreditation Council for Graduate Medical Education and dental schools by the American Dental Association specify the learning objectives associated with instruction in areas of behavioral health. Given that trainees in other health care professions are not being trained to practice clinical health psychology, it is obvious that supervising students from these disciplines will require less depth in most of the competency areas described in this book.

Recognizing that a bulk of foundational skill development in professional training programs is accomplished through course work and related experiences that typically focus on assessing and treating mental health problems, it is critical that clinical health psychology supervisors anticipate the "speed bumps" that will predictably occur as trainees translate their "broad and general" clinical and counseling skills into practicing within the broader health care arena. For example, working with a dying patient will present challenges for trainees who are accustomed to employing cognitive-behavioral interventions that provide hope for an optimistic future. Or implementing psychological assessments within the fast-paced primary care environment will challenge trainees who desire to perform comprehensive evaluations of cognitive and personality functioning. Competent supervisors anticipate these hurdles and address them as they are occurring.

In clinical service or research environments, clinical health psychologists often supervise trainees across all levels, including fairly novice learners all the way up to credentialed but junior professionals. In the health care setting, it is critically important to manage these trainees well and assign them tasks that fall within their areas of competence. Across almost all supervisory settings of this type, the attending clinical health psychologist could easily perform designated tasks more competently than the junior trainees. However, by doing everything oneself, the clinical health psychologist prevents trainees from acquiring any new skill-based competencies. In this regard, it is important to manage a balance between providing high-quality patient care and opportunities to facilitate autonomy among the trainees on the team.

As members of interdisciplinary treatment teams, clinical health psychologists are frequently called upon to supervise behavioral health provision conducted by trainees from other health professions. Although few acquire competency in this area through formal courses, this skill often can be acquired via simple modeling; if the supervisor possesses effective skills in respecting other professionals on the health care team, more often than not, trainees acquire these skills by watching and learning. There are times, however, where more directive feedback is needed to modify trainee behaviors during team meetings or working with another member of the health care team. Needless to say, these sorts of situations call for some balance of tact and grace, particularly when supervising the work of physicians-in-training.

There is no doubt that medical center environments are structured hierarchically, and that physicians hold the positions with the highest authority. As doctoral-level members of the health care team, clinical health psychologists hold a certain amount of prestige, but we rarely, if ever, are in the position of accepting primary responsibility for patient care or program development in hospital or academic medical center settings. This stands in direct contrast to the private practice of psychology or the provision of services via community mental health centers or counseling centers, where psychologists often direct patient care autonomously. In this regard, skill in supervising the development of professional autonomy and identity in an environment that never really provides complete autonomy is a challenge for trainees as well as their supervisors.

The last competency in the area of supervision in clinical health psychology is comprehension of the tension between health care provision and training that often exists in health care settings. Although health sciences centers are optimal places for acquiring foundational and functional competencies in clinical health psychology, they are also administratively complicated institutions with multiple missions (e.g., research, training, and patient care). It goes without saying that these missions do not always align for purposes of assigning value of the daily activities of professionals who work in them. Often, professional activities that are the most valuable from a training perspective are the least billable or reimbursable from a patient care perspective. Clinical health psychologists need to understand the institution's competing goals when (notice we did not say "if" here) these situations arise and devise strategies to optimize the quality of the instructional activity without compromising patient care.

ACQUISITION OF TEACHING AND SUPERVISION COMPETENCIES IN CLINICAL HEALTH PSYCHOLOGY

Returning to the "see one, do one, teach one" model of competency development mentioned at the beginning of this chapter, it is clear that competencies in teaching and supervision come later in the sequence of training than some other competency areas. This is likely true for most clinical health psychologists, because one needs to acquire a breadth of knowledge and/or a range of skills before developing the competence to teach them. Although some of the knowledge-based competencies in the area of teaching and supervision begin to accrue during doctoral training years, most of the skill-based competencies are not fully acquired until post-doctoral work. This is not to say that skill-based competencies cannot be learned earlier in training. Certainly, doctoral students with interests in clinical health psychology would be capable of teaching an undergraduate course in health psychology or stress and health. In contrast, doctoral students or psychology interns would not be able to supervise the clinical or research work of medical residents or fellows. These assignments are likely to be reserved for faculty members or at the very least advanced postdoctoral fellows.

Due to the primary focus on clinical training during the internship year, few opportunities typically exist for developing formal teaching competencies. Psychology interns are occasionally called upon to make professional presentations at departmental grand rounds and during their didactic seminars, but they rarely have opportunities for developing formal teaching skills during the internship year. In contrast, psychology interns often have opportunities to supervise the clinical work of less advanced trainees during their internship year, including supervision of psychometricians or practicum students from local doctoral programs. In this regard, opportunities to acquire skill-based competencies in supervision are frequently available during the capstone internship experience prior to receipt of the doctoral degree.

Postdoctoral fellows are often sought out to provide guest presentations and conduct supervision of the research and/or clinical work of less advanced trainees. After all, they have doctoral degrees, which provide them with the credentials to engage in teaching activities more autonomously. However, because postdoctoral fellows are considered "temporary" employees that often relocate upon completion of their fellowships, any long-term teaching arrangements are typically going to be offered to more permanent employees of the institution. Furthermore, some states disallow supervision for licensure by licensed psychologists with less than 2 or 3 years of experience, so that clinical supervision by postdoctoral fellows may not count for purposes of licensure. This is unfortunate, because postdoctoral fellows, having just completed their doctoral training, have knowledge of the most recent advances in professional practice and would likely be excellent supervisors. For example, with the current emphasis on primary care psychology, it would be a shame to disallow supervision by a postdoctoral fellow, well trained in the delivery of primary care psychology, when very few qualified supervisors exist in most regions of the world. Without access to clinical health psychology supervisors, the mechanism through which we train the next generation of health care evaporates. In this regard, it is good for the longevity of the specialty area to see increased efforts made in hiring clinical health psychologists in health science center settings as well as other health care venues that possess education in their mission statements.

The specialized competencies in teaching and supervision emerge more slowly over the training life span of the clinical health psychologist, with most opportunities for developing competencies in clinical teaching and supervision occurring during the internship and postdoctoral years. Through regular continuing education efforts and a commitment to life-long learning, clinical health psychologists continue to develop as instructors and supervisors, and consequently, their value to the institutions that employ them steadily increases.

FIFTEEN

Management, Administration, and Advocacy

As students emerge from their undergraduate years with their bachelor's degrees in psychology in hand, they eagerly anticipate future careers as psychologists, physicians, attorneys, educators, or members of other chosen professions. Many envision themselves as researchers discovering findings that support or refute prevailing psychological theories, as educators teaching students at various levels of education, or as service providers helping those with significant health or mental health needs. On rare occasions, a student might dream of administering a program to assist those in need or developing policies that might impact a larger group of people, but never will one hear a recent psychology graduate report a desire to manage an academic department or administer a health care system. Despite the relative lack of interest in management and administration early on in one's career, many professional psychologists apply for and ultimately obtain leadership positions administering programs, departments, and even entire academic or health care institutions. Their academic credentials in areas of research and clinical service provision, coupled with their interpersonal skill sets, make them particularly strong candidates for these leadership positions. It is also important to consider that there are several daily functions associated with being a professional psychologist in any setting that involve administrative competencies, like managing a grant project, interacting with a health maintenance organization to procure an authorization to see a patient, maintaining a positive working relationship with office support staff, or completing paperwork in a timely manner. Indeed, all venues for the professional practice of psychology rely in some way on competency in the area of management and administration.

Competencies in advocacy represent another "hidden" competency that often goes unnoticed. In fact, advocacy was not included at all in the cube model for competency development (Rodolfa et al., 2005). Suffice it to say, however, that no profession of any kind survives without advocacy, and those professions that advocate well grow in size, earn their constituent professionals more money, and maintain a more prestigious status in the eyes of the public. Unfortunately, advocacy among professional psychologists is not an area of competency that comes naturally. As a group, we are not boastful or quick to take credit for outcomes that we had a significant role in generating. In fact, for years we have been "giving away" our discipline such that now behavioral health service providers from all divergent fields receive at least some training in interventions and techniques originally developed by psychologists. Thus, it is not surprising that advocacy was considered critically important by the Competency Benchmarks Work Group and included as a required functional area of competence for all entry-level professional psychologists.

Competencies in management, administration, and advocacy are equally important for psychologists in nonapplied areas of psychology (e.g., experimental psychology, behavioral neuroscience). Organizational structures and their accompanying rules and regulations affect all who work in the immediate environment—those with clinical/applied as well as basic science or educational interests. In this regard, competency in management and administration applies to both students in professional psychology training programs and those in experimental fields of study. Grant budget management, managing a laboratory team, recording and assigning student grades, developing a training curriculum—even figuring out billing systems and methods to obtain reimbursement for services—all involve skills in management and administration. Systems in which health care providers do not attend to proper billing protocols, complete their paperwork in a timely manner (including treatment plans and progress notes), or complete required training programs (e.g., HIPAA training, research integrity), would be very short lived in the current health care environment, and practitioners' tenure in those systems would be even shorter. Although most graduate students do not take courses in leadership or administration (and, in fact, few departments even offer such courses), fundamental competencies in these areas are required to become a competent psychologist. Psychologists without these competencies experience substantial difficulties in establishing and maintaining programs of research, educational and training experiences, and managing a successful clinical practice in today's health care arena.

Because of the complexities associated with practicing, conducting research, or training within health sciences center settings, some additional competencies in management, administration, and advocacy have been included in the most recent list of competencies for entry-level practice in clinical health psychology (see Table 15.1). These distinctive competencies for clinical health psychologists above and beyond those

TABLE 15.1 **Competencies and Behavioral Anchors in Management, Administration, and Advocacy Unique to Clinical Health Psychology**

A. MANAGEMENT/ADMINISTRATION/LEADERSHIP

1. Knowledge of mission and organizational structure, relevant historical factors, and position of psychology in the health care organization and system[a]
   - Recognizes appropriate chains of communication to initiate a change in local systems of care
   - Understands current reporting lines for psychologists within the health care organization
   - Demonstrates knowledge of globalization and technological advances and how these factors influence management of clinical practice[b]
2. Knowledge of appropriate methods to develop a clinical health psychology practice, educational program, and/or program of research[b]
   - Works with organizational leaders to ensure appropriate resources are available for an effective clinical health psychology practice[a]
   - Creates business plans that track costs and quality associated with integration of behavioral health care within the health care environment[a]
   - Conducts a needs assessment that employs both a focus on the needs of the health care system and the perceived needs of patients and their families
   - Develops and implements standards for evaluating prospective behavioral health care providers in the health care setting
3. Able to conduct the business of health psychology practice, educational program, and/or research management[b]
   - Successfully manages a budget of an interdisciplinary research project
   - Understands electronic coding and management of records
   - Recruits and retains appropriate staff to provide behavioral health care services
   - Develops policy and procedures manuals
   - Uses Health and Behavior Codes when applicable
   - Monitors income and expenses to assure the practice lives within its annual budget
4. Leadership within an interprofessional team or organization in the health care setting[b]
   - Integrates talents and skills of professionals from different disciplines and different levels of training (e.g., masters, doctoral) to optimize treatment
   - Administers clinical programs that fully utilize the skills of the providers hired to be part of the treatment team
   - Plans and implements ongoing in-services and continuing education offerings to maintain and improve skills of providers

B. ADVOCACY

1. Recognition that advocacy to improve population health involves interacting with a number of systems (e.g., the health care system, local funders, federal funders, etc.)[a]
    • Demonstrates understanding that transitions of care (e.g., inpatient to home) are influenced by funding, caregiver availability, and patient capacity
    • Recognizes the unique and sometimes competing interests of different stakeholders in the health care system (e.g., patients, providers, payers, employers, and government)
 2. Advocates for increased resources for research and training in clinical health psychology at local, state, and federal levels[a]
    • Serves on advisory boards of community agencies
    • Engages in active outreach efforts and to policy makers to deliver message
    • Works with the state psychological association on a coordinated effort to train psychologists in clinical health psychology

[a]Adapted from Competencies for Psychology Practice in Primary Care. Interorganizational Workgroup on Competencies for Primary Care Psychology Practice (2013, pp. 18–23).
[b]Adapted from Competencies in Clinical Health Psychology. France et al. (2008, p. 579).

established by the Competency Benchmarks Work Group are described in the following sections.

MANAGEMENT AND ADMINISTRATION COMPETENCIES IN CLINICAL HEALTH PSYCHOLOGY

The Competency Benchmarks Work Group (Fouad et al., 2009) defined four domains of competency in management and administration: (a) knowledge and skills in the direct delivery of services; (b) knowledge and skills in administering organizations, programs, or agencies; (c) knowledge and skills in leadership; and (d) knowledge and skills in evaluating management and leadership efforts. All four domains involved the acquisition of knowledge-based competencies prior to skill-based competencies as professional psychologists-in-training proceeded from the early years of graduate training to completing their degrees. Because all professional psychology training programs possess an organizational structure with a specified leader and program rules and regulations, the training experience provides a perfect environment for observing and acquiring these management and administration competencies. Trainees who complete their paperwork in a timely fashion, register for the proper sequence of courses, and participate on departmental committees or those in professional organizations are acquiring important management and administration skills that will serve them well as they enter the profession. Behavioral anchors associated with competencies in the areas of management and administration are provided in detail in the Competency Benchmarks document (Fouad et al., 2009, pp. S23–S24). It should be noted that in contrast to the Benchmarks document that focused solely on competencies in management and administration of clinical service activities, the specialized competencies in clinical health psychology extend beyond the area of clinical service provision into areas of managing external grants or research team activities as well as administering and managing educational training programs. Additionally, the management and administration competencies listed by the Competency Benchmarks Work Group paid little attention to the coordination of care required to function within interdisciplinary health care settings, a feature that was recognized in the specialty competencies in clinical health psychology initially drafted at the Tempe Summit (France et al., 2008). The knowledge-based and skill-based competencies distinctive to clinical health psychology are discussed in the following sections.

Knowledge-Based Competencies in Management and Administration

The first two competencies of management and administration in clinical health psychology are based on acquiring knowledge of psychology's role in the health care organization and broader health care system (item 1 in Table 15.1) and methods for establishing and managing a practice, training program, or program of research within the health care environment (item 2 in Table 15.1). In contrast to other types of professional psychologists, clinical health psychologists need to know how the health care system operates both locally and globally. We already live in a global economy, where financial decisions made in other countries influence our domestic markets, including the business of health care. Even more problematic, contagious diseases that even just a few years ago may have remained isolated in one or two regions of the world now spread worldwide quickly given our mobile and global travels and businesses. As a result, clinical health psychologists need to be aware of global health issues as well as prevailing trends in health care systems and health policy around the world in addition to those that operate in the health care environment where they work. Through frequent interactions with administrative staff members of the local health care environment, essential knowledge of policies and procedures is gained that will permit the navigation of the layers of bureaucracy that exist in health care environments. Understanding exactly which groups or subgroups need to approve credentialing for work with patients, to authorize human subjects' approvals for research, or developing accredited training programs will facilitate getting work done more efficiently.

Compliance rules and regulations, both fiscal and pragmatic, often prove to be challenging to navigate to professionals just beginning their careers. This runs the gamut from knowing what can and what cannot be billed to a grant (and how to justify the expense, or what the consequences are if the expense is disallowed) to understanding the health and behavior codes or diagnoses appropriate for billing in the specific health care setting. Fortunately, few individuals have to deal with lawyers and legal issues associated with billing for services during training to minimize risk to one's practice. However, this prevents trainees from acquiring these knowledge-based competencies that they need to have while conducting clinical work or research in complex medical systems. Failure to comply with these rules and regulations often results in huge penalties from both federal and local agencies (e.g., HIPAA, certain Homeland Security violations associated with technology); as a result, most health care environments devote significant resources to ensure compliance. Being aware of aspects of one's practice associated with compliance issues, and learning early how to manage risk and how to assess for risk in both patient and research encounters are important skills in the area of practice management in health care environments.

Skill-Based Competencies in Management and Administration

In addition to the knowledge-based competencies in management and administration, clinical health psychologists are expected to have two unique skill-based competencies in order to function in the modern health care arena. The first skill-based area of competence (item 3 in Table 15.1) involves the application of the knowledge-based competencies in management described in the previous section. Although it is important to possess the knowledge of how to navigate through the health care environment for purposes of establishing a clinical practice or development of a program of research, it is more important to know how to do the navigation itself. Unfortunately, courses in this area are not commonly taught in training programs at any level and few practicum experiences are available that provide opportunities for developing these skills. It is important, however, for clinical health psychologists-in-training to learn how to apply for and maintain hospital privileges, access and utilize electronic medical recordkeeping systems, and navigate working with third-party vendors to pay for direct patient care services. Depending on the setting where the professional research, education, and service provision activities of the clinical health psychologist are provided, this can become an extremely time-consuming enterprise, time that cannot typically be reimbursed directly. Regarding programs of education or research, seemingly basic tasks take on considerable complexity when conducting projects in health care settings, including hiring and managing of staff and related support personnel, procuring equipment and services needed to complete the project, and simply paying for advertising and student or participant recruitment efforts.

The other skill-based competency in the area of management and administration extends the benchmark competency of leadership into the daily functioning of a clinical health psychologist (item 4 in Table 1). Based upon our skills in functioning on interdisciplinary treatment teams, these venues provide excellent opportunities for developing leadership skills. It is not uncommon for all other members of the treatment team to look toward the clinical health psychologist whenever any "psychosocial" issues arise in managing particular patients. In this regard, the clinical health psychologist becomes the resident expert for any emotional or behavioral health issues that arise during the course of medical treatment—even those that may reflect the emotional responses of the health care team itself. It is important to remember that being an effective leader does not require that one knows everything; rather being an effective leader requires making clear decisions calmly in difficult situations. It also involves facilitating the decision making of other individuals or groups in the health care team, particularly when there may be conflict regarding which option is best. Therefore, demonstrating leadership on health care teams involves operating within the boundaries of one's competence and requesting consultation from other health care professionals when needed.

PROFESSIONAL ADVOCACY IN CLINICAL HEALTH PSYCHOLOGY

Two competency domains in the area of advocacy were identified by the Competency Benchmarks Work Group (Fouad et al., 2009): (a) knowledge of the social, political, economic, or cultural factors that influence individuals and empowering them to engage in action; and (b) under-standing processes involved in system change and promoting change when desirable. It is important to note that the behavioral anchors associated with competencies in advocacy (see Fouad et al., 2009, pp. S24–S25) do not specify the avenues through which professional psychologists advocate on behalf of their patients or the broader health care community. Rather, the competencies in advocacy assert that professional psychologists stand up and say something (or empower others to say something) when a systems-level problem is identified that harms patient care or the health of the community. The decision to engage in personal efforts in advocacy or becoming involved in larger professional advocacy groups is left to the individual professional psychologist.

Competencies in advocacy were not considered at the Tempe Summit (France et al., 2008). However, since that time, groups of educators that have examined both broad professional competencies (HSPEC, 2013) as well as specialty competencies (CCHPTP, 2013; Inter-Organizational on Competencies for Primary Care Psychology Practice, 2013) have reaffirmed the important role of knowledge and skills in professional advocacy. To these ends, the current list of entry-level competencies for practice in clinical health psychology includes two competencies in advocacy distinctive to our specialty area (see Table 15.1).

The first of these two advocacy competencies reflects knowledge of the various levels where advocacy to improve population health occurs and the related attitude that advocacy is a constructive activity for the clinical health psychologist. There are various positions regarding what constitutes legitimate health care services and for which ones payment should be made, and unfortunately, psychologists are rarely in positions to be making these decisions. For the most part, these decisions are made by health care system administrators and health care payment organizations, including insurance companies, health maintenance organizations, and federal payment programs. Although almost all psychologists strongly believe that behavioral health care services should be an essential component of any health care system, there are many who are not aware of the evidence that supports including behavioral health care services into any health care system and who view it as a nice but nonessential element. As a profession, it is clear that our inclusion in the health care system requires a commitment on the part of every clinical health psychologist to understand the various agencies where such advocacy efforts could be made, including the health care system in which they work, local funders for clinical health psychology services, and state and federal systems that oversee health care systems and payment for services.

The second advocacy competency complements the first. While the first competency involves the knowledge of systems of care and payment for care as well as an appreciation and value of advocacy efforts, the second focuses on engagement in advocacy for research, training, and service provision in clinical health psychology at local, state, and federal levels. It should be noted that demonstration of this competency does not require that clinical health psychologists visit their state or federal legislators or send money to their political campaigns. Professional advocacy can be done in many ways, including serving on advisory boards of community agencies, engaging in outreach efforts to improve health behaviors among youth, and working with professional organizations to work with one another to change the way health care is delivered.

ACQUISITION OF MANAGEMENT, ADMINISTRATION, AND ADVOCACY COMPETENCIES IN CLINICAL HEALTH PSYCHOLOGY

Knowledge-based competencies in management, administration, and advocacy are important to develop fairly early during doctoral training, while their skill-based counterparts are often acquired later in training during postdoctoral experiences. Part of the reason for the delayed skill development of these competency areas relates to the simple fact that most trainees express little desire to engage in management and administrative experiences. Indeed, if one approaches an upper-level graduate student and gives him or her a choice between a practicum assignment where advanced competencies in intervention or administration could be acquired, preference would clearly be given to the former assignment. As a result of student preferences and their desire to "optimize" opportunities to obtain face-to-face clinical hours, efforts to acquire skills in program management, evaluation, and administration tend to receive lower priority. Additionally, like the functional competencies in areas of consultation and supervision, competencies in management and administration are easier to acquire with some professional maturity. Beginning trainees are not often asked to serve as consultants or supervisors, nor would they be asked (or should they be asked) to manage a research project or administer a clinical program. Accordingly, skill-based competencies in management and administration are among the last competencies to achieve during the training years.

Some of the best opportunities for developing management and/or administration skill-based competencies for trainees occur through participation in efforts to establish new research collaborations or provide new clinical services. Although time consuming and often frustrating, building these collaborations or services from scratch exposes clinical health psychologists-in-training to most of the essential competencies in practice or research program development that they will utilize throughout their professional careers. Unfortunately, these opportunities arise at irregular intervals throughout training, and there is no guarantee that such opportunities will arise during a particular phase of training, if at all. For example, consider a case where a treatment team on an oncology service desires behavioral health services to be fully integrated into their standard treatment protocols. Imagine the attending oncologist contacted a clinical health psychologist who agreed to supervise services provided by advanced graduate students-in-training or psychology interns. Assuming this arrangement was successful and was maintained for several years, many young professionals could receive excellent training in this setting and acquire competencies in assessment and treatment in health care environment as a result. However, the very first trainee supervised in this setting obtained an experience no others that followed obtained: the experience of developing the program itself. Although supervisory experiences of later trainees were sure to operate more smoothly than those of the first student on the service, the program development opportunity the first student received more than compensated. Due to the irregularity of these opportunities, it is advisable for trainees at all levels to keep an eye open for them and be quick to volunteer their time and assistance when they arise. There are other ways, of course, for developing skill-based competencies in management and administration, but this sort of program development experience is invaluable.

Every training program (doctoral, internship, and postdoctoral) has a set of operating rules and regulations that specify things like how to apply to graduate; when to submit forms for tuition waivers; when quarterly, semesterly, or annual evaluations need to be completed; and how to assemble a dissertation committee. Accompanying the operating rules and regulations is usually an extensive list of approved forms that often require an advisor's signatures at various time intervals during training. These rules, regulations, and forms represent years of administrative work and experience in program development, and all require occasional review and modification. At a basic level, awareness of and adherence to program rules and regulation represents a fundamental administrative competency and one that all trainees should maintain throughout years of training. Becoming involved in bringing about program change or modifying program rules and regulations represents a somewhat higher level of management and administrative competency. For trainees with career aspirations in administration, involvement in committees of prominent national organizations linked to health psychology represents another method for developing and refining solid management and administrative competencies.

Although frequently overlooked, competencies in advocacy are an important focus for trainees at all levels. Often, some of the most vocal advocates for a given profession are those who are in training to enter that profession. This makes intuitive sense because their chosen careers are imminently at risk if nobody advocates for their profession. One only has to examine the efforts of the American Psychological Association of Graduate Students (APAGS) to see the influence they have had in shaping issues for consideration by the broader professional organization. Once the American Psychological Association changed its bylaws to define psychology as a health care profession (Anderson, 2003), it was very apparent that advocacy efforts within clinical health psychology had played a significant role in promoting this new direction for the entire field of professional psychology.

Competencies in management, administration, and advocacy receive much less emphasis during graduate and postgraduate training. However, developing and maintaining a successful career as a clinical health psychologist depends upon acquiring and continuing to build competencies in these areas throughout one's professional career. Trainees should be aware of opportunities for developing their competencies in these areas as they present themselves irregularly throughout one's professional development.

PART IV

Summary and Conclusions

SIXTEEN

The Future of Clinical Health Psychology Competencies

Among all specialty areas, clinical health psychology was the first to articulate competencies associated with entry-level practice in their specialty area. Other specialty areas have followed suit: Competencies for practice in rehabilitation psychology (Hibbard & Cox, 2010) and clinical geropsychology (Knight, Karel, Hinrichsen, Qualls, & Duffy, 2009) have been drafted and disseminated, and the competencies for practicing psychology in primary care settings have recently been enumerated (Inter-Organizational Workgroup of the Practice of Psychology in Primary Care, 2013). Competencies to conduct various types of therapy, including cognitive-behavioral therapy (Newman, 2010), psychodynamic therapy (Sarnet, 2010), and humanistic-existential therapy (Farber, 2010), have also been described. Given the importance of defining competencies among specialty practice areas in today's professional climate, it is almost a certainty that other specialty areas will approach this task shortly. For a specialty area in psychological practice to neglect this activity would make it quite difficult to protect the public from professional psychologists who claim to possess competencies to practice in the designated specialty area but in fact do not. Only by identifying and defining competencies and methods for their assessment can a specialty area distinguish those who are competent to practice in the specialty area from those who are not.

Thankfully, considerable work has already been done in articulating competencies associated in the general professional practice of psychology (Fouad et al., 2009; Kaslow, 2004; Rodolfa et al., 2005), and these efforts provided the organizational structure within which specialty competencies could be considered. It goes without saying that specialty competencies build upon the foundational and functional competencies for the general practice of psychology as a health service profession. Similar to medical training, all professional psychologists need to acquire the general competencies described in the Competency Benchmarks document (see Fouad et al., 2009) and more recently in the Blueprint for Health Service Psychology document (HSPEC, 2013), but only those who choose to pursue advanced training in a specialty area need to acquire the specialty competencies articulated in this book and the other books in this series. As Nash and Larkin (2012) note in their recent article on the various pathways to obtaining specialty competencies, it is now the norm that psychologists-in-training are obtaining both broad and general clinical competencies and specialty competencies simultaneously beginning early during graduate study. Failure to begin specialty competency acquisition during graduate study in doctoral programs results in reducing a student's competitiveness for matching with an internship program with strong rotations in the designated specialty area. This state of affairs exists in the specialty area of clinical health psychology, where there are simply too many highly qualified clinical health psychologists-in-training competing for valuable clinical internships and postdoctoral fellowships.

SPECIALTY COMPETENCIES IN CLINICAL HEALTH PSYCHOLOGY

Like other areas of specialization, clinical health psychologists need to acquire both broad and general competencies associated with the professional practice of psychology and the competencies associated with the specialty of clinical health psychology. The chapters in Parts II and III of this book have described each of these specialty competencies in detail. A summary of the distinctive foundational and functional competencies required for the entry-level practice of clinical health psychology is shown in Table 16.1.

A significant area of competency unique to the practice of clinical health psychology that appears across several of the competencies (research, teaching, supervision, professional relationships, clinical service provision) summarized in Table 16.1 involves developing productive relationships with members of the health care team from other disciplines. Although many people believe that interdisciplinary practice is a recent development in health care that coincided with the passage of the Patient Protection and Affordable Care Act in 2010, its importance has

TABLE 16.1 **Summary of Specialty Competencies Distinctive to Clinical Health Psychology**

FOUNDATIONAL COMPETENCIES

1. Adoption of a professional identity as a clinical health psychologist
2. Skill in self-assessment of competency in the many roles of the clinical health psychologist, including promotion of self-care of all health care providers
3. Broad knowledge of scientific bases of health and disease using a biopsychosocial framework in psychology as well as other health care disciplines
4. Knowledge and skills in interprofessional communication, including functioning on interdisciplinary teams
5. Knowledge and skills in understanding social and cultural factors that influence health and obtaining health care
6. Knowledge of ethical and legal issues distinctive for practicing in health care settings

FUNCTIONAL COMPETENCIES

1. Knowledge and skill associated with psychological assessment using a biopsychosocial approach in health care settings
2. Implement evidence-based interventions and prevention programs for individuals and systems in health care settings and evaluation of outcomes
3. Knowledge and skill in consultation in health care settings
4. Skill in conducting research in health care settings, including conducting research on interdisciplinary teams
5. Effective evaluation of clinical services in health care settings, including quality improvement programs
6. Teach and supervise psychology trainees in health care settings
7. Teach and supervise trainees from other health care disciplines
8. Knowledge and skill in administering and managing programs/practices in health care settings
9. Leadership skill on interdisciplinary teams
10. Advocacy for clinical health psychology research, education, and practice

been recognized for decades. In fact, the first meeting coordinated by the then newly founded Institute of Medicine (IOM; founded in 1970) was a conference on Interrelationships of Educational Programs for Health Professionals held in Washington, D.C., in October of 1972. The report of that conference (Institute of Medicine, 1972) called for, among other things, that health care settings in which interdisciplinary educational and practical experiences occurred should be developed, opportunities for faculty to be trained in interdisciplinary skills should be developed, and that social and behavioral research into the origins of diseases should be conducted by interdisciplinary teams. According to the IOM, such an approach would reduce tensions among health professions, and guidelines to facilitate learning about the roles and contributions to health care of various providers would emerge. Thus, the idea of integrating behavioral health care into health care settings is not new; however, professional psychology's interest in it probably is.

The IOM defined five core competencies that they believed applied to all health professionals, including clinical health psychologists (Greiner

& Knebel, 2003). These included (a) the provision of patient-centered care; (b) the ability to work in interdisciplinary teams; (c) the utilization of evidence-based practice; (d) the ability to employ quality improvement methods and strategies; and (e) the ability to utilize informatics. According to the IOM, then, the competencies in clinical health psychology described in this book overlap almost perfectly with the core competencies articulated by the IOM. It is quite clear that the nation's health care system is starting to resemble the blueprint provided by the IOM over a decade ago, and that clinical health psychology will be asked to play a significant role in it.

ASSESSMENT OF COMPETENCIES IN CLINICAL HEALTH PSYCHOLOGY

Constructions of lists of competencies do little good if they are not accompanied by a description of methods for assessing them reliably. Attesting to the importance of competency assessment, the Competency Benchmarks document was published with a complementary Competency Assessment Toolkit (Kaslow et al., 2009). In this regard, students-in-training as well as educators and credentialing bodies that evaluate them during training and prior to licensing, respectively, not only had access to lists of the competencies they should be evaluating but some clues regarding how to conduct these assessments. In contrast to the work that has been conducted on general professional competencies for all psychologists, the work initiated at the Tempe Summit and continued during the annual meetings of CCHPTP has focused more on defining specialty competencies than describing methods for assessing them. Presumably, competencies could be self-reported as well as observed and evaluated more objectively by professional educators and/or supervisors. To assist in the assessment of clinical health psychology competencies, an evaluation tool for this purpose has been developed by CCHPTP (see Appendix). The evaluation form contained in the Appendix can be used by the trainee for purposes of self-assessment and evaluation, by educators for evaluating competency acquisition during training, or by credentialing bodies (e.g., licensing boards, ABPP examination boards) to assure that only those who possess the entire array of clinical health psychology competencies identify themselves as clinical health psychologists.

Although many rating systems could be used for evaluating competencies, we prefer the approach developed by Benner (1984) and modified for use by Hatcher and Lassiter (2007) for purposes of evaluating practicum competencies. In an attempt to understand how humans develop complex cognitive processes associated with expertise, this system enumerates five steps of competency development from early beginners (i.e., Novices) to credentialed specialists (i.e., Experts). Although the exact label associated with each level of development has evolved over time, the following descriptions outline the typical process of acquisition of competence as initially proposed by Dreyfus and Dreyfus:

Novice: The beginning stage of competency acquisition, characterized by rigid rule following with no capacity to adapt behavior to different situational contexts. Little capacity is evidenced for dealing with complexity and practicing independent judgment, and consequently, close supervision of professional activity is required.

Advanced Beginners (Hatcher & Lassiter named this level "Intermediate"): Trainees at this level continue to be characterized by rule following, but with experience, they can now detect how their behavior needs to be modified depending upon the situational context. Basic tasks can be completed independently, but more complex problems require supervision. Generalization of skills to new areas is limited.

Competent (Hatcher & Lassiter named this level "Advanced"): Autonomous functioning of basic and advanced skills has been fully achieved by those providers at this level. Because the strategy of rule-following becomes cumbersome for efficient practice (i.e., there are too many rules to apply for managing every potential situation), competent providers make rational decisions based on development of relevant organizing principles or "perspectives." Having considerable experience, providers at this level understand the long-term outcomes of their professional actions and accept full responsibility for them.

Proficient: Pattern recognition is fully achieved among proficient providers as they can easily view a situation holistically and separate the pertinent from impertinent issues in solving problems. Depth of knowledge and skill is evident and decisions are made without difficulty.

Expert: Individuals who achieve the level of expert go beyond the rational decision making seen in all previous levels by adding intuitive knowledge in solving problems. Analytic problem-solving methods can still be used to deal with complicated problems, but for the most part, experts no longer rely on rules, guidelines, or maxims and their decisions are made effortlessly.

Using this developmental model, self-assessment and/or assessment by independent observers can be conducted for purposes of measuring professional competence. In the following sections, strategies for assessing specialty competencies in clinical health psychology are described for trainees, educators, and credentialing agents.

Clinical Health Psychology Trainees

For clinical health psychologists-in-training, this evaluation form can be used to conduct a self-assessment of the competencies required for entry-level practice. The form is designed to monitor progress on competency acquisition of knowledge, skills, and values associated with broad and general professional psychology competencies (on the left portion of the form) as well as specialty competencies in clinical health psychology (on the right portion of the form). Presumably, self-ratings as a novice will be the norm for most of the competency areas of students as they enter doctoral training programs. It is quite possible that some of the general professional psychology competencies will already have been acquired prior to entry into graduate training. For example, progress on foundational competencies in professionalism (e.g., integrity, deportment, concern for the welfare of others), scientific knowledge and methods, and skills in interpersonal relationships will likely be factors considered by admissions' committees, and prospective candidates who already possess them will be more likely to receive offers of admission.

As trainees complete courses and related practical experiences that comprise their graduate training programs, self-ratings as a novice will presumably decline and progress toward the advanced beginner level will occur. As noted earlier, during these training years, most budding clinical health psychologists will be acquiring general professional competencies and clinical health psychology specialty competencies simultaneously. Hopefully, most areas of competency of these trainees will be at the advanced beginner level by the time they are ready to apply for their clinical internships. Directors of internship training programs play a significant role in promoting competency development from the advanced beginning level to the competent provider level, but they really do not perceive their role as working with trainees at the novice level. In fact, upon accepting a trainee at novice competency levels into a clinical internship, the trainee will invariably not possess the requisite competencies for successful completion of the internship, and the quality of the internship experience will decline among the cohort of interns who must complete their training year with a peer at a lower level of competence.

Upon completion of the requirements for the doctoral degree (including completion of the clinical internship), trainees should achieve self-ratings at the competent level, at least with respect to the broad and general professional competencies, prior to application for licensure as a psychologist. For those whose self-assessment reveals that they are still functioning at lower levels of competency acquisition, some remedial attention is indicated before applying for licensure. For the trainee who has acquired competent ratings for all specialty competencies at this point in time in the sequence of training, accepting entry-level positions as clinical health psychologists is an option. For those who desire to either advance their level of competency to the level of proficiency or who need to complete some gaps in procuring competent ratings that were apparent upon degree completion, postdoctoral fellowships in clinical health psychology settings are an attractive option. Using this form as a self-assessment tool, clinical health psychologists-in-training can easily track their progress in acquiring the competencies needed in order for them to function as clinical health psychologists in today's workforce.

Clinical Health Psychology Trainers

Although self-assessment of competency is a hallmark attribute of any profession, those who direct, teach, or supervise trainees in the area of clinical health psychology know that assessment should be multimodal. As such, assessment of competencies should not rely entirely on self-report ratings. Objective methods of assessment of competencies are often recommended to complement self-assessment (e.g., Kaslow et al., 2009), including direct observation of professional activities and observations of performance during standardized testing (e.g., interviewing standardized patients, structured clinical assessments, and interacting with patient avatars using virtual technologies). Although some training programs have made creative use of these types of assessment, most rely on the direct observations of research advisors and clinical and teaching supervisors.

Rating systems used for purposes of evaluating competency acquisition vary; there are probably as many different rating systems as there are training programs. Consequently, it is difficult to aggregate these data across programs and even more challenging to compare trainees' competency acquisition in one program with those from another program. Given this state of affairs, it is difficult to evaluate the applicant's strengths and weaknesses at key points during the sequence of training (e.g., readiness for practicum, readiness for internship, readiness for entry to practice, readiness for board certification). However, should programs adopt a uniform method for evaluating competency acquisition, such challenges can be surmounted. In this regard, training programs could use the evaluation form in the Appendix as a tool to track acquisition of competencies that would be quite useful, particularly as students make the transition from doctoral programs to internships and from internships to postdoctoral fellowship programs. At these key transition points, training plans could be more efficiently created if programs admitting students had a decent assessment of their baseline competencies. For example, if a given student's training had not provided any exposure to supervising entry-level trainees or trainees from another profession, training plans of internships or postdoctoral fellowships could be devised to ensure that opportunities to acquire these competencies during the training experience were available.

Ratings of competency acquisition by educators who direct, teach, and supervise clinical health psychology programs are best done if data from all professionals who had contact with the trainee are available. Optimally, the evaluation is conducted at a meeting when all potential evaluators could openly discuss the competency acquisition of the trainee and varying perspectives could be shared. This is a time-consuming method, but it assures that all potential sources of information regarding each student's progress are considered. Other methods involve obtaining written evaluations from all teachers and supervisors who had contact with a given student. Through using an evaluation form directly linked to the essential competencies required for the successful practice of clinical health psychology, student evaluations can be done more systematically.

An additional advantage for using a standard method for evaluating competency acquisition is that training programs could then use these data for ongoing program evaluation. Should a few years go by in which all trainees failed to acquire a particular competency area, the program would quickly realize that a modification in curriculum may be warranted. For example, if none of a given program's students acquires knowledge of interdisciplinary functioning and teamwork prior to applying for internship, the program would recognize that increased effort to cover this essential competency area needs to be made in order to assure that their students possess the requisite competencies to compete for clinical internships and postdoctoral fellowships later during their training years.

Credentialing Bodies of Clinical Health Psychologists

Because generic licensing as psychologists is the norm across all 50 states in the United States and the Canadian provinces, regional credentialing bodies for clinical health psychologists do not exist. This is to say that we are licensed as "psychologists," not as clinical health psychologists. As such, it can be difficult to monitor and regulate whether those who call themselves clinical health psychologists actually possess the competencies to practice in this specialty area. Licensing boards request information regarding an applicant's self-assessed areas of competence, and applicants are required to demonstrate how they achieved competency in the area they are declaring. In this regard, an applicant who applies to be licensed as a psychologist with a strong background and training in clinical health psychology would be permitted to refer to himself or herself as a clinical health psychologist once licensed. Presumably, an applicant for licensure who did not complete any training in clinical health psychology but who attempted to declare it an area of competence would be restricted from doing so by the licensing body. Of course, applicants who seek out additional training in a given specialty area and then demonstrate competence in the area to the licensing board are then permitted to add it to their list of areas of competence. In this regard, the credentialing licensing boards have some control over who calls themselves clinical health psychologists once they are licensed to practice.

Although licensing boards play a role in regulating specialty areas of practice in every state, there are no uniform guidelines that they can use to distinguish those who are competent clinical health psychologists from those who are not. To complicate matters, because boards of psychology are typically comprised of individuals appointed by governmental agencies and/or elected officials, there is no guarantee that any board member will possess knowledge of the requisite competencies to practice in each specialty area, including in clinical health psychology. In this regard, the list of competencies depicted in the form in the Appendix could provide credentialing bodies, like licensing boards, with important knowledge to help them make these determinations. Furthermore, they could use the form as an evaluation tool to determine whether applicants who profess to have competence in clinical health psychology actually do so. Presumably, applicants for licensure would need to obtain ratings of "competent" in all of the general and specialty competency areas listed.

The ultimate credential for documenting professional identification as a clinical health psychologist is receipt of board certification from the American Board of Professional Psychology (ABPP) in the area of clinical health psychology. Technically, it is the only credential available to distinguish oneself as a clinical health psychologist. Presumably, the ABPP evaluation of a candidate's record of distinction could also make use of the evaluation tool depicted in the Appendix. Of course, some ratings higher than "competent" would be expected in some of the specialty competency areas at the time of application for board certification.

In sum, through adoption of a uniform assessment tool, self-assessment of clinical health psychologists-in-training, educators of training programs in clinical health psychology, and bodies that credential clinical health psychologists can provide reasonable assurance to the public that those who call themselves clinical health psychologists have acquired the competencies to do so. By establishing this standard, the future of clinical health psychology has considerable promise, particularly as the nation's health care system, and the world health care system beyond, emphasizes the importance of behavioral expertise in solving the major leading causes of death, disease, and disability that afflict us. Through careful consideration of the competencies that distinguish the specialty area of clinical health psychology, we have provided a blueprint in this volume that outlines the steps we need to take individually and collectively to help solve our biggest health care problems.

APPENDIX: COMPETENCY TRACKING FORM FOR SPECIALTY COMPETENCIES IN CLINICAL HEALTH PSYCHOLOGY

Cluster 1: Science

Rating: N = Novice; AB = Advanced Beginner; C = Competent; P = Proficient; E = Expert

BENCHMARKS COMPETENCIES	RATING	CLINICAL HEALTH COMPETENCIES	RATING
1. Scientific Knowledge and Methods		**1. Scientific Knowledge and Methods of Clinical Health Psychology**	
1A. Scientific Mindedness			
Independently applies scientific methods to practice			
1B. Scientific Foundation of Psychology			
Demonstrates advanced-level knowledge of core science (i.e., scientific bases of behavior)		Knowledge of pathophysiology of disease and biomedical treatments specific to medical specialty or environment in which the practice will occur	
		Knowledge of the pathways and reciprocal interactions among psychosocial (cognitive/affective/behavioral) and biological phenomena as they relate to health promotion, illness prevention, and disease progression	
		Knowledge of life span developmental and social-environmental factors associated with health behavior, illness, and disease	
		Knowledge of the interactions among populations and contextual variations (e.g., age, gender, ethnicity, culture, religion, etc.) and the impact on health behavior and health outcomes	
		Knowledge of the scientific foundations and research methods of other health disciplines (e.g., epidemiology, biostatistics)	
1C. Scientific Foundation of Professional Practice			
Independently applies knowledge and understanding of scientific foundations independently applied to practice		Knowledge of relevant scientific literatures as they bear on health care and the ability to conceptualize and generate new issues, concerns, and questions based on that knowledge	

2. Research/Evaluation

2A. Scientific Approach to Knowledge Generation
Generates knowledge

2B. Application of Scientific Method to Practice
Applies scientific methods of evaluating practices, interventions, and programs

2. Research/Evaluation

Application of diverse methodologies to scientifically examine psychosocial and biological processes as they relate to health promotion, illness prevention, and disease progression

Selection, application, and interpretation of quantitative and qualitative data analytic strategies that are best suited to the diverse research questions and levels of analysis characteristic of health psychology

Formulation and implementation of health-related research using interdisciplinary research teams

Accurate and efficient communication of research findings in ways that can be understood by fellow psychologists, professionals from other disciplines, and lay audiences

Use of research skills to evaluate the effectiveness and quality of clinical health psychology services within health care settings, including participation in quality improvement efforts

Cluster 2: Professionalism

1. Professionalism

1. Professional Values and Attitudes

1A. Integrity
Monitors and independently resolves situations that challenge professional values and integrity

1B. Deportment
Conducts self in a professional manner across settings and situations

1C. Accountability
Independently accepts personal responsibility across settings and contexts

1D. Concern for the Welfare of Others
Independently acts to safeguard the welfare of others

1E. Professional Identity

BENCHMARKS COMPETENCIES	RATING	CLINICAL HEALTH COMPETENCIES	RATING
Displays consolidation of professional identity as a psychologist; demonstrates knowledge about issues central to the field; integrates science and practice		Professional identity as a clinical health psychologist Flexibility in approaching problems and issues encountered in the health care setting Knowledge to address issues and challenges unique to working in health care settings	
2. Individual and Cultural Diversity		**2. Individual and Cultural Diversity**	
2A. Self as Shaped by Individual and Cultural Diversity Independently monitors and applies knowledge of self as a cultural being in assessment, treatment, and consultation		Knowledge of self and others as cultural beings in health care settings, including knowledge of health disparities across a number of different diversity-related characteristics	
2B. Others as Shaped by Individual and Cultural Diversity and Context Independently monitors and applies knowledge of others as cultural beings in assessment, treatment, and consultation			
2C. Interaction of Self and Others as Shaped by Individual and Cultural Diversity and Context Independently monitors and applies knowledge of diversity in others as cultural beings in assessment, treatment, and consultation			
2D. Applications Based on Individual and Cultural Context Applies knowledge, skills, and attitudes regarding dimensions of diversity to professional work		Application of knowledge of the relations between social and cultural factors and the development of health problems to patient care, including access to health care	
3. Ethical Legal Standards and Policy		**3. Ethical Standards in Health Care Settings**	
3A. Knowledge of Ethical and Legal Standards and Guidelines Demonstrates advanced knowledge and application of the APA Ethical Principles and Code of Conduct and other relevant ethical, legal, and professional standards and guidelines		Knowledge of ethical and legal ramifications of biopsychosocial assessment, intervention, and research/quality improvement strategies in addressing health conditions seen in health care settings	
3B. Awareness and Application of Ethical Decision Making Independently utilizes an ethical decision-making model in professional work			
3C. Ethical Conduct Independently integrates ethical and legal standards with all competencies		Identification and ability to address the distinctive ethical issues encountered in clinical health practice, particularly if these are in conflict with the ethical code of other members of the health care team Knowledge of policies that regulate the delivery of services in health care systems	

4. Reflective Practice/Self-Assessment/Self-Care

4A. Reflective Practice
Demonstrates reflectivity both during and after professional activity; acts upon reflection; uses self as a therapeutic tool

4B. Self-Assessment
Accurately self-assesses competence in all competency domains; integrates self-assessment in practice; recognizes limits of knowledge/skills and acts to address them; has extended plan to enhance knowledge/skills

4C. Self-Care
Self-monitors issues related to self-care and promptly intervenes when disruptions occur

4D. Participation in Supervision Process
Independently seeks supervision when needed

4. Reflective Practice/Self-Assessment/Self-Care

Knowledge of importance of self-assessment in clinical health settings

Facilitation of self-care, including healthy lifestyles, of health professionals in clinical health settings

---

Cluster 3: Relationships

1. Relationships

1A. Interpersonal Relationships
Develops and maintains effective relationships with a wide range of clients, colleagues, organizations, and communities

1B. Affective Skills
Manages difficult communication; possesses advanced interpersonal skills

1C. Expressive Skills
Verbal, nonverbal, and written communications are informative, articulate, succinct, sophisticated, and well integrated; demonstrates thorough grasp of professional language and concepts

1. Relationships

BENCHMARKS COMPETENCIES	RATING	CLINICAL HEALTH COMPETENCIES	RATING
		2. Interprofessionalism	
		2A. Values/Ethics	
		Values and appreciates the interprofessional team approach to care	
		Encouragement of behavior that demonstrates appropriate respect for the professional autonomy of other health care professionals	
		2B. Interprofessional Roles/Responsibilities	
		Knowledge of strengths and potential pitfalls of role relationships that characterize interdisciplinary collaborative activities (e.g., research, education, clinical care, administration)	
		Knowledge and appreciation of the role and primary responsibilities of other health care professionals (e.g., physicians, nurses, social workers) in providing care both in general and specific medical settings	
		Ability to access, evaluate, and utilize information from other health care providers, including use of methods that include new and emerging health technologies (e.g., EHR)	
		2C. Interprofessional Communication	
		Development of facilitative and collaborative relationships with professionals from a variety of health care disciplines, including medicine, nursing, physical therapy, social work, etc.	
		Ability to interact with fellow health care professionals in ways that facilitate improved treatment implementation based on the unique contributions that clinical health psychology can make in the health care setting	
		Communication that cultivates mutual understanding regarding problems among individuals from diverse disciplines, including those that involve research and patient care	
		2D. Team and Teamwork	
		Ability to assess team dynamics and coach teams to improve functioning	
		Implementation of empirically supported health promotion, prevention, treatment, and rehabilitation in the context of the interdisciplinary team	

1. Evidence-Based Practice
1A. Knowledge and Application of Evidence-Based Practice
Independently applies knowledge of evidence-based practice, including empirical bases of assessment, intervention, and other psychological applications, clinical expertise, and client preferences

2. Assessment
2A. Knowledge of Measurement and Psychometrics
Independently selects and implements multiple methods and means of evaluation in ways that are responsive to and respectful of diverse individuals, couples, families, and groups and context

2B. Knowledge of Assessment Methods
Independently understands the strengths and limitations of diagnostic approaches and interpretation of results from multiple measures for diagnosis and treatment planning

2C. Application of Assessment Methods
Independently selects and administers a variety of assessment tools and integrates results to accurately evaluate presenting questions appropriate to the practice site and broad area of practice

1. Evidence-Based Practice

2. Assessment
Ability to evaluate the presenting problem and to select and administer empirically supported biopsychosocial assessments appropriate for the patient's physical illness, injury, or disability

Knowledge and understanding of biological assessment strategies and their results used in health care settings
Knowledge and understanding of psychological assessment strategies used in health care settings
Knowledge and understanding of social and environmental assessment strategies used in health care settings

Ability to conduct a comprehensive biopsychosocial interview and evaluate objective biological and psychosocial findings related to physical health or illness, injury, or disability
Ability to assess biopsychosocial and behavioral risk factors for the development of physical illness, injury, or disability
Ability to assess environmental factors that facilitate or inhibit patient knowledge, values, attitudes, and/or behaviors affecting health functioning and health care utilization
Ability to assess biopsychosocial factors affecting adherence to recommendations for medical and psychological care

BENCHMARKS COMPETENCIES	RATING	CLINICAL HEALTH COMPETENCIES	RATING
2D. Diagnosis Utilizes case formulation and diagnosis for intervention planning in the context of stages of human development and diversity		Ability to assess the biopsychosocial impact of medical procedures (including screening, diagnostic, and intervention/prevention procedures) Ability to solicit input of significant others in the assessment process as indicated	
2E. Conceptualization and Recommendations Independently and accurately conceptualizes the multiple dimensions of the case based on the results of assessment			
2F. Communication of Assessment Findings Communicates results in written and verbal form clearly, constructively, and accurately in a conceptually appropriate manner		Ability to communicate the results of assessments to both professional and lay audiences in the health care setting	
3. Intervention		**3. Intervention**	
3A. Intervention Planning Independently plans interventions; case conceptualizations and intervention plans are specific to case and context		Ability to access, evaluate, and utilize information in designing and implementing treatment, health promotion, and prevention interventions using new and emerging health technologies	
3B. Skills Displays clinical skills with a wide variety of clients and uses good judgment even in unexpected or difficult situations		Implementation of individual- or family-level evidence-based treatment interventions to treat health and mental health–related issues	
3C. Intervention Implementation Implements interventions with fidelity to empirical models and flexibility to adapt where appropriate		Implementation of evidence-based interventions for individuals and populations along a continuum from acute clinical need to subclinical problems to prevention and wellness	
3D. Progress Evaluation Independently evaluates treatment progress and modifies planning as indicated, even in the absence of established outcome measures		Ability to evaluate, select, and administer appropriate assessments for the purpose of monitoring and evaluating the process and outcomes of treatment and rehabilitative services	

4. Consultation

4A. Role of Consultant

Determines situations that require different role functions and shifts roles accordingly to meet referral needs

4B. Addressing Referral Question

Demonstrates knowledge of and ability to select appropriate and contextually sensitive means of assessment/data gathering that answers consultation referral question

4C. Communication of Consultation Findings

Applies knowledge to provide effective assessment feedback and to articulate appropriate recommendations

4D. Application of Consultation Methods

Applies literature to provide effective consultative services (assessment and intervention) in most routine and some complex cases

4. Consultation

Knowledge of own and others' professional roles and expectations within the context of intradisciplinary and interdisciplinary consultation in the health care setting

Conceptualization of referral questions that bear on human behavior (including an understanding of the client's, other providers', or the health system's role)

Translation and communication of relevant scientific findings as they bear on the health care consultation/liaison questions

Ability to work with professionals from other disciplines to increase the likelihood of appropriate early referral for consultation with clinical health psychologists as opposed to "last resort" referrals

Cluster 5: Education

1. Teaching

1A. Knowledge

Demonstrates knowledge of didactic learning strategies and how to accommodate developmental and individual differences

1B. Skills

Applies teaching methods in multiple settings

1. Teaching

Recognition of the range and type of students/trainees learning in health care settings, the potential skills they possess, and their necessary competencies

Instruction in clinical health psychology to psychologists and psychology trainees

Instruction in clinical health psychology or methods and procedures for conducting health-related research to other health care professions (interprofessional education)

BENCHMARKS COMPETENCIES	RATING	CLINICAL HEALTH COMPETENCIES	RATING
2. Supervision		**2. Supervision**	
2A. Expectations and Roles			
Understands the ethical, legal, and contextual issues of the supervisor role			
2B. Processes and Procedures			
Demonstrates knowledge of supervision models and practices; demonstrates knowledge of and effectively addresses limits of competency to supervise			
2C. Skills Development			
Engages in professional reflection about one's clinical relationships with supervisees, as well as supervisees' relationships with their clients			
2D. Supervisory Practices			
Provides effective supervised supervision to less advanced students, peers, or other service providers in typical cases appropriate to the service setting		Supervision of clinical health psychology skills, conceptualizations, and interventions for psychologists, psychology trainees, and behavioral health providers from other health professions	
		Awareness of conflicts between training and service in health care settings and negotiation for the optimal integration and reimbursement of these activities	

Cluster 6: Systems

BENCHMARKS COMPETENCIES	RATING	CLINICAL HEALTH COMPETENCIES	RATING
1. Interdisciplinary Systems		**1. Interdisciplinary/Interprofessional Systems (see Interprofessionalism Competencies in Cluster 3)**	
1A. Knowledge of the shared and distinctive contributions of other professions			
Demonstrates awareness of multiple and differing worldviews, roles, professional standards, and contributions across contexts and systems; demonstrates intermediate-level knowledge of common and distinctive roles of other professionals			
1B. Functioning in multidisciplinary and interdisciplinary contexts			
Demonstrates beginning, basic knowledge of and ability to display the skills that support effective interdisciplinary team functioning			

1C. Understands how participation in interdisciplinary collaboration/consultation enhances outcomes

Participates in and initiates interdisciplinary collaboration/ consultation directed toward shared goals

1D. Respectful and productive relationships with individuals from other professions

Develops and maintains collaborative relationships over time despite differences

2. Management/Administration

2A. Appraisal of Management and Leadership

Develops and offers constructive criticism and suggestions regarding management and leadership of organization

2B. Management

Participates in management of direct delivery of professional services; responds appropriately in management hierarchy

2C. Administration

Demonstrates emerging ability to participate in administration of service delivery programs

2D. Leadership

Participates in system change and management structure

3. Advocacy

3A. Empowerment

Intervenes with client to promote action on factors impacting development and functioning

3B. Systems Change

2. Management/Administration/Leadership

Knowledge of mission and organizational structure, relevant historical factors, and position of psychology in the health care organization and system

Knowledge of appropriate methods to develop a clinical health psychology practice, educational program, and/or program of research

Able to conduct the business of health psychology practice, educational program, and/or research management

3. Advocacy

Leadership within an interprofessional team or organization in the health care setting

3. Advocacy

BENCHMARKS COMPETENCIES	RATING	CLINICAL HEALTH COMPETENCIES	RATING
Promotes change at the level of institutions, community, or society		Recognition that advocacy to improve population health involves interacting with a number of systems (e.g., the health care system, local funders, federal funders, etc.) Advocates for increased resources for research and training in clinical health psychology at local, state, and federal levels	

Sources: Revised Competency Benchmarks for Professional Psychology (2011). American Psychological Association (adapted from Fouad et al., 2009). Available at http://www.apa.org/ed/graduate/competency.aspx. Clinical Health Psychology Competencies (2013). Council of Clinical Health Psychology Training Programs. Available at http://www.cchptp.org/.

REFERENCES

Accardi, M. C., & Milling, L. S. (2009). The effectiveness of hypnosis for reducing procedure-related pain in children and adolescents: A comprehensive methodological review. *Journal of Behavioral Medicine, 32*, 328–339. doi:10.1007/s10865-009-9207-6

Accreditation Council for Graduate Medical Education. (2007). *ACGME program requirements for graduate medical education.* Chicago, IL: Author.

Adler, N. E., & Rehkopf, D. H. (2008). U.S. disparities in health: Descriptions, causes, and mechanisms. *Annual Review of Public Health, 29,* 235–252. doi:10.1146/annurev. publhealth.29.020907.090852

American Psychological Association. (1958). Standards of ethical behavior for psychologists: Report of the committee on ethical standards of psychologists. *American Psychologist, 13,* 266–271.

American Psychological Association. (2002). Ethical principles of psychologists and code of conduct. *American Psychologist, 57,* 1060–1073. doi:10.1037/0003-066X.57.12.1060

American Psychological Association. (2011). Petition for the recognition of a specialty in professional psychology for clinical health psychology. In *Minutes from the Annual Report of the Commission for the Recognition of Specialties and Proficiencies in Professional Psychology (CRSPPP).* Washington, DC: Author.

American Psychological Association Task Force on Health Research. (1976). Contributions of psychology to health research: Patterns, problems, and potentials. *American Psychologist, 31,* 263–274. doi:10.1037/0003-066X.31.4.263

Anderson, N. B. (2003). Psychology as a health profession. *APA Monitor on Psychology, 34,* 9.

Andrasik, F., Goodie, J. L., & Peterson, A. (Eds.). (2014). *Biopsychosocial assessment in clinical health psychology: A handbook.* New York: Guilford Press.

Barnes, P. M., Bloom, B., & Nahin, R. L. (2008). *Complementary and alternative medicine use among adults and children: United States, 2007.* National Health Statistics Reports (No. 12). Hyattsville, MD: National Center for Health Statistics. Available at: http://www.cdc.gov/nchs/data/nhsr/nhsr012.pdf

Belar, C. (2003). Models and concepts. In S. Llewelyn & P. Kennedy (Eds.), *Handbook of clinical health psychology* (pp. 7–19). New York, NY: Wiley.

Belar, C. D. (2008). Changing educational needs of psychologists: Do we need more medical knowledge, basic science and more psychological science? *Journal of Clinical Psychology in Medical Settings, 15,* 12–17. doi:10.1007/s10880-008-9097-8

Belar, C. D., Brown, R. A., Hersch, L. E., Hornyak, L. M., Rozensky, R. H., Sheridan, E. P.,...Reed, G. W. (2001). Self-assessment in clinical health psychology: A model for ethical expansion of practice. *Professional Psychology: Research and Practice, 32,* 135–141. doi:10.1037/0735-7028.32.2.135

Belar, C. D., & Deardorff, W. W. (2009). *Clinical health psychology in medical settings: A practitioner's guidebook* (2nd ed.). Washington, DC: American Psychological Association.

Benner, P. (1984). *From novice to expert: Excellence and power in clinical nursing practice.* Menlo Park, CA: Addison Wesley.

Birk, L. (1973). *Biofeedback: Behavioral medicine.* New York, NY: Grune & Stratton.

Blount, A. (2003). Integrated primary care: Organizing the evidence. *Families, Systems, and Health, 21,* 121–133. doi:10.1037/1091-7527.21.2.121

Bogart, L. M., Wagner, G., Galvan, F. H., & Banks, D. (2010). Conspiracy beliefs about HIV are related to antiretroviral treatment nonadherence among African American men with HIV. *Journal of Acquired Immune Deficiency Syndromes, 53,* 648–655. doi:10.1097/QAI.ob013e3181c57dbc

Bogart, L. M., Galvan, F. H., Wagner, G., & Klein, D. J. (2011). Longitudinal association of HIV conspiracy beliefs with sexual risk among black males living with HIV. *AIDS and Behavior, 15,* 1180–1186. doi:10.1007/s10461-010-9796-7

Brase, G. L., & Richmond, J. (2004). The white-coat effect: Physician attire and perceived authority, friendliness, and attractiveness. *Journal of Applied Social Psychology, 34,* 2469–2481. doi:10.1111/j.1559-1816.2004.tb01987.x

Cannon, W. B. (1932). *Wisdom of the body.* New York, NY: Norton.

Carr, J. E., Emory, E. K., Errichetti, A., Bennett Johnson, S., & Reyes, E. (2007). Integrating behavioral and social sciences in the medical school curriculum: Opportunities and challenges for psychology. *Journal of Clinical Psychology in Medical Settings, 14,* 33-39. doi:10.1007/s10880-006-9049-0

Centers for Disease Control and Prevention (CDC). (1999). Achievements in public health, 1900-1999: Control of infectious diseases. *Morbidity and Mortality Weekly Report, 48*(29), 621–629.

Centers for Disease Control and Prevention. (2006). *Behavioral Risk Factor Surveillance System: operational and user's guide.* Atlanta, GA: U.S. Department of Health and Human Services, Centers for Disease Control and Prevention.

Centers for Disease Control and Prevention. (n.d.). *Leading causes of death, 1900-1998.* Retrieved April 2012, from http://www.cdc.gov/nchs/data/dvs/lead1900_98.pdf

Cobigo, V., Ouellette-Kuntz, H., Balogh, R., Leung, F., Lin, E., & Lunsky, Y. (2013). Are cervical and breast cancer screening programs equitable? The case of women with intellectual and developmental disabilities. *Journal of Intellectual Disability Research, 57,* 478–488. doi:10.1111/jir.12035.

Cohen, S., Kessler, R. C., & Underwood Gordon, L. (Eds.). (1997). *Measuring stress: A guide for health and social scientists.* New York, NY: Oxford.

Commission on Accreditation. (2007). *Guidelines and principles for accreditation of programs in professional psychology.* Washington, DC: American Psychological Association.

Commission on Dental Accreditation. (2010). *Accreditation standards for dental education programs.* Chicago, IL: American Dental Association.

Craig J. V., & Smyth, R. L. (Eds.). (2007). *The evidence based practice manual for nurses* (2nd ed.). New York, NY: Churchill Livingstone.

Craske, M. G., & Barlow, D. H. (2008). Panic disorder and agoraphobia. In D. H. Barlow (Ed.), *Clinical handbook of psychological disorders* (4th ed., pp. 1–64). New York, NY: Guilford Press.

Cruess, S. R., Johnston, S., & Cruess, R. L. (2004). Profession: A working definition for medical educators. *Teaching and Learning in Medicine, 16,* 74–76. doi:10.1207/s15328015tlm1601_15

Cuff, P. A., & Vanselow, N. A. (Eds.). (2004). *Improving medical education: Enhancing the behavioral and social science content of medical school curricula.* Washington, DC: National Academies Press.

Dacy, J. M., & Brodsky, S. L. (1992). Effects of therapist attire and gender. *Psychotherapy, 29,* 486–490. doi:10.1037/h0088555

Division 38 (Health Psychology) of the American Psychological Association. (2012). *Mission statement.* Retrieved June 2012, from http://www.health-psych.org/AboutMission.cfm.

Engel, G. L. (1977). The need for a new medical model: A challenge for biomedicine. *Science, 196,* 129–136.

Evidence-Based Medicine Working Group. (1992). Evidence-based medicine. A new approach to teaching the practice of medicine. *Journal of the American Medical Association, 268*(17), 2420–2425. doi:10.1001/jama.268.17.2420

Fadiman, A. (2012). *The spirit catches you and you fall down: A Hmong child, her American doctors, and the collision of two cultures.* New York: Farrar, Straus and Giroux.

Farber, E. W. (2010). Humanistic-existential psychotherapy competencies and the supervisory process. *Psychotherapy Theory, Research, Practice, Training, 47*(1), 28–34.

Fouad, N. A., Grus, C. L., Hatcher, R. L., Kaslow, N. J., Hutchings, P. S., Madson, M. B., ... Crossman, R. E. (2009). Competency benchmarks: A model for understanding and measuring competence in professional psychology across training levels. *Training and education in Professional Psychology, 3*(Suppl.), S5–S26. doi:10.1037/a0015832

France, C. R., Masters, K. S., Belar, C. D., Kerns, R. D., Klonoff, E. A., Larkin, K. T., ... Thorn, B. E. (2008). Application of the competency model to clinical health psychology. *Professional Psychology: Research and Practice, 39*(6), 573–580. doi:1037/0735-7028.39.6.573

Friedman, H. S., & Adler, N. E. (2007). The history and background of health psychology. In H. S. Friedman & R. C. Siler (Eds.), *Foundations of health psychology* (pp. 1–18). New York, NY: Oxford University Press.

Goodheart, C. D., Kazdin, A. E., & Sternberg, R. J. (2006). *Evidence-based psychotherapy: Where practice and research meet.* Washington, DC: American Psychological Association.

Gosling, R., & Standen, R. (1998). Doctor's dress. *British Journal of Psychiatry, 172,* 188–189. doi:10.1192/bjp.172.2.188c

Greiner, A. C., & Knebel, E. (Eds.). (2003). *Health professions education: A bridge to quality.* Retrieved May 2012, from http://www.nap.edu/catalog/10681.html.

Hannay, H. J. (1998). Proceedings of the Houston Conference on specialty education and training in clinical neuropsychology. *Archives of Clinical Neuropsychology, 13,* 157–249. doi:10.1093/arclin/13.2.157

Hatcher, R. L., & Lassiter, K. D. (2007). Initial training in professional psychology: The practicum competencies outline. *Training and Education in Professional Psychology, 1,* 49–63. doi:10.1037/1931-3918.1.1.49

Health Service Psychology Education Collaborative. (2013). *A blueprint for health service psychology education and training.* Washington, DC: American Psychological Association.

Hessol, N. A., & Fuentes-Afflick, E. (2012). The impact of migration on pregnancy outcomes among Mexican-origin women. *Journal of Immigrant and Minority Health*. E-published online – December, 2012. doi:10.1007/s10903-012-9760-x

Hibbard, M. R., & Cox, D. R. (2010). Competencies of a rehabilitation psychologist. In R. Frank, M. Rosenthal, & B. Caplan (Eds.), *Handbook of rehabilitation psychology* (2nd ed., pp. 467–475). Washington, DC: American Psychological Association.

Holroyd, K. A., Cottrell, C. K., O'Donnell, F. J., Cordingley, G. E., Drew, J. B., Carlson, B. W. & Himawan, L. (2010). Effect of preventive (β blocker) treatment, behavioural migraine management, or their combination on outcomes of optimised acute treatment in frequent migraine: Randomised control trial. *British Medical Journal, 341*, 1–12.

Institute of Medicine. (1972). *Educating for the healthcare team: Report of a conference*. Washington, DC: National Academy of Sciences.

Inter-Organizational Work Group on Competencies for Primary Care Psychology Practice. (2013). *Competencies for psychology practice in primary care*. Washington, DC: American Psychological Association.

Interprofessional Education Collaborative Expert Panel. (2011). *Core competencies for interprofessional collaborative practice: Report of an expert panel*. Washington, DC: Interprofessional Education Collaborative.

Jung, C. G. (1971). Psychological types. In *Collected works* (Vol. 6, trans. G. Adler & R. F. C. Hull). Princeton, NJ: Princeton University Press. (First German edition, 1921)

Kanfer, F. H., & Schefft, B. K. (1988). *Guiding the process of therapeutic change*. Champaign, IL: Research Press.

Kaslow, N. J. (2004). Competencies in professional psychology. *American Psychologist, 59*(8), 774–781. doi:2004-20395-022 [pii] 10.1037/0003-066X.59.8.774

Kaslow, N. J., Borden, K. A., Collins, F. L., Jr., Forrest, L., Illfelder-Kaye, J., Nelson, P. D., & Willmuth, M. E. (2004). Competencies conference: Future directions in education and credentialing in professional psychology. *Journal of Clinical Psychology, 60*(7), 699–712. doi:10.1002/jclp.20016

Kaslow, N. J., Grus, C. L., Campbell, L. F., Fouad, N. A., Hatcher, R. L., & Rodolfa, E. R. (2009). Competency assessment toolkit for professional psychology. *Training and Education in Professional Psychology, 3*(Suppl.), S27–S45. doi:10.1037/a0015833

Kawachi, I., Daniels, N., & Robinson, D. E. (2005). Health disparities by race and class: Why both matter. *Health Affairs (Project Hope), 24*, 343–352. Available at: http://content.healthaffairs.org/content/24/2/343.full

Kennerly, R. C. (2002). *A brief history of the origins of behavioral medicine*. Retrieved May 2012, from http://psychologyforyouandme.com/LECTURES/behavioral%20medicine/A%20Brief%20History%20of%20the%20Origins%20of%20Behavioral%20Medicine.doc.

Kerns, R. D., Berry, S., Frantsve, L. M. E., & Linton, J. C. (2009). Life-long competency development in clinical health psychology. *Training and Education in Professional Psychology, 3*(4), 212–217. doi:10-1037/a0016753

Khoury M. J., Gwinn, M., Yoon, P. W., Dowling, N., Moore, C. A., & Bradley, L. (2007). The continuum of translation research in genomic medicine: How can we accelerate the appropriate integration of human genomic discoveries into health care and disease prevention? *Genetics in Medicine, 9*(10), 665–674. doi:10.1097/GIM.0b013e31815699do

Kleinman, A., Eisenberg, L., & Good B. (1978). Culture, illness, and care: Clinical lessons from anthropological and cross-cultural research. *Annals of Internal Medicine, 88,* 251–258. doi:10.7326/0003-4819-88-2-251

Klonoff, E. A. (2009). Disparities in the provision of medical care: An outcome in search of an explanation. *Journal of Behavioral Medicine, 32,* 48–63. doi:10.1007/s10865-008-9192-1

Klonoff, E. A., & Landrine, H. (1999). Do blacks believe that HIV/AIDS is a government conspiracy against them? *Preventive Medicine, 28,* 451–457. doi.org/10.1006/pmed.1999.0463

Knight, B. G., Karel, M. J., Hinrichsen, G. A., Qualls, S. H., & Duffy, M. (2009). Pikes Peak model for training in professional geropsychology. *American Psychologist, 64*(3), 205-214. doi:2009-04471-004 [pii] 10.1037/a0015059

Kuhn, T. S. (1962). *The structure of scientific revolutions.* Chicago, IL: The University of Chicago Press.

Landrine, H., & Klonoff, E. A. (2004). Culture change and ethnic minority health-behavior: An operant theory of acculturation. *Journal of Behavioral Medicine, 27*(6), 527–555.

Larkin, K. T. (2009). Variations of doctoral training programs in clinical health psychology: Lessons learned at the box office. *Training and Education in Professional Psychology, 3*(4), 202–211. doi:10-1037/a0016666

Larkin, K. T. (2014). The blueprint for building psychology into a health care profession: Retaining our foundation in science while expanding breadth of training. *Training and Education in Professional Psychology, 8*(1), 18–21. doi:10.1037/tep0000013

Lehrer, P. M., Vaschillo, E., Vaschillo, B., Lu, S. E., Scardella, A., Siddique, M., & Habib, R. H. (2004). Biofeedback treatment for asthma. *Chest, 126,* 352–361.

Macintosh, T., Desai, M. M., Lewis, T. T., Jones, B. A., & Nunez-Smith, M. (2013) Socially-assigned race, healthcare discrimination and preventive healthcare services. *PLoS One, 8*(5), e64522. doi:10.1371/journal.pone.0064522

Masters, K. S., France, C. R., & Thorn, B. E. (2009). Enhancing preparation among entry-level clinical health psychologists: Recommendations for "best practices" from the the first meeting of the Council of Clinical Health Psychology Training Programs (CCHPTP). *Training and Education in Professional Psychology, 3*(4), 193–201. doi:10.1037/a00116049

Matarazzo, J. D. (1980). Behavioral health and behavioral medicine: Frontiers for a new health psychology. *American Psychologist, 35,* 807–817. doi:10.1037/0003-066X.35.9.807

McDaniel, S. H., Grus, C. L., Cubic, B., Hunter, C., Kearney, L., Schuman, C. C., …& Bennett-Johnson, S. (2014). Competencies for psychology practice in primary care. *American Psychologist, 69*(4), 409–429. doi:10.1037/a0036072

Miller, N. E. (1957). Experiments on motivation: Studies combining psychological, physiological, and pharmacological techniques. *Science, 126,* 1271–1278.

Miller, N. E. (1983). Some main themes and highlights of the conference. *Health Psychology, 2*(5), 11–14. doi:10.1037/h0090285

Murphy, S. L., Xu, J., & Kochanek, K. D. (2012). Deaths: Preliminary data for 2012. *National Vital Statistics Report, 60*(4). Retrieved April 2012, from http://www.cdc.gov/nchs/data/nvsr/nvsr60/nvsr60_04.pdf.

Nash, J. M., & Larkin, K. T. (2012). Geometric models of competency development in specialty areas of professional psychology. *Training and Education in Professional Psychology*, 6, 37–46. doi:10.1037/a0026964

Nash, J. M., McKay, K. M., Vogel, M. E., & Masters, M. S. (2012). Functional and foundational characteristics of psychologists in integrated primary care. *Journal of Clinical Psychology in Medical Settings*, 19(1), 93–104. doi:10.1007/s10880-011-9290-z

Newman, C. F. (2010). Competency in conducting cognitive-behavioral therapy: Foundational, functional, and supervisory aspects. *Psychotherapy Theory, Research, Practice, Training*, 47, 12–19.

Nicholas, D. R., & Stern, M. (2011). Counseling psychology in clinical health psychology: The impact of specialty perspective. *Professional Psychology: Research and Practice*, 42(4), 331–337. doi:10.1037/a0024197

National Institutes of Health (2010). Interdisciplinary research. Retrieved on April 14, 2014 from https://commonfund.nih.gov/Interdisciplinary

Painter, A. F., & Lemkau, J. P. (1992). Turning roadblocks into stepping stones: Teaching psychology to physicians. *Teaching of Psychology*, 19, 183–184. doi:10.1207/s15328023top1903_20

Palermo, T. M., Janicke, D. M., McQuaid, E. L., Mullins, L. L., Robins, P. M., & Wu, Y. P. (2014). Recommendations for training in pediatric psychology: Defining core competencies across training levels. *Journal of Pediatric Psychology*, [Epub online]. doi: 10.1093/jpepsy/jsu015

Patterson, D. R. (2010). *Clinical hypnosis for pain control*. Washington, DC: American Psychological Association.

Peek, C. J. (2011). *A collaborative care lexicon for asking practice and research development questions*. Rockville, MD: Agency for Healthcare Research and Quality, US Department of Health and Human Services.

Penwell, L. M., Larkin, K. T., & Goodie, J. L. (2014). Biopsychosocial assessment of coping. In F. Andrasik, J. L. Goodie, & A. Peterson (Eds.), *Biopsychosocial assessment in clinical health psychology: A handbook*. New York, NY: Guilford Press.

Perez, M. A., & Luquis, R. R. (Eds.) (2008). *Cultural competence in health education and health promotion*. San Francisco, CA: Jossey-Bass.

Peterson, R. L., Peterson, D. R., Abrams, J. C., & Stricker, G. (1997). The National Council of Schools and Programs of Professional Psychology educational model. *Professional Psychology: Research and Practice*, 28, 373–386. doi:10.1037/0735-7028.28.4.373

Pomerleau, O. F. (1982). A discourse on behavioral medicine: Current status and future trends. *Journal of Consulting and Clinical Psychology*, 50(6), 1030–1039. doi:10.1037/0022-006X.50.6.1030

Quittner, A. L., Modi, A. C., Lemanek, K. L., Levers-Landis, C. E., & Rapoff, M. A. (2008). Evidence-based assessment of adherence to medical treatments in pediatric psychology. *Journal of Pediatric Psychology*, 33(9), 916–936. doi:10.1093/jpepsy/jsm064

Rodolfa, E. R. (2010, August 12). *Editor's report*. Fourth Editorial Board Meeting, Training and Education in Professional Psychology, San Diego, CA.

Rodolfa, E. R., Bent, R. J., Eisman, E., Nelson, P. D., Rehm, L., & Ritchie, P. (2005). A cube model for competency development: Implications for psychology educators and regulators. *Professional Psychology: Research and Practice*, 36, 347–354. doi:10.1037/0735-7028.36.4.347

Rozansky, A., Blumenthal, J. A., & Kaplan, J. (1999). Impact of psychological factors on the pathogenesis of cardiovascular disease and implications for therapy. *Circulation, 99*, 2192–2217.

Rozensky, R. H., Sweet, J. J., & Tovian, S. M. (1997). *Psychological assessment in medical settings*. New York, NY: Plenum Press.

Sackett, D. (1996). Evidence-based medicine: What it is and what it isn't. *British Medical Journal, 312*, 71–72.

Sarnet, J. (2010). Key competencies of the psychodynamic psychotherapist and how to teach them in supervision. *Psychotherapy Theory, Research, Practice, Training, 47*, 20–27.

Schön, D. (1983). *The reflective practitioner: How professionals think in action*. New York, NY: Basic Books.

Schofield, W. (1969). The role of psychology in the delivery of health services. *American Psychologist, 24*, 565–584.

Schwartz, G. E., & Beatty, J. (Eds.). (1977). *Biofeedback: Theory and research*. New York, NY: Academic Press.

Schwartz, G. E., & Weiss, S. M. (1978a). Yale Conference on Behavioral Medicine: A proposed definition and statement of goals. *Journal of Behavioral Medicine, 1*, 3–11. doi:0160-7715/78/0300-0003$05.00/0

Schwartz, G. E., & Weiss, S. M. (1978b). Behavioral medicine: An amended definition. *Journal of Behavioral Medicine, 1*, 249–251. doi:0160-7715/78/0900-0249$05.00/0

Selye, H. (1956). *The stress of life*. New York, NY: McGraw-Hill.

Shavers, V. L., Fagan, P., Jones, D., Klein, W. M., Boyington, J., Moten, C., & Rorie, E. (2008). The state of research on racial/ethnic discrimination in the receipt of health care. *American Journal of Public Health, 102*, 953–66. doi:10.2105/AJPH.2012.300773

Sheppard, V. B., Mays, D., LaVeist, T., & Tercyak, K. P. (2013). Medical mistrust influences black women's level of engagement in BRCA 1/2 genetic counseling and testing. *Journal of the National Medical Association, 105*, 17–22.

Smedley, B. D., Stith, A. Y., & Nelson, A. R. (Eds.) (2003). *Unequal treatment: Confronting racial and ethnic disparities in health care*. Washington, DC: National Academies Press.

Simon, J. M. (1999). Evidence-based practice in nursing [Editorial]. *Nursing Diagnosis, 10*, 3.

Stone, G. C., Weiss, S. M., Matarazzo, J. D., Miller, N. E., Rodin, J., Belar, C. D., ... Singer, J. E. (Eds.). (1987). *Health psychology: A discipline and a profession*. London, UK: The University of Chicago Press.

Society of Behavioral Medicine. (n.d.). *Definition of behavioral medicine*. Retrieved March 2014, from http://www.sbm.org/resources/education/behavioral-medicine.

Sokhadze, T. M., Cannon, R. L., & Trudeau, D. L. (2008). EEG biofeedback as a treatment for substance use disorders: Review, ratings of efficacy, and recommendations for further research. *Applied Psychophysiology and Biofeedback, 33*, 1–28.

Thorn, B. E. (2004). *Cognitive therapy for chronic pain: A step-by-step guide*. New York: Guilford Press.

Truman, B. I., Smith, C. K., Roy, K., Chen, Z., Moonesinghe, R., Zhu, J., Crawford, C. G., & Zaza, S. (2011). Rationale for regular reporting on health disparities and inequalities – United States. *Morbidity and Mortality Weekly Report, 60*, 3–10.

Tulkin, S. R. (1987). Health care services. In G. C. Stone, S. M. Weiss, J. D. Matarazzo, N. E. Miller, J. Rodin, C. D. Belar, ... & Singer, J. E. (Eds.), *Health psychology: A discipline and a profession* (pp. 122–135). Chicago, IL: The University of Chicago Press.

Turk, D. C., & Melzack, R. (Eds.). (2001). *Handbook of pain assessment* (2nd ed.). New York, NY: Guilford Press.

Wallace, W. A., & Hall, D. L. (1996). *Psychological consultation: Perspectives and applications.* Pacific Grove, CA: Brooks/Cole.

Wallston, K. A. (1996). *Healthy, wealthy, and Weiss: A history of division 38 (Health psychology).* Retrieved May 2012, from http://www.health-psych.org/PDF/DivHistory. PDF

Ward, K. D., Vander Weg, M. W., Kovach, K. W., Klesges, R. C., DeBon, M. W., Haddock, C. K., ... & Lando, H. A. (2002). Ethnic and gender differences in smoking and smoking cessation in a population of young adult air force recruits. *American Journal of Health Promotion, 16,* 259–266. doi: http://dx.doi.org/10.4278/0890-1171-16.5.259

Weiss, S. M. (1978). News and developments in behavioral medicine. *Journal of Behavioral Medicine, 1,* 135–139. doi:10.1007/BF00846587

Working Group on Predoctoral Education / Doctoral Training (1983). *Health Psychology, 2* (Supplement), 123–130. doi:10.1037/h0090310

World Health Organization (WHO). (2013). *Top 10 causes of death in the world, 2011.* Retrieved April 2014, from http://www.who.int/mediacentre/factsheets/fs310/en/index.html.

KEY TERMS

Affordable Care Act: federal legislation that is the foundation of a new health care system that provides coverage for all Americans and controls health care costs.

American Board of Professional Clinical Health Psychology: national professional organization charged with evaluating competencies of clinical health psychologists for purposes of board certification. To be board certified, applicants must possess adequate credentials in clinical health psychology, demonstrate work samples of competence, and pass an oral examination.

Arden House Conference: location of the National Working Conference on Education and Training in Health Psychology, held in 1983, with funding by the Carnegie Foundation, the MacArthur Foundation, and the Kaiser Family Foundation. It was a hallmark meeting that defined the education of health psychologists as occurring in either science (health psychology) or scientist-practitioner (clinical health psychology) tracks.

Behavioral medicine: the interdisciplinary field concerned with the development and integration of behavioral, psychosocial, and biomedical science knowledge and techniques relevant to the understanding of health and illness, and the application of this knowledge and these techniques to prevention, diagnosis, treatment, and rehabilitation (Schwartz & Weiss, 1978b).

Biopsychosocial interview: comprehensive patient assessment that involves an evaluation of how the patient's physical condition (e.g., body mass index, HbA1c, out-of-range lab values), thoughts, emotions, behaviors, habits, interpersonal relationships, and environment influence the identified problem and current level of functioning.

Biopsychosocial model: the conceptual foundation of health psychology and clinical health psychology that involves consideration of biological, psychological (behavioral, cognitive, and emotional), and social factors in understanding health and health behaviors. It was initially articulated by Engel in 1977 in an effort to expand our understanding of factors contributing to the primary causes of death and disability beyond the biomedical model. The biopsychosocial model includes having a "broad understanding of biology, pharmacology, anatomy, human physiology and pathophysiology, and psychoneuroimmunology," "how learning, memory, perception, cognition, and motivation influence health behaviors; are affected by physical illness/injury/disability; and can affect response to and recovery from illness/injury/disability," and "the impact of social support, culture, physician-patient relationships, health policy, and the organization of health care delivery systems on health and help-seeking" (American Psychological Association, 2011, p. 10).

Clinical health psychology: the application of the scientific foundations of health psychology with patients diagnosed with medical and other health-related problems.

Collaborative behavioral health care: behavioral health and primary medical providers collaborate in providing care for patients with regular communication between clinicians (Peek, 2011).

Co-located behavioral health care: behavioral health provider accepts referral from primary medical provider and provides services within the primary care facility with minimal contact with primary medical provider (Peek, 2011).

Commission on Accreditation (CoA): body of psychologists recognized by the US Department of Education that is responsible for the review of doctoral programs, internships, and postdoctoral fellowship programs for purposes of accreditation.

Competencies: the essential knowledge, skills, and attitudes required for practice of a profession.

Competency Assessment Toolkit: a compendium of strategies for assessing knowledge- and skill-based competencies (Kaslow et al., 2009).

Competency Benchmarks Work Group: an assembly of educators representing all levels of the entire training community that outlined the foundational and functional competencies for all professional psychologists. The group sought extensive feedback from the training community and published the benchmarks competency list in 2009 (see Fouad et al., 2009).

Coordinated behavioral health care: behavioral health and primary medical providers practice separately within their respective systems (not necessarily in the same system). Information on mutual patients is shared as needed, but collaboration is limited following the initial referral (Blount, 2003; Peek, 2011).

Council of Chairs of Training Councils (CCTC): a group comprised of the chairs of all of the training councils that meets twice yearly to address issues common across all areas of training and all levels of training. This group receives support from the Education Directorate of the American Psychological Association and has been instrumental in supporting efforts to disseminate the lists of benchmarks competencies, addressing the internship imbalance, and advocating for the highest standards for the practice of psychology.

Council of Clinical Health Psychology Training Programs (CCHPTP): a nonprofit training council organized at the Tempe Summit in 2007 with the purpose of developing and maintaining training standards and guidelines for training programs in clinical health psychology.

Council of Health Psychology: the original training council established at the Arden House Conference that included both health and clinical health psychology training programs. This council conducted very little business since the 1980s and was replaced by CCHPTP in 2007.

Deportment: professional conduct, including appropriate attire and personal hygiene as well as appropriate communication and use of language.

Division 38 (Health Psychology): a division of the American Psychological Association that was founded in 1978 devoted to the research and practice of health psychology. Members include both psychologists who conduct health psychology research and who practice the application of evidence-based practice in medical and health care settings. The Division publishes the journal *Health Psychology* and the newsletter *The Health Psychologist*.

Electronic health record (EHR): the health record accessible to and shared by all providers in a given health care system via a secure, encrypted network.

Ethical Principles and Standards of Conduct: a set of ethical guidelines that govern psychologists. It was first published in 1958 by the American Psychological Association.

European Health Psychology Society (EHPS): the European complement to Division 38 of the American Psychological Association. EHPS publishes *Psychology and Health* as well as *Health Psychology Review.*

Evidence-based practice: making decisions on the best available evidence in the context of patient characteristics and desires and the clinical setting.

Examination for Professional Practice of Psychology (EPPP): standardized examination used to test knowledge of the field of psychology and the ethical standards that govern it. The examination is administered during application for licensure as a psychologist, and receiving a passing score is required for licensure in all states in the United States and provinces in Canada.

Health disparities: differences in the incidence, prevalence, access, treatment, morbidity, and mortality of illness, disease, and symptoms associated with belonging to one group versus another (Truman et al., 2011).

Health Insurance Portability and Accountability Act (HIPAA): a federal law that sets standards regarding access, security, and release of protected health information (PHI).

Health psychology: the scientific discipline aimed at examining the relation between behavior and health. "Health psychology is the aggregate of the specific educational, scientific, and professional contributions of the discipline of psychology to the promotion and maintenance of health, the prevention and treatment of illness, and the identification of etiologic and diagnostic correlates of health, illness and related dysfunction and to the analysis and improvement of the health care system and health policy formation" (Wallston, 1996, p. 10).

Health service psychologist: psychologists who historically have characterized themselves as clinical, counseling, or school psychologists, and who have sought licensure to practice in the health care environment.

Health Service Psychology Education Collaborative (HSPEC): group of professional psychologists that developed *A Blueprint for Health Service Psychology Education and Training* to guide the future of psychology as a health profession (2013; Washington, DC: American Psychological Association).

Integrated behavioral health care: tightly integrated onsite teamwork including both behavioral health and medical providers with a unified care plan for shared patients (Blount, 2003). Because most patients arrive at primary care settings with both behavioral and medical problems, or their medical problem is influenced by behavioral factors (e.g., stress, health behaviors, psychological disorders), cost-effective treatments require access to providers with expertise in both behavioral and medical health provision (Peek, 2011).

Interdisciplinary treatment team: health care teams in which treatment involves care provided by professionals from several disciplines. In contrast to multidisciplinary teams, aspects of the treatment plan can be shared by various team members (e.g., clinical health psychologists may treat depression to both improve mood and adherence to a medical regimen).

Inter-Organizational Work Group on Competencies for Primary Care Psychology Practice: a group of psychologists with expertise in the practice of psychology in primary care settings were invited by Suzanne Bennett-Johnson, president of the American Psychological Association, to articulate competencies for practice in primary care settings. The resulting list of competencies was published in the *American Psychologist* in 2014.

Interprofessional Education Collaborative (IPEC): a collaborative group with representatives from numerous health care professions with the purpose of articulating interprofessionalism competences that are shared across fields of nursing, pharmacy, medicine, dentistry, public health, psychology, physician's assistants, and physical therapy.

Institute of Medicine: nonprofit organization founded in 1970 by the National Academy of Sciences to provide advice on health and medical sciences and promote the overall health of the United States.

Interprofessionalism: knowledge of other health care professions, understanding the importance of each health professional's roles and boundaries of competence, and skills in interacting with health professionals trained in other disciplines, including medicine, nursing, physical and occupational therapy, social work, dentistry, and so on.

Mind-body dichotomy: suggested by Descartes in the 17th century, the mind and the body represent separate systems. Although the functioning of the body was mechanistic, the workings of the mind could not be explained by the laws of nature.

Multidisciplinary treatment team: health care teams in which professionals from different disciplines jointly treat patients in health care environments. In contrast to an interdisciplinary team, various professionals provide care to the patient independently only on elements of the treatment plan in their area of expertise (e.g., clinical health psychologists may treat depression without monitoring how it impacts adherence to a medical regimen).

Precepting: the teaching/supervision that occurs when a beginning student is permitted to observe and participate in the clinical activities of an experienced professional health care provider. Precepting is primarily a teaching activity, and students in these roles are closely supervised and only assigned activities that are very limited in scope.

Profession: "an occupation whose core element is work based upon the mastery of a complex body of knowledge and skills... used in the service of others. Its members are governed by codes of ethics and profess a commitment to competence, integrity and morality, altruism, and the promotion of the public good within their domain" (Cruess, Johnston, & Cruess, 2004, p. 74).

Psychosomatic medicine: A subfield of medicine that focused on understanding the causes and treatments of mind-body disorders. It was initially based on psychoanalytic conceptualizations of illness but later embraced the biopsychosocial model more broadly.

Quality improvement (QI): Ongoing evaluations conducted in all modern health care facilities aimed at evaluating clinical practices and procedures with the goal of making ongoing improvements.

Reflection-in-action: cognitive processing or review of one's functioning in the moment, characterized as "thinking on one's feet" (Schön, 1983).

Reflection-on-action: cognitive processing or review of one's functioning following an encounter with a patient, student, or colleague (Schön, 1983).

Riverfront Conference: a small meeting held in Jacksonville, Florida, in 2010 for the purposes of preparing clinical health psychology's petition to maintain clinical health psychology as a specialty by APA's Commission for the Recognition of Specialties and Proficiencies in Professional Psychology. Meeting participants reaffirmed the model of training for clinical health psychology that was established at the Arden House Conference.

Scientific mindedness: a way of knowing that involves an appreciation for the scientific method and conclusions derived from empirical data.

Scientist-practitioner model of training: the model of training that serves as the foundation for clinical health psychology. It involves training clinical health psychologists as competent researchers and competent health service providers. It was initially stated at the Arden House conference in 1983 and reaffirmed at the Riverfront Conference in 2010.

Self-assessment template: a tool for clinical health psychologists to assist in evaluating one's strengths and weaknesses in order to establish the boundaries of one's area of practice (Belar et al., 2001).

SOAP (Subjective, Objective, Assessment, Plan) format: the typical format used for writing progress notes in health care settings. Subjective information is what the patient states; Objective information is based on the observations of the care provider; Assessment provides results of any assessment, including diagnostic information; and Plan focuses on future steps in patient care.

Society of Behavioral Medicine: an interdisciplinary professional organization that dates back to the Yale Conference on Behavioral Medicine in 1977. Members include a variety of health professionals, including medicine, nursing, pharmacy, dentistry, and public health to name a few. The Society of Behavioral Medicine publishes the journal *Annals of Behavioral Medicine* and a newsletter *the Outlook.*

Society of Pediatric Psychology: an American Psychological Association division (Division 54) that is comprised of psychologists who conduct research and practice with patients in pediatric settings.

Tempe Summit: the Tempe Summit on Education and Training in Clinical Health Psychology was held in 2007 with funding by Division 38 (Health Psychology) of the American Psychological Association.

Transdisciplinary treatment team: health care teams in which professionals from different disciplines not only jointly treat patients in health care environments but train and/or supervise those from other health care disciplines (including trainees).

Translational research: programs of research that extend empirical effort from "bench" findings in the laboratory to the "bedside" of actual patients with diagnosed health problems.

Wellness model: an extension of the typical disease model that includes methods of maintaining health as well as prevention of disease.

Yale Conference on Behavioral Medicine: a conference held in 1977 that defined the interdisciplinary field of behavioral medicine, distinguished it from existing mental health–related disciplines of clinical and counseling psychology, and defined the scope of problems of concern to behavioral medicine. The foundation of the Society of Behavioral Medicine and the *Journal of Behavioral Medicine* can be traced back to this conference.

INDEX

f denotes figure; *t* denotes table

ABOUT THE AUTHORS

Kevin T. Larkin, PhD, ABPP, received his doctorate in psychology from the University of Pittsburgh in 1986. He joined the faculty at West Virginia University as an assistant professor that year and was promoted to the rank of associate professor with tenure in 1992 and to the rank of professor in 2002. He served the department for 13 years as director of clinical training and was appointed department chair in 2013. He is board certified in the area of clinical health psychology from the American Board of Professional Psychology and served as the chair of the Council of Clinical Health Psychology Training Programs (CCHPTP) from 2007 to 2013.

Elizabeth A. Klonoff, PhD, ABPP, received her PhD in clinical psychology from the University of Oregon. She has served as member of the faculty in the Departments of Psychiatry and Obstetrics and Gynecology at Duke University School of Medicine, in the Departments of Psychiatry and Neurology at Case Western Reserve University School of Medicine, and in the Department of Psychology at California State University, San Bernardino. Currently, she is professor of psychology at San Diego State University (SDSU) and professor of psychiatry at University of California San Diego, where she serves as the SDSU codirector of the Joint Doctoral Program in Clinical Psychology. She is board certified in both clinical and clinical health psychology by the American Board of Professional Psychology, and she has served as President of APA Division 38 (Health Psychology) and as a board member for the Council of Clinical Health Psychology Training Programs.

ABOUT THE SERIES EDITORS

Arthur M. Nezu, PhD, ABPP, is professor of psychology, medicine, and public health at Drexel University and special professor of forensic mental health and psychiatry at the University at Nottingham in the United Kingdom. He is a fellow of multiple professional associations, including the American Psychological Association, and is board certified by the American Board of Professional Psychology in cognitive and behavioral psychology, clinical psychology, and clinical health psychology. Dr. Nezu is widely published, is incoming editor of the *Journal of Consulting and Clinical Psychology,* and has maintained a practice for three decades.

Christine Maguth Nezu, PhD, ABPP, is professor of psychology and medicine at Drexel University, and special professor of forensic mental health and psychiatry at the University at Nottingham in the United Kingdom. With over 25 years of experience in clinical private practice, consultation/liaison, research, and teaching, Dr. Maguth Nezu is board certified by the American Board of Professional Psychology (ABPP) in cognitive and behavioral psychology and clinical psychology. She is also a past president of ABPP. Her research has been supported by federal, private, and state agencies, and she has served as a grant reviewer for the National Institutes of Health.